24 December 1996

Roberta,

Thank you for sending the prisms- so I can take credit for having such good ift sources. ☺ And especially thanks for the nifty book... I've an interest in glass but don't know anything about it- until now. You've set yourself up to answer a lot of silly questions, but, you started it.

Enjoy the Alaska stories... my contribution makes me out to be a (potential) felon on the loose. Oh well. The other stories are good...

Sorry 'bout not getting this out earlier....

alaska
passages

Whoa! ALASKA Deofus Stories -
what'll they think of next?
Ya'll need to take a closer look at
the situations described herein -
they're neat. And, I offer all
my time and resources to that end -

alaska passages

20 voices
from above the
54th parallel

edited by susan fox rogers

SASQUATCH BOOKS
SEATTLE

For Cyndie and Nancy, for sharing Alaska—
and more

Printed in the United States of America.
Distributed in Canada by Raincoast Books Ltd.

00 99 98 97   4 3 2 1

Cover and interior design: Karen Schober.
Cover photograph: Paul Souders/Tony Stone Images
Composition: Blue Fescue Typography & Design

Library of Congress Cataloging Publication Data
Rogers, Susan Fox.
Alaska passages : 20 voices from above the 54th parallel / edited by
    Susan Fox Rogers.
        p. cm.
    ISBN 1-57061-046-0 (trade paper)
    1. Alaska—Social life and customs.   2. Adventure and adventurers–
    –Alaska.   3. Alaska—Biography   I. Rogers, Susan Fox.
    F910.5.R65 1996
    979.8 ' 05—dc20   96-19611

Sasquatch Books
615 Second Avenue
Seattle, Washington 98104
(206)467-4300
books@sasquatchbooks.com
http://www.sasquatchbooks.com

Sasquatch Books publishes high-quality adult nonfiction and children's books related to the Northwest (San Francisco to Alaska). For information about our books, contact us at the above address, or view our site on the World Wide Web.

Contents

Acknowledgments

Thanks to: Gary Luke for this project, and his humor and encouragement throughout. My father, Thomas Rogers, for exploring Alaska with me. My mother, Jacqueline Rogers, for letting us go. Linda Smukler for support through it all. And especially to all of the writers who sent me their stories and to the twenty gathered here.

Introduction

Like many who live in the Lower 48, I have spent a lot of time dreaming and reading about Alaska. It's a land that fascinates, takes hold of our imaginations. So when I was asked to edit this collection of essays on Alaska, I was thrilled: Here was an opportunity to indulge my dreams.

"Don't give me an anthology that is twenty stories on the Iditarod," my editor warned me.

"Promise," I said. And as I gathered manuscripts for this collection, I realized I was drawn not to the Iditarod or Denali stories, but rather to those that expanded my view of Alaska, that revealed the complexity and uniqueness of this place. I was taken by tales that surprised me and made me think about what is Alaska, what is Alaskan: a teachers' strike in Anchorage, a Christmas celebration in the bush, an encounter with spirits on the land. What I wanted to read were stories that gave me an Alaska that was less familiar. And so that is what I offer here: no Iditarod, no Denali. But, still, Alaska.

The twenty essays gathered here create a portrait of Alaska that goes beyond the expected or predictable, and the voices and perspectives are as varied as the landscape: serious and funny, whimsical and professorial.

All portraits are personal, and so too is this one. In the shades of dark and light are reflected the interests of this editor, and so I certainly won't pretend that this one is complete—Alaska is far too diverse and large a land to cover in one book. But this anthology does create, I think, a rich portrait, and each of these essays provides a taste of Alaska, a vivid encounter with the land or people or life there. There are writings by both men and women; some are experienced writers and others have never been published. But all have experienced this place and have transformed that experience into words. This, I learned, is not an easy task.

Alaska is an inspiring landscape, but it is a challenge to contain that or to transform it into words. Most people, when asked what Alaska is like, will say amazing or beautiful. And then fumble for a few more equally broad words to try to paint an abstract picture of this land. Stephen Binns, in his rambling narrative of driving through Alaska, tries to describe Mounts Hayes, Deborah, and Hess as viewed from the Denali Highway. "I can't describe it," he finally writes. "I give up. It's neat." Most people really do give up because it is difficult to describe a land so suffused with superlatives: the highest mountains, the coldest temperatures, the shortest and longest days and nights.

Some of the writers in this collection do tackle these extremes. Douglas Yates describes the power of negative temperatures during those legendary Alaskan winters. And Jenifer Fratzke takes us out on a snow machine to hunt musk ox, bringing us close to ancient animals in an incredibly cold and flat landscape that can be seen as either bleak or beautiful. Mary Hussman, while kayaking in Glacier Bay for two weeks, was careful to take photographs that would somehow give her a perspective of this land and of herself within this landscape.

Of course, not all of the writers approach the bigness of Alaska; some describe experiences that could happen anywhere. David Abrams writes of his experience fly fishing with his father. Migael Scherer tenderly writes of visiting a friend who is sick with cancer. In both of these tales, Alaska as background adds to the experience. The landscape pushes Abrams to relate to his father differently, and the beauty and strength of Alaska—a land where everyone is perpetually young and healthy—makes the loss of Scherer's friend all that more poignant.

But most of the experiences described here are uniquely Alaskan. Jennifer Brice takes us to visit with a couple and their two sons who have homesteaded at Deadfish Lake. She sees how they live such a life with as little as possible and questions why they stay.

Linda Davis offers a very different portrait of bush life as she describes the lack of friends, toys, and traditional schooling in her daughter Jenny's life. She wonders if such a life is fair to a child.

And then, of course, there's no reason to take life too seriously. Writer Ted Kerasote makes us laugh at the extremes of bush life, as he describes his experience with an eager dog team at minus forty degrees. What *do* you do with a caribou hair stuck behind your contact lens? And Jessica Maxwell's wry tale reveals the humor in the bigness of Alaska—from the big fish to the big waves to men who are larger than life.

Next to these people who live to survive are Alaskans who simply throw themselves at physical challenge, because, well, it's there. Sherry Simpson describes a sailing race around Admiralty Island that "offers most elements of the best Alaskan contests: potential disaster, a test of skills undervalued by society, the chance to be pummeled by awful weather, a certain grandeur of vision, and relative pointlessness." Such ventures are, to some Alaskans, "practically irresistible."

One of the great joys of working on this collection was the opportunity to travel in Alaska for an extended period of time. I was in search of writers, but I was also trying to get a better sense of the land and the people.

It was the land that struck me first as I traveled up the Inside Passage, entering Alaska slowly via the Alaska Marine Highway ferry. There was so much land, so much wildlife, and yet, as two essays in this collection warn, this land and all of its abundance cannot be taken for granted. Geneen Marie Haugen takes a raft trip in Arctic National Wildlife Refuge, a profoundly remote land filled with wildlife (her encounter with a grizzly bear is both scary and comical), and threatened again and again by oil development. In her essay, Susan Ewing describes a grassroots artist's efforts to save the wonderful forests in Southeast Alaska.

During my travels, I was intrigued by what Sheryl Clough calls Alaskan manners—how Alaskans will go out of their way to help and are generous and often open. I was given a ride from Denali National Park to Fairbanks by Michelle and Tim, offered a couch by Sheryl in Anchorage, taken in for a week by Cyndie and Nancy in Fairbanks. In seeing their lives, I realized that life in Fairbanks is a lot like my life: during the summer Cyndie and Nancy tended to their garden; they went mountain biking and hiking. Yet I knew that their choice to work as teachers in Fairbanks was different than if they were teachers in New Jersey, and I wanted to know how. Sheryl Clough's dramatic essay about a teacher's strike in Anchorage points out how work in Alaska is different, how the stakes are raised in a land of both abundance and scarcity.

All of these people told how they came to live in Alaska: accident, luck, birth, or most often, a strong dose of wanderlust. This is the narrative that binds Alaskans, and most are proud they have figured out how to navigate the land. Yet in some ways, the terrain is similar to others. When Kay Landis is approached by a lone man bird-watching off a trail near Anchorage, she vacillates between fear and trust as a woman would anywhere.

The Alaskan spirit I found is also one of creativity and independence, so I had no problems finding writers. I tacked up my call for submissions everywhere I went and the manuscripts poured in. Frank Soos said he saw my call for submissions at the Laundromat in Talkeetna, and from him came an essay that embodies the freewheeling and intelligent, comic yet serious perspective that I met again and again in my travels.

I stuck to the usual destinations, and I know I missed a lot by not traveling farther afield. In a sense there are two worlds in Alaska: the life in the cities or larger towns that are connected by roads and electricity, and the life in towns that are reached only by plane or boat, and then only during certain times of the year. How these two worlds do not relate is viewed by Melissa S. Green, who writes about the laws for juvenile delinquents created by Congress in Washington, D.C. How can these possibly apply to the inhabitants of Aniak or Alakanuk?

This convergence of lives or cultures is seen in other essays included here. Mary Lockwood describes leading a blind Native woman home from the store—literally guiding her through the intersection of a Native's cache economy with the dollar economy of much of the country. And Naomi Warren Klouda, involved with a Sugpiak fisherman from Kodiak Island wonders, *How do you take yourself into another culture?* (And yet his children say to her, We look like you.) Through his spiritual encounters with the "little people," Steve Chamberlain, living with and among Native peoples, comes to know how some of them are more connected to the land.

As part of my travels, I went into Denali park for seven days of solo hiking and camping. Of course, one is rarely solo in Denali, despite the vastness of the park. People congregate at the campgrounds, talking over oatmeal and instant dinners while swatting away mosquitoes.

At the end of my trip, I found myself sharing a picnic table with an older woman, Charlotte, who was camped at Wonder Lake for a few weeks. This was an annual pilgrimage of hers, and everyone knew her. When I told her about this collection, she pointed me toward a dozen books. Like many Alaskans, she knew her history, treasured it, and wanted to be sure I knew it as well. She also had a lot to say about every bad book written on Alaska. She seemed to take these books as a personal offense; bad history is worse than no history. Charlotte was not the only Alaskan I met who was protective of her history and her land, which made me worry that Alaskans would not trust me with their stories. So I want to thank all of the writers who sent me their work, and especially the twenty writers here who entrusted me with their tales.

When I left the park, I noticed Charlotte was on the bus with me, out for a ride to see the land that she knew and loved. When we stopped at a rest area, she cornered me.

"Don't make a hash of Alaska, Susan," she said staring at me.

"I'll try not to," I promised. I felt the weight of her warning throughout this editorial process. I read and selected with care, and now offer twenty writers who, I believe, illuminate, define, and share Alaska through their beautiful writings. I hope Charlotte agrees.

Circumnavigation

Sherry Simpson

We were sitting in the Breakwater Bar, the sailors and I, planning the upcoming race around Admiralty Island. We had drilled ourselves hard during sprint races up and down Gastineau Channel, shaking down *Lyric* and ourselves. We had jibed and tacked, raised sails and lowered them, flung ourselves from port to starboard.

I was not a sailor. I was along as a reporter, an observer, an initiate. The sailors promised to teach me something about sailing, and I promised not to fall overboard. My mind still fumbled with the purer science of sailing, with the idea that sails sculpt wind to draw power. Every time the sailors spoke of aerodynamic force, hull resistance, drag ratios, and thrust, I nodded, but I heard only math not magic.

Now my arms ached as if I had been hoisting bags of cement. Broken blisters oozed on my palms. I washed the taste of brine from my lips with ale, recalling the way *Lyric* coursed around the stodgy tugboats, nipped under the towering bow of an anchored ocean liner.

I asked the sailors casually, "Why race around Admiralty Island?" It is something they do every summer solstice, launching themselves on a 210-mile circumnavigation around the huge island and back to Juneau. They sail night and day, pausing only for an overnight stop at Baranof Warm Springs. For a week they run away to sea, deserting families, jobs, identities. They call the race the Spirit of Adventure, and it's true it offers most elements of the best Alaskan contests: potential disaster, a test of skills undervalued by society, the chance to be pummeled by awful weather, a certain grandeur of vision, and relative pointlessness. It is practically irresistible.

The sailors considered my question, and then, in the intimate manner of the mildly intoxicated, one of them leaned against me and said the race illustrates the three essential conflicts she learned about in high school literature. She ticked them off against her fingers: Man against man. Man against nature. Man against self.

Bullshit, said her fellow sailor, the one drinking Jack Daniels—*it's all about terror and ecstasy.* That seemed right. We all raised our glasses to terror and ecstasy.

On the morning of the race, I lugged my waterproof duffel down the causeway of Harris Harbor. Swaddled in fog and drizzle, the world dissolved around the edges. The town of Juneau glistened and pulsed like a mirage, houses and buildings fading in and out. Douglas Island appeared to be drifting away from the mainland. Nothing resembled the certain lines of charts and maps I had studied the night before, hoping to memorize the outlines of the place we were sailing to.

From childhood on, I had explored local waters in all manner of vessels—as large and utilitarian as the state ferries, as small as my thirteen-foot skiff. On the water, I always moved slowly and gently, as if in the company of a wild animal whose attention I didn't wish to attract. They were the best days, those spent fishing for ocean-bright salmon coursing at unknown depths, or searching for whales near Shelter Island, or visiting uninhabited islands no larger than a high school gymnasium. Marine charts flag known dangers—lurking reefs, the thrust of rocks, unexpected shoals. But what I worried about was not marked on any chart I had ever seen. No navigational symbols warned of the absolute and utter way the sea can claim you, the complete indifference of its force. Even in the finest weather, I never forgot how quickly it can change—how fast wind can rise, how steadily waves can beat themselves higher and higher until, suddenly, returning to shore becomes a matter not of will but of absolute attention. And luck. Luck never hurts.

I descended the slippery gangway carefully, holding back against the steep cant. The tide was out. Boats of all character nudged the creaking docks like restless horses in a stable. Ravens hunched in the mist, one to a piling. In this unpromising dawn, I felt reluctant to abandon land's sweet and certain hold, so it was a relief to glance up and see three great blue herons floating overhead, their wings as silent and ashen as the clouds. A good omen, I thought. Forget the charts. Cling to portents.

Lyric rocked and swayed as the sailors stowed gear and unsnapped sail covers. A twenty-seven-foot Catalina, she was shaped like the camber of a gull's wing. But framed by the slip, she seemed cramped and slight among the comfortable houseboats, the sturdy, smelly fishing boats, the gleaming pleasure vessels. *Lyric's* spars looked reedy and bare without sails. The five of us stepped carefully around each other; the cabin was smaller than a college dorm room, the cockpit smaller yet. Except for the married couple who owned the boat, none of us knew each other well. I wondered if we would be speaking to each other at race's end.

The sailors checked lines and hoisted sails as we motored out of the harbor and into Gastineau Channel. A stiff breeze snapped the white cloth until we trimmed the sails tight as drumheads by hauling on the sheet ropes. The boat vibrated, strummed by wind and motion. With fourteen other sailboats, most larger than *Lyric,* we circled the bobbing markers like sharks, waiting for the 8 a.m. start flag. The sailors shouted insults at other boats cutting across our bow as skippers maneuvered for a good opening. My nervousness evaporated in the high spirits.

When the red flag shot up the start boat's mast, we surged into a commotion of sails and bows and cheers. At the mark, *Lyric* tacked sharply across the channel, but boats in better positions outpointed us, sailing closer to the wind and quickly gaining distance. Our enthusiasm ebbed as we fell behind. We were not the last boat, but we were not far ahead of it. A lot can happen in this race, the sailors told each other. *Just wait. We'll catch up.*

We split into two shifts, and the other watch went below, beginning the schedule of three hours on, three hours off. A steady head wind lulled us into a rhythm of tacking back and forth across the channel, but the tide flowed against us, and we didn't actually seem to be going anywhere. Mesmerized by the scrolling waves, I lapsed into a cottony reverie. A fair-weather boater only, I have always tethered myself close to shore, allowing only my imagination to hover over the abyss. Long ago this coast was named and charted, but I yearned to feel what the early explorers did as they slipped into bays, rounded dark islands, searched the unfamiliar sky and water for omens. Everything they encountered became a revelation. Seldom in our lives do we have the chance to set sail toward a new world.

Not everyone returns, even from the most modest of expeditions. Boats are found drifting, or never found at all. Wreckage washes up on empty shores. Bodies float low like waterlogged driftwood, nibbled into anonymity by the sea and its creatures. From the safety of land we invent fates for those who don't come back. Sea lions capsized their kayaks. He hit his head and fell overboard. A rogue wave crashed over the stern. Lost at sea, we say, they are lost at sea. Once I read about a lighthouse keeper who, with his partner, took his small boat to cut a Christmas tree near Cross Sound. But the engine died, and the ocean carried him away. His partner last saw him sitting in the skiff with arms akimbo, as calm as if he had already accepted the great blankness that awaited him. Fishermen who searched for him finally found the empty boat a hundred miles away.

A thump against the hull startled us. I turned to gauge how far we had sailed in the past few hours, but grayness had closed behind us. Ahead, Gastineau Channel opened into a great bowl of sea rimmed by shadowy islands. We looked about for whatever knocked against the boat—driftwood? a loose buoy?—until the best sailor emerged from the cabin, recognized the sloppy way the mainsail spilled air, and shouted at us. Under bracing gusts of curses, we tightened the sails and ourselves. He seized the tiller, and the boat quickened under his sure hand.

Just as we broke the tide's grip and slipped into Stephens Passage, a southeasterly wind gulped us whole. Before, it had all seemed so familiar: the same endless trinity of ocean, mountain, and forest. Suddenly, I recognized nothing. Whitecaps curled as four-foot seas climbed up each other. Spray whipped off waves the way blowing snow streams from mountain peaks. Like a bully in a schoolyard fight, thirty-five-knot winds shoved *Lyric* over, testing how far she would heel without capsizing. Hard rain stuttered across the water. The boat surged and tossed, and waves spewed over the bow.

My stomach churned, from motion sickness and perhaps panic. I had never taken the wind so personally. Somehow I felt that my fear had invoked this storm. I should have known better than to venture into waters I didn't know, with people who were strangers, on a boat I didn't really understand. All I could do was crouch in the stern and stare at the mainland, trying to fix my eyes on something stable.

Time lost hold of us as *Lyric* beat on long tacks that drew us close to Admiralty Island's rocky, log-strewn shores, then swept us away. We swung on the end of a pendulum, motion without progress. The sails bellied and strained with too much wind, overpowering the boat. Eventually, the sailors climbed into neon-orange survival suits and strapped on lifelines. Two of them staggered onto the foredeck to reef the mainsail, diminishing its size to reduce the wind's effect. For the first time, I realized there was no spare survival suit for me. I cast about, thinking of things that float. Ice chest? Seat cushions in the cabin? I tried to remember if anyone had showed me where the life jackets were stowed.

I stopped worrying about flotation devices when I realized the port side rails lining the deck were dashing over and over into the foaming black water. Instinctively, I leaned away from that side of the boat. In our practice runs, the captain assured me that he had never dipped the side rails. I thought hard about this, trying to understand exactly what he meant. Surely he hadn't lied. But could this actually have been the first time the boat had heeled over that far? Did that mean this was the worst storm he had ever sailed in? Did he really know what he was doing? Watching the rails submerge repeatedly, I tried to sense through the hull that fulcrum beyond which the boat would not roll upright again.

The sailors returned to the mast and braced themselves against the heaving foredeck. They ducked their heads against the rain as they dropped the mainsail in jerks and prepared to raise a smaller one. The wind shrouded them in canvas, and they struggled against the wet sail while trying to keep their footing. When they shoved the mainsail toward us to stuff into the cabin, I studied their faces for signs of fear, or worse, but I saw only ferocious concentration and a crazed kind of exhilaration.

As the gale continued and the sailors tired, they decided to conserve strength by returning to our watch schedule. I gathered my helplessness and went below. The others dug themselves into sleeping bags and instantly dozed. I slumped on a berth and stared through the opposite porthole, captured by the way the pitching window presented alternating views of clouds before it plunged below the green-black water. Sky, then sea. Sky, then sea.

The cabin was close and humid, and my dread escaped the mental choke hold I had clamped upon it. I imagined being trapped below deck should the boat capsize. Then I saw myself in my yellow slicker, struggling toward dim green light above. Frigid water poured into my boots and flooded my overalls, dragging me below. I swallowed the sea. It filled my mouth and lungs and belly. Down and down I drifted, hands limp and white, hair floating upward. My eyes remained open in the darkness, the cold ocean pressing against them.

And now I dwelled on my private horror: crabs settling on my body, flounders writhing across me, colonies of small creatures slipping under my clothes and then under my skin, picking and chewing and gnawing.

I mourned my husband, as if he were lost to me and not I to him.

The intense desire to throw up shoved panic away. I felt almost grateful. Surely I couldn't be so far gone if I feared the humiliation of puking in the cabin more than drowning in it. Climbing topside, I reeled to the stern and vomited in wrenching bursts. The sailors didn't notice. I was glad; it's one thing to die, but another to die as a known coward. I leaned against the gunwale, head hanging overboard, and watched the way waves folded into each other, green marble skeined by white foam. Cold rain soaked my head and sopped my jacket collar. Even the insides of my ears were wet. I was too miserable to pray, so over and over I pictured the morning's three herons and the solemn way they winged out of the fog.

I don't know when I realized the gale was subsiding, the sound of high weather fading like a distant radio station. I would have been relieved if I were not so tired, so bruised by fear. This is only the first day, I thought; what else could happen during our journey? I longed to be home, back in my ordinary life.

At 9 p.m., the watch changed, and it was time to be useful. My shift tried to regain lost time by harvesting failing winds to power *Lyric* across the strait. How peaceful, this serene motion across a calming sea. Our tasks seemed so simple after the afternoon's frantic efforts.

One sail floated behind us, a white signal against the dimming light. For all our impotent motion, we were still not last. The other ships forged ahead along the storm's edge. Later, when we heard that *Arrogant's* mainsail blew out and *Casa Mia's* seacocks flooded with water, I felt absurdly satisfied knowing that my fear wasn't misplaced.

Across the passage, darkness flowed from sea into sky. When it was time to go below, I wedged myself into a bunk, still wearing wet clothes that twisted and rubbed uncomfortably against the damp sleeping bag. Sleep was a wave rolling me over and over against the shore. When the sailor who wanted my bunk shook me awake for the 3 a.m. to 6 a.m. shift, I mumbled, "Okay," but the absence of motion confused me. For several dazed moments, I didn't know where I was.

On deck, cool salty air washed against my face. Indistinct shapes crowded the horizon. Far off—impossible to say how far in this flat light—icebergs as big as houses glowed with their own faint blue auras. I propped myself against the gunwales and drowsed, tucking my hands under my arms for warmth. My head dangled painfully, lolling against my shoulder as I drifted off, then jerked awake. Across the water, I heard wordless singing and the sound of people murmuring. Someone was calling me, I thought, struggling to make out the words. Perhaps I dreamed.

In the slow swell of dawn, the sea stretched before us like time, large enough to swallow all history, legend, desire, imagination. I felt the burden of my own story floating away, as if I had rolled up yesterday's fear like parchment, tucked it into a bottle, and sent it off on some other current, not knowing who might read it and understand. We sailed on an ocean awash in the stories of all those who came before us in cedar canoes, sloops of war, merchant schooners, steamers, freighters, fishing boats, dories. In the ghostly light, they moved with us—the Tlingit Indians; the Russian, British, and American explorers; the seafarers and traders; the settlers and sailors; everyone who ever imagined themselves, like me, to be the first to witness this place.

I had studied charts with creases worn soft as flannel, read chronicles and folklore, and now I felt us slipping by secret harbors where bear hunters lived and foreign sailors sought refuge. I peered at reefs where ships foundered and their passengers with them. We passed abandoned Tlingit forts, lost villages, and all the unmarked places where Natives found marble for polishing wood and stone carvings, or raked up green ribbons of kelp pearled with herring roe, or set halibut hooks carved with human faces down at the bottom of the sea.

Sorrow and loss washed up along these shores, too. The wind pushed us beyond islands where fox farms rot into the forest, past the crooked inlet where a cross marks the place where mother and child drowned, away from the killing rock where Tlingits sacrificed slaves for potlatches.

During our journey, history crested in wave after wave, ebbing into myth, dissolving into time like handfuls of salt tossed into the sea. There were ways to mark our passage, methods of triangulation and calculation that could reveal exactly where we were. There were chronicles that could fix us squarely in the flow of events. I preferred to let the metronome of tides measure out the journey.

In the storm's wake, sunny skies brought air so still that for two days we drifted becalmed and fell still further behind the race leaders. The slightest breeze wrinkling across the water provoked *Lyric's* crew into a frenzy. They raised the filmy spinnaker to make a kind of sail called a drifter, a silken square so fine it captured any exhalation. Light glowed through the cloth like rays through stained glass. We slipped from one rippled patch of water to another, craving motion, no matter how meager. Ghosting, the sailors called it.

The change in weather was not received well by the sailors. They languished in a sort of mental doldrums, cross because we had mired in dead air. They quarreled good-naturedly about which sail to try next, what we should have done at the starting line, which shift was more skilled, whose boat would win. They cursed the winds, their luck, each other. They rarely spoke of themselves or of anything besides sailing. Their ordinary existence was stranded on the other side of the storm.

I left some part of myself behind, too. The race no longer mattered to me. My notes grew ever more cryptic with the kind of sightings and observations that would fill the log of someone lost at sea: "Wind slight. Nursed spinnaker along for three hours." Or "Halyard's jammed. Captain went up in bosun's chair." I felt pleasantly doomed, but *Lyric's* sailors never gave up. If they could have paddled the boat with hands and feet, they would have. They drank canned beer, adjusted ropes and rigging, and imagined all the ways they could still win. I dangled my feet over the side and spit at my wavering shadow. The spit moved faster than we did.

I supposed they had fiercer hearts than I. I liked not being afraid. I liked these long hours of reflected heat and light. I was becalmed, too, as if I had entered some strange latitude where false tranquility stills all desire and motion. But fear remained something I could taste on my lips, a briny, bitter tang I could lick from my skin. Some people seek a sense of peace in Alaska, but it is fear that binds me to this landscape—fear of what I might find or lose, fear of what might find or lose me, out here where everything seems familiar and foreign, all at once. Alaska is big enough to cradle every true fear and hope we can bear. Why else would I have been out there, far from every safe harbor I've ever known?

For hours I studied the impassive shoreline of Admiralty Island, looming like an undiscovered continent to starboard. Through binoculars I peered at reticulated beaches, bays folded into ciphers, the toothy jaws of mountains clapped against the sky. Thick, deep forest draped the slopes, and sometimes the green scent of spruce and hemlock trees enveloped us. Knowing that brown bears and deer roamed the shoreline just beyond sight, I felt their eyes upon us. If I stepped onto the shore of the enormous island, the forest would have swallowed me as surely as the ocean.

All day long, creatures flew or swam past on their own unknowable journeys. Harbor porpoises inscribed perfect arcs. Ravens flapped overhead, every stroke of their black wings thunderous in the quiet. For once they said nothing and merely cocked their heads to see us clinging to flotsam. A few hundred yards away, two humpback whales fanned scalloped flukes before diving. A sea lion rolled past, turning brimming eyes toward us, calling in a garbled tongue that unsettled me.

I shielded my face from the sun's painful light and gazed into mossy green depths, trying to picture the underwater landscape we passed over like a small cloud casting shadows. Schools of fingerlings flashed and twisted in eerie unison. Orange globular jellyfish contracted and expanded like lungs. Rafts of brown rockweed and strips of bull kelp threatened to entangle us. I leaned over too far, and my sunglasses slid off my face and spiraled into darkness.

On the third morning we passed Yasha Island, a tiny speck that marked the entrance to Chatham Strait on the western flank of Admiralty. Bald eagles owned the island, two score perched in spruce trees or hunkered on the rocks. Suddenly, a sailor shouted and pointed. An eagle plummeted to the water's surface to snatch at something, but something snatched it. The bird struggled, wings smashing and beating as it sank below the surface. We watched, but the eagle did not reappear. The sailors wondered what could seize such a powerful bird. I pictured the eagle soaring underwater, bubbles trailing from its feathers as it descended.

At night, when all aspects of land, sea, and sky merged, splashings and murmurings and gurglings became urgent mysteries. I expected fabulous sea creatures to rise thrashing from below and crush us in their beaks, tentacles, jaws. Decades ago, at the junction of Chatham and Peril Straits, two Juneau men of impeccable reputation claimed they had spotted a sea serpent three hundred feet long gliding in the water. They peppered the greenish-blue monster with gunfire, and it sank, writhing. The men waited for its carcass to float to the surface, but returned to Juneau with nothing but legend. It was not enough to see a monster; they had to own it, too.

I had no need to invent dangers. It was enough to think of unmarked reefs, sudden storms, collisions with other vessels. I had no need to invent dangers, but I did, in those smothering moments before exhaustion dragged me into unconsciousness. And when the fantastic did appear, when humpback whales snorted and heaved around the boat, I floated so far away in sleep that my companions could not call me back.

So we drifted, suspended on the cusp between heaven and sea, sea and earth, between what is above and what is below.

⊚

On the fifth day, the wind rose. We saw it coming in the way the seas gathered in a black line along the horizon, like the shadow of an eclipse racing toward us. For a moment, I was afraid. Not another storm, I thought. But then I realized how much I craved wind and motion after the long, silent hours. No worse fate for sailors than stillness.

We leapt about, yanking ropes, raising sails, making the ship ready. Waves arrived first, smacking against the hull. Then wind rolled over the boat, strumming the rigging, billowing the canvas, infusing us with a blue desire. Silence fell behind as the bow hissed and sails hummed. *Lyric* quickened. This was what she was made for.

When the sailors felt sated by the wind, they urged me to take the helm, to understand their complicated joy. Already they knew that despite their longing and skill, they would not win this race. They could afford to be generous. You are ready, they told me. It was my turn to sail.

I did not steer the boat; I gave myself over to a physics of ·intuition. Through my hands, I discovered the invisible place where the boat bound together wind and sea and glided along the seam it created with each moment. Air surged around me, and finally pierced me.

And when, too soon, the wind faltered, sails fluttered and fell limp, and the boat subsided, the world settled into an unfortunate equilibrium. I realized that most of the time, I think too much.

We sail in search of terror and ecstasy, the sailor said, and he was right.

⊚

In Southeast Alaska, there exist more bays, more inlets, more islands than you can imagine. As one of the last blank spaces on eighteenth-century maps, the archipelago became a promising destination for those making their imperial voyages of discovery. Three times Spanish mariners stepped ashore to claim this territory for their crown. Once, they had barely returned to their ship when they saw the Tlingits dragging away the large white cross the Spaniards had just erected to signify possession and benediction of the New World by the Old.

As the outlines of land and sea took shape on charts, others followed. Traders swept through, exchanging trinkets for furs. Captain George Vancouver surveyed the coastline inch by inch, searching for the Northwest Passage. He scattered like party favors the names of sovereigns, relatives, and people worth flattering: Seymour Canal, Stephens Passage, Chatham Strait, and hundreds of others. The Russians took what was never theirs and sold it to the Americans. The Americans sent soldiers, missionaries, tourists. For a long while, the Tlingits resisted these various occupations, and many still do.

In Southeast Alaska, there exist more beaches, more mountains, more secrets than I can ever know. How many others before me impaled themselves against these rocks, slipped gratefully below the surface, drifted out to sea? I stared at charts, sounded the depths, marked the hazards, and still I had to accept the rapture of the deep, a darkness I could never penetrate, a chaos I will never control. I didn't want to look into the abyss, and I couldn't help but look. I relinquished the useless fantasy of possession, realizing there is only surrender. This is how the lost lighthouse keeper must have felt as he floated away toward his destiny.

At midnight on our last night at sea, I apprenticed myself to air. I lay flat against the foredeck, each hand wrapped around a rope that controlled an edge of the drifter. The sail spread above me, slight as a whisper, radiantly paned in summer twilight. A minnow of air wriggled over the boat. I cast the drifter like a gentle net. The cloth trembled, luffed. I teased the ropes that leashed the sail that held the air. The boat answered. All along my body, I sensed it stirring below me. We ghosted.

For hours I submerged myself in this simple task, anticipating the breeze, gathering and easing the sail in response. I breathed through my hands. Remembering the storm, I finally understood that the sailors did not fight the wind. They embraced it. They shaped the boat and themselves to it.

The sailors said nothing to me. I was in another place, and in that place, I did not need their help or their words. A cruise ship steamed by to port, glowing like a chandelier, and I barely glanced. Nothing seemed so filled with light as that sail. The sky deepened into indigo clarity, but I refused to be swallowed. The sail, the wind, the rasp of rope against my palms—this seemed enough.

Then, a humpback whale moaned. It pealed like a clapper struck against the dark bell of the ocean. It was a foghorn, a tuning fork, the purest note that harmonizes longing and fulfillment. It was the edge of the world. I fell.

The Tangle River

David Abrams

In my father's house, fly-fishing was often discussed but seldom practiced, just as my father preached from the pulpit each Sunday about humility, kindness, and occasionally love but rarely put them to good use either.

It wasn't until years later, the summer we came together in Alaska, that his rabid self-defense of both piety and angling first cracked, and I caught a glimpse of something soft and quivering—pink as a just-birthed mammal—within the Abrams armor. Of course, the light slanting off the central Alaska landscape could have had a lot to do with it. The Last Frontier has an unnerving effect on even the most careful of charlatans, a group for which my dear father was high priest for many years.

He built his reputation as a fly-fisherman from the weekly newspaper column he wrote for seven years in our small Wyoming town: "Outdoors with Dan Abrams." Below the standing headline each week, a pen-and-ink fisherman stood hip-deep in a mountain stream.

That fisherman was not my father. He sat at home in his recliner where, when he reclined, he could look at the antelope head mounted on the living room wall above him. He read every magazine that came in the mail—*Outdoor Life, Sports Afield, Field and Stream*—working himself into a fever of machismo, a hot lather of inspiration. Then he spent weeks planning for his outdoor odysseys—hunting, fishing, or camping in two-day bursts—from which he drew three months of newspaper columns. When members of his Baptist church asked how he sandwiched so much adventure between weddings, funerals, and sermon-writing, he never lied. "It's not easy," he sighed.

My father won numerous newspaper awards for writing about the best ways to dress big game animals, backpack in the Wind River Mountains, and match dry fly patterns to the insect hatch. Once, he even won the Outdoor Writers Association of America's prestigious Buck Knife Award for a nostalgic article about the time he and I hunted sage grouse near Riverton.

It was one of the few times we hunted together. I shot wild and high when the grouse exploded from the prairie, and we drove home empty-handed. He never mentioned my poor aim in his prize-winning article.

On another hunting trip, this time through waist-deep snow in a fruitless search for elk, I carried his candy bars and rifle like a jungle safari porter.

We'd moved to northern Wyoming when I was eight years old and, after an initial, euphoric blitz on the area's rivers, my father's daily trips to the Snake, the Firehole, and the Yellowstone dwindled to weekends, then monthly excursions, then only on national holidays; and finally he made a showy spectacle over wetting his line on opening day in April. By the time I was in sixth grade, he spoke of the wild waters the way a parent wistfully talks about a wayward child he hasn't seen in years.

As much as my father enjoyed the Rocky Mountains of the Lower 48, he panted like a horny schoolboy for the Upper 49th. If Wyoming was a fisherman's paradise, then Alaska was something higher than heaven, a fish-filled stratosphere of ecstasy. He could never afford the time or money for his great northern safari, and so he had to resign himself to living on the banks of what were universally agreed to be the best trout waters of Wyoming, Idaho, and Montana.

"Someday," he said to us in a husky whisper, "someday I'll make it to Alaska." We believed him like we'd believe the Publishers Clearing House folks were standing outside our front door with an oversized check and a balloon bouquet.

We watched my father with pity as, with eyes closed and a smile misting his lips, he made invisible casts from his recliner, all the time dreaming he was on the banks of the Gulkana or on the decks of a Valdez fishing charter. The salmon leapt into his lap like manna from heaven.

Fish swam throughout my father's Sunday services in schools of metaphors. He peppered his sermons with images that described predestined salvation as "God's well-timed cast" landing upstream where we, as "unsuspecting trout," waited to be "hooked into the kingdom of God." Instead of saying productive Christians should "bear good fruit in keeping with their faith," he altered the passage to include something about "a creelful of keepers." Few people sitting in the pews suspected he hadn't got his waders wet in months.

In those guileless days of my middle childhood, I admit he trapped me in his spell. I read his fishing articles and believed he spent his spare time wandering the banks of local rivers. And when I do remember My Father the Angler, these are my landmark images: the nicks in his hands from embedded hooks, the smell of fish oil filtering from his clothes. The times he caught fish—as infrequent as national holidays—he stood at the sink, poking heads, tails, and fins into the garbage disposal, and his eyes sparkled as the whole house filled with the heavy perfume of trout.

I waited for him to teach me the mysteries of fish, to lead me by the hand along the Snake River, pointing out the character of the current. Nothing happened.

The one time we came together for a casting lesson, it was not on the banks of the Snake but in our backyard.

I stood with my hands in my pockets as he strung up the nine-foot graphite rod and tied a barbless streamer fly to the end of the leader. "You pass the line through the eye of the hook, then wrap the end back around the leader," he explained, braiding the monofilament. "Then you make a loop, pass it through, then once again through the other loop, pull it tight, and there you have it." His voice was quick and complicated as an instruction manual, and he finished the clinch knot before I could even see what his fingers were doing.

"Now, let's pretend that crabapple tree over there is a pool in the stream you're casting to," he said and placed the fly rod in my hands. The cork handle squeaked against my sweaty palm. I was twelve years old and still believed I could please him.

I pulled orange line from the reel and whipped the rod from side to side. I remembered the motion from reading one of his newspaper columns.

"No, no," he said. "Here, like this." He stepped behind me, circled his arms around my body, and started casting vigorously as my right hand clenched the butt of the rod, trying to feel that secret rhythm of casting. "You bring it to the ten o'clock position and stop. Count to three, then snap the wrist forward."

The line whistled through the air, the fly popping at the end of each cast as he took control of the rod and my hands. The cork squeaked in my hand and my teeth clacked as he pumped my arm back and forth.

"Ten o'clock, stop, snap! Ten o'clock, stop, snap!"

I went to bed that night mumbling the magic formula over and over, my right arm throbbing. I dreamed of lines knotted and kinked by the wind, of trout swimming through the grass of my backyard, and of my father standing on the opposite bank of an impossibly wide river.

Many years later, I left home and, like the prodigal son, went my own way. That is to say, I became a practicing fisherman.

I moved to Oregon, Montana, and, yes, Alaska, in which places I fished the Willamette, the Madison, and the Chatanika Rivers. When I took my first tentative step into the Madison River and was nearly swept downstream, I realized how little I knew about water. Undaunted, I taught myself how to wade icy streams, navigating the slippery rocks as if I'd been doing it for years. I learned to choose the most trout-tempting fly patterns, to tie secure knots, and to remove hooks from the jaws of madly flipping fish.

I did not purposefully look for traces of my father as I walked the cobblestone banks, but still I heard his condescending voice in the gurgling current telling me the best way to read the river.

When I mentioned my new interest in fishing during a phone conversation, I received a package in the mail two weeks later. Inside were boxes of flies, reels, leaders, diagrams of knots, and a three-page single-spaced letter of fishing tips. I vowed not to bring this on myself again.

Once—when I was married, fathering my own children and living in Eugene, Oregon, with a cushion of miles between my father and me—I went fishing with a friend whose father was also a self-proclaimed sportsman. My friend knew as little about catching trout as I did, and we both approached the fishing trip with impatience and aggression. The day before, we packed our gear and vowed, "Come hell or high water, we're going fishing." Flames danced in our eyes when we talked about the trout we'd bring home.

We drove down the interstate, turned onto a state highway, and finally pulled off at a single-lane logging road that led us to a spot on the McKenzie River where my friend had heard the biting was good.

We tied our flies to the line with fingers as thick and clumsy as sausages. When we cast out on the water, our lines scrambled in a network of knots and confusion.

We fished for an hour. Our flies were on the water for, at the most, twenty minutes. The rest of the time they were hooked on the dark pines behind us, wrapped around our legs, or snagged on underwater hazards.

Exhausted from the strain of not catching anything, my friend and I sat on the banks and ate cold ham sandwiches and talked about work, children, God—anything but our fathers. We could be honest about many things, but not when it came to the real reason we'd just spent half a day in anger and frustration on the water. Our fathers lurked like logs under the surface.

Half an hour before we left, we looked upstream and watched, stunned, as an osprey swooped along the river channel toward us. Neat as a sanitation worker stabbing a piece of trash, the osprey sank its talons in the river and came up with a fish.

My friend and I drove home, trembling with excitement and anger. That week, when I talked to my father on the phone, I purposefully did not mention being skunked by a bird. The very thought of hearing his voice say the word "hook" depressed me.

Years later, when my father came to Alaska for a visit and we camped along the banks of the Tangle River, I strung up my rod without saying a word, unsure how to act around him as he busied himself with his gear. He'd begun planning this trip six months earlier, when five tons of snow lay heavy on the waters and the fish slumbered beneath the ice.

There was unmistakable tension between us. After all, I'd entered paradise before him. I'd moved to Fairbanks in the dead of winter seven months before my father's visit, and already I'd cut holes in the ice of Harding Lake and pulled warm trout from the dark water below. Several times that spring, I'd haunted the shores of that same lake, gently assassinating the fish who came to feed at the edge of the ice during breakup. And then there was the early-season salmon trip to Montana Creek that I didn't even have the heart to mention to my father during our long-distance phone conversations. His voice was already distorted with jealousy. The forty-five-pound king I wrestled out of Montana would surely break his spirit.

But now here he was, on the banks of the Tangle River and bristling like a child on Christmas Eve.

"Take it easy, Dad," I said. "We've got all day and most of the night."

"I'm fine, I'm fine," he said, blowing on the drab fly to fluff the hackle. Nervous spittle from his mouth clung to the tips of the elk hairs.

His fishing vest bulged with nail clippers, hooks, coiled tippets, and enough flies to make him look like a wild fur-and-feather beast. He said his new graphite rod cost more than four hundred dollars, and by the amount of time he spent attaching the reel and fitting the sections together, I saw he was determined to get his money's worth.

Finally, he said in a voice that chimed like bells, "Let's go hit the water."

The Tangle River is less than two miles long, a short, snake-shaped stretch of water connecting Long Tangle Lake to Round Tangle Lake in central Alaska near the town of Paxson. The lakes and their umbilical river lie in one of those shallow valleys for which Interior Alaska is famous. The terrain has been scooped by bulldozing glaciers, yes; but it's also been smoothed and patted back into a gentle undulation of eskers, muskeg, and puddle lakes. The landscape couldn't have been more different from the jagged upthrust of the Wyoming Rockies in my father's backyard.

Grayling and lake trout frolicked in the Tangle River, spawning in its glacial waters like hormone-crazy teenagers. The word "tangle" is a descriptive term for the maze of lakes and streams in the drainage system. In the seven square miles sur-rounding us, hundreds of braided channels and melted glaciers outnumbered patches of dry land where we could be sure of our footing. As my father and I walked with our fly rods held high, it was hard to think of the water as anything but metaphor.

The land around us glittered with the thousand waters of the state's year-round moisture. The bog slowed us down, sucked at our boots. I turned to warn my father about lacing up tighter, but his face was already wrapped in a dreamy, foggy gaze. He was looking at the New Jerusalem rising from the Alaskan tundra. Any minute now, the Four Horsemen would come galloping across the muskeg.

Instead of the Book of Revelation, I thought of Genesis: this was something closer to Noah, wringing out his clothes after the ark ride.

It was nearly ten o'clock at night when we approached the Tangle River. At two hours short of midnight, the sun still burned brightly. My father, unaccustomed to the twenty-four-hour daylight of Alaska's summers, blinked and shaded his eyes as he searched the water for what he called "dimples," places where the trout rose to gulp insects from the surface but never fully broke the tensile strength of the water. A dimple is to a fly-fisherman what rustling vegetation is to a hunter. For one brief moment, he can pinpoint the feeding fish before it submerges again to the riverbed. Though hunting requires proper aim and gentle trigger squeeze, fly-fishing involves not only aiming and casting but also grace—breathing life into a feather-and-tinsel fly through fifty feet of line.

My father pulled line from his reel with a sharp ratcheting sound and flung his fly halfway to the opposite bank. When it hit the water, he sighed—a sound of exhilaration, long pent up inside his chest. I watched as he pulled the line back with his left hand, the fly skimming the slow current like a surfer. A white wake trailed the hook.

"The idea is to work the whole stream," he said.

I nodded, biting my lip, and moved upriver away from him.

I stood at the mouth of the river, where Long Tangle Lake emptied southward. Here, the current was warm and nearly silent, save for the spots where it brushed against the long grass of the banks. The shallow river gradually deepened as it moved away from the parental lake. Grayling the size of minnows flitted among the small rocks. These were the immature fish, the ones who'd bite at anything as they swam in schools less than a hundred feet from the lake where they'd hatched. As I watched the river, twenty mouths the size of pencil tips broke the surface like a short violent hailstorm. A caddis fly, dipping too near the river, had just fallen prey to the feeding frenzy. I thought of casting, but knew that even the smallest hook in my box of flies would be larger than the heads on most of these fish.

I heard a sharp "Hey! Got one!" and turned to see my father set the hook. He brought his arms up like a referee calling a touchdown and a five-inch grayling flew over his head, landing in the dirt ten feet behind him.

As I walked downstream to my father, he twisted the hook out of the grayling's mouth. A tiny ooze of blood seeped from one corner of its jaw. The fish was young and soft. One firm squeeze from my father's hand would mash it to a pulp of scales, fins, and bones.

"Not worth keeping, is he?" my father said as he dunked the fish back into the water. "We might as well throw him back."

I thought of my father's sermon on the prodigal son. The same cycle of sermons was resurrected every five years, and I'd heard his commentary on the New Testament parable at least four times. I pictured him leaning over the pulpit, purposefully not looking at me sitting in the back pew. As I stood on the banks of the Tangle River, I tried to remember the tone of his voice when he preached that sermon but found I couldn't. I wondered if he'd found fault with the father who let his son go out into the corrupt world or with the child who rejected the love and security of his family.

There were, I realized, layers upon layers of invitation and promise in my father's voice (and I'm speaking now of his Sunday voice, which, as with most men of the cloth, is different than his Monday-through-Saturday voice). For that hour each week, his baritone was barbed with the mysteries of mercy, the promise of salvation, and, as I was now realizing, the tease of a paradise like Alaska.

Suddenly, I remembered its high, lingering pitch. I could almost hear it mixed into the current of the Tangle River and wondered, with a stab of guilt, if I'd been the one to short-change the relationship with my father.

Together, we watched the young grayling swim to the middle of the river. "He'll be fine," my father said, staring at the water long after the grayling was gone.

"Let's move downstream," I said, hoping we'd find larger, more athletic fish in the stronger current.

"It's worth a try," he said. It was a cool evening, but his forehead glistened with sweat. The mosquitoes were out in full force, diving in and out for his blood, but he didn't even seem to notice their stings. He moistened his lips and looked at the river, as if the two of them were lovers reunited after a long absence. I led the way as we walked along the riverbank, keeping pace with the current. I tried to imagine myself doing this when I was nine years old but couldn't. My father followed close behind, brushing loudly through the grass.

In that moment, I felt an invisible pane of glass break inside me and a flood of conflicting emotions, strong as the current at our feet, rush and tumble from my heart to my head and back again. Mixed with my bitterness was an unfamiliar feeling of sorrow for my father, for all the moments like this he'd missed. This and every other river in the world had always been here, flowing over the rocks and mud and grass at the same unwavering pace, waiting for him, for us. All the words he'd ever written or spoken had failed to bring us any nearer to the water.

It had taken the land, Alaska in all its prehistoric barrenness, to bring us together. Prehistory. That was it. Maybe this was the river of Genesis, the first river of the world. I stopped walking, caught up short at the irony of the thought.

My father also paused, raised his head. "What is it, son?"

I looked at him, trying to put the land into words. The water sang, the mosquitoes hummed. "This place..."

"Sure is something, isn't it?" He cocked his head and eyed the low sun.

"Something," I said. "Yeah, something."

"Well," he shook himself...as if he, too, had seen the chink in the armor. "Those grayling are waiting for us."

When the Tangle River crossed under the Denali Highway bridge, it took on an entirely different character of water and fish. My father and I walked to a spot where the river was narrow and mean, lashed to a gray froth like an ocean in the winter. Here the sound of a million drops of water roaring across the submerged rocks drowned out all but the most necessary words between us. "There," he said and pointed at an exposed flat rock, large as a table, ten feet from shore.

I analyzed the architecture of the river with my self-trained eye. I would have picked something a little closer, where I could drop my fly off the rod tip straight into the water and let the current wash it downstream. I'd worked this kind of water before and never had much success. I was frustrated by how quickly my dry flies got sucked under after hitting the choppy riffles. No trout would be tempted by a soggy hunk of feathers and deer hair, I thought.

Just below the rock the river smoothed briefly before breaking up again.

"That's where the fish are," my father said, standing at my elbow. I flinched at the sound of his voice. He'd watched me study the river. "Go ahead," he said. "See where the stream divides around that rock? That's where you want to put your fly, then let it float down to the pool." I hesitated and he said, "It's okay if your fly goes under the surface."

I looked at him, my face pinching sharply. A drenched dry fly? I didn't remember reading that technique in any of his newspaper articles.

"Trust me," he said.

I took the fly between my fingers and blew on the hackle to dry it, then tossed it into the river and stripped out line, enough to reach the rock. Since I was surrounded by a dense ring of willows, I couldn't bring the rod tip up to the ten o'clock position, so I tried a roll cast. With a tight swirl of my rod, the line spiraled out, flipping the fly upstream of the rock.

"Nice cast," my father said. He stood on the bank with his rod in his hands. He raised his eyebrows and jutted out his lower lip in genuine surprise at the success of my cast. I'd worked for months to find the right rhythm of the roll cast.

Just as I feared, my fly dipped below the surface, caught in the tug of the river. But then, at the base of the rock, it did a very surprising thing. Instead of sinking to the bottom, it popped back up like a cork and hovered in the pool for several seconds before the line, also caught in the current, dragged it downstream. I knew those few moments on the surface of the pool were enough to catch the attention of any fish below.

"Hey," I said. "It works."

"Of course it does."

I lifted the tip of my rod and cast upstream again and again, working the same lane of the river until finally, on the one perfect trip around the rock, we saw a small splash and the fly completely disappeared.

I heard my father say, "Now!" But I didn't need to be coached. I pulled down on the line with my left hand and raised the rod with my right hand. The line filled with an electric tension that hummed between my fingers. If I'd touched my father, I could have zapped him with a shock.

"Bring him in close and I'll grab him." My father leaned out over the water, reaching for the leader. Wrapping it between his fingers, he pulled the fish onto the bank and we both stared at the two-pound grayling. It was a vision of wild beauty. It flipped once, then stilled under my father's hand as he spread its large, sail-like dorsal fin.

"Look at that," he said. "This is one of the biggest ones I've ever seen."

I didn't doubt him for a second.

He pulled a buck knife from his fishing vest and sliced through the belly. I helped him scoop out the heart, the stomach, the gills and within minutes we both reeked of fish musk.

I held the gutted grayling between my hands and my father took a picture.

"Well," he said as he washed his hands in the stream, "let's see you do that again."

"What about you, Dad? Don't you want to fish, too?"

"Oh, maybe I will a little later on. But first let's see you catch some more." There was a wary catch in his voice—not the confident baritone of Sunday mornings, but the troubled tenor of someone shoved up against a lie.

He nestled his fly rod in the crook of a nearby tree, then lowered himself to the ground. I looked at him, then nodded without saying anything else. I realized my father had come all the way to Alaska, marched the whole distance to his glacial Zion, to watch me fish. He was counting on me to catch my limit, to soak my hands in fish oil.

I blew on the fly and tossed it in the water again, conscious of my every move. I felt his eyes on my wrists, my rod, my fly. I thought of his hands covering mine that day in the backyard as he and I cast toward the crab apple tree. "That's it," he'd said, then and now. "That's it."

Another fish hit my fly. And another. And another. My creel filled with fish—fat grayling, the wily ones who had eluded fishermen for many summers. My father spent most of his time watching my roll casts spiral upstream, the wet thin line sparkling in the sun.

At the end of the day, he said, "I'll say this much, you've turned out to be a darn good caster." I barely heard his voice above the roar of the water.

After so many years the words were unexpected, like a hook snagging a rock in an otherwise easy stretch of water. I knew it was the highest praise he'd ever give me. I turned upstream so he couldn't see my face and all that rippled on its surface. After all, in my father's house the things that mattered most were seldom expressed.

Dead Fish and Dreams

Jennifer Brice

In the clearing stands a young woman wearing a flannel nightgown over gape-tongued leather boots. Behind her rise the unfinished walls of a cabin. She cradles a rifle in one arm and a baby in the other. Her right foot is propped, with artful casualness, on the carcass of a black bear.

Earlier that spring morning in 1984, a maundering bear had rousted the Hannans from sleep, and Jill had shot it. Before skinning out the carcass, she mugged for her husband Dennis's camera. The image captures something of the innocence and energy with which the Hannans set about making a life for themselves on five wilderness acres near the geographic center of Alaska. Into a region that bureaucrats had bleakly described as "seldom if ever seen," the couple brought images drawn from history texts and Jack London novels of how a settler was supposed to look. They were less certain of how one ought to be.

A decade after the picture was taken, I held it up to a vein of sunlight pulsing through the Hannans's window. The day before, a photographer named Charles Mason and I had flown to their remote homesite on the shore of Deadfish Lake to begin documenting a way of life no longer possible: by an act of Congress, the sweat-equity settlement of federal land in America ended forever in 1986. Turning Jill's photograph this way and that, I barely recognized the woman posing with the baby and the bear. In a way, she has never existed. Like the sepia-tinted photographs one commissions from an old-time booth at the county fair, this one has the stillness of an artifact without the authenticity.

Why is it that the past always seems both simpler and more meaningful than the present? As a child, my favorite author was Laura Ingalls Wilder, and I often wished I'd been born a century earlier, into a time when (it seemed to me) the drama of daily life was pitched higher. In a sense, it was the tug of my own dreams that led me to the closing of the American frontier. In an essay on the subject of biography, Sven Birkerts wrote, "We can't help mapping our experiences alongside those of others." Even if we no longer hunt moose or harvest potatoes or pick berries, even if we no longer sew hats out of fur or build houses from logs or educate our children in the ways of the forest, we somehow find meaning when we observe, either firsthand or vicariously, the lives of those who do.

Outlined by frost as early as August, Deadfish Lake is roughly three-quarters of a mile long and a half-mile wide. On aviation maps, it is unnamed, a pinprick in a valley bounded to the south by the Mount McKinley massif, with the highest peak (20,320 feet) in North America, and to the north by the snow-spackled mountains of the Kuskokwim Basin. Seen from the air, the leaves of birch trees riffle in the wind like gold braid against malachite spruce. Umber tundra is sieved with lakes and crisscrossed by drainages as crooked as fault lines.

The boreal forest adheres to a beauty of scale: typically, the greater the scale, the greater the beauty. Seen up close, the black spruce trees grow as slender as bamboo, only a few inches in diameter. The name of the lake derives from the oily black fish that bob to the surface every spring, either asphyxiated by noxious gases or starved of oxygen. Not even the Hannans's dogs will eat them. During the summer, a Monet-like coverlet of lily pads hides quicksand, microscopic mussels, and leeches. "This is hungry country," Jill says.

There are no roads within a hundred miles, and the nearest city is more than two hundred miles away. One can reach Deadfish Lake only by floatplane or ski plane, and virtually not at all during the spring or fall, when ice on the surface of the lake is melting or forming. In wilderness this profound, a ruptured appendix or the slip of an axe could prove fatal. The Hannans get by without running water, electricity, a telephone, or power tools. They travel on foot in summer, by dogsled in winter. Drinking water is hauled from the lake in buckets, then filtered twice. To settle at Deadfish Lake, as Dennis and Jill Hannan have, is to live on the cusp of the twenty-first century as though it were the nineteenth—to be blown, like the angel in one of Laurie Anderson's songs, "backwards into the future."

From the outside, the Hannans's cabin resembles a grassy hummock with a stovepipe sticking out. By digging in, the family benefits from earth's insulating properties: the cabin is cool in summer, warm in winter, and always alee of the north wind. Shored up by hand-peeled spruce logs as bony as a young girl's wrist, the interior walls form roughly a sixteen-by-twenty-foot rectangle. The floor is plywood, the only window a south-facing slit.

Virtually every item in the Hannan household adheres to a rigid code of functionality. One of the few exceptions is an ornately carved cuckoo clock with wrought-iron weights that chimes on the half hour. In a household where everyone wears a knife and no one a wristwatch, the clock, a gift that Dennis's mother hand-carried home from a trip to Germany, seems out of place. There is a rhythm to everyday life here, one governed less by the hours in a day than by the hours of daylight.

On the last day of moose-hunting season in 1993, Dennis stalked into the woods early in the morning with the couple's only good rifle. In nearly a decade at Deadfish Lake, he and Jill had been skunked only once, and they dreaded the prospect of heading into winter without fresh meat. Jill was home helping the boys, aged nine and eleven, with their correspondence lessons. It was a clear day without wind, so nothing muffled the nearby sound of a huge animal battling through underbrush. Jill and the boys looked up sharply from the workbook-strewn table. The noise came from the south, in the opposite direction from Dennis. Jill grabbed the second-best rifle, one with a broken sight, and scooted out the door. Her heart thudded as she paddled across the lake. She'd never shot a moose. After beaching the canoe as close as she dared to the thrashing bushes, she scraped the wooden paddle against the trunk of a tree. The unseen beast froze at her imitation of a rival bull marking territory. "There was a point," she told Dennis afterward, "where I just couldn't back out."

The moose charged. Jill later estimated its weight at fifteen hundred pounds. She held her ground. With the broken rifle, she needed a target too big to miss. At thirty yards, when she could see the whites of its eyes, she fired. The second shot dropped the moose. Later Dennis discovered two bullet holes, two inches apart; one had penetrated the heart.

To generalize about human nature, or the nature of one human, has always struck me as reckless because it reduces to roughly the same degree that it informs. Yet even the most casual observer of the Hannan household would probably concur that Jill is a doer and Dennis a thinker. The first time Charles and I flew into Deadfish Lake, it was she who waded, grinning, into the stagnant, hip-deep water to grab the rope and anchor the float-plane. Dennis hung back, arms akimbo, eyes inscrutable. He is like that in conversation as well. For every hundred words of Jill's, he contributes one or two. Often, Jill's sentences begin like promising veins of ore that peter out when she succumbs to self-consciousness or distraction. For instance, describing how moved she felt on returning to the lake after several months' absence, she said: "We got off the plane, and the loon was trilling, and the swans..." Dennis's sentences, by contrast, are lean, linear, artic-ulate. They have closure. A writerly quality infuses his arguments. Inflamed by the self-righteous, romantic rhetoric of animal rights activists, he says, "Trapping's not nice, but those animals aren't going to die in a bed somewhere. They're going to starve or something's going to eat them."

Neither Jill nor Dennis has ever voted, collected welfare, participated in a census, purchased an insurance policy, or used a credit card to order something from a catalog company. Even if they wanted to, they couldn't get credit because they have no credit record. This is a paradox: Money is hard to come by in the wilderness, so it means everything to the Hannans; money is useless in the wilderness, so it means nothing to them. Terms such as "standard of living" lack relevance in a place where no standard exists. When you live this close to the bone, living well and just plain living are pretty much the same thing. Although the Hannans subsist well below the federal poverty line of $12,500 per year for a family of four, such conventional categories of poverty and wealth fail to encompass their way of life. "We live better than most of the world," Dennis says. "People living in Manhattan making a hundred thousand dollars a year...I wouldn't want to live like that even if I could. I'm happier here making four or five thousand."

When Shaun and his younger brother, Stormy, were both toddlers, Jill washed as many as a dozen cloth diapers per day by hand. Disposable diapers were too expensive and, ironically, too undisposable. The already cramped cabin could not accommodate a clothesline, so the diapers hung out to dry year-round. In winter, they froze stiffer than a nun's wimple.

"I told Dennis, when I'm done with diapers, I'm done with babies," Jill said.

City life tends to divorce practicality from responsibility in the sense that responsible behavior—the use of cloth diapers or cotton grocery bags, taking the time to recycle or compost—is not always practical. The poet Charles Olson once remarked, "We are alien from everything that was most familiar." By this he meant that we no longer grow the cotton to make our clothes, or grind wheat into flour, or scrub our bodies in the river, or cut down trees to build our cabins. Because our lives are no longer strenuous, we squeeze running or aerobics into our daily schedules. As society evolves, what was once most familiar to us—the creation of food, clothing, and shelter through physical labor—has become unfamiliar. Yet, no matter how much we have, we tend to define ourselves by what we want: a bigger house, a fancier car, a more prestigious job, wittier friends. In the wilderness, by contrast, it is not only possible but necessary to behave as though one's simplest gesture has significance. Trash must be recycled, toilet paper burned, water filtered, leftovers preserved, wood chips hoarded. While the rest of us worry about how much we can get, the Hannans ask themselves how little they need. I was curious about what, if anything, they missed by not living near a city.

"I don't miss anything," Dennis said.

Jill was more wistful: "I used to miss talking to my friends and my mom when the kids were young. And I miss playing softball."

For breakfast, Jill tucked a cranberry coffee cake into the stovepipe oven and sliced the fresh fruit Charles and I brought with us from Fairbanks. The scent of cranberries and brown sugar is as strong as memory. A sliver of glass hanging above the kitchen counter suffices as the cabin's only mirror. As Jill cut into honeydew melon and nectarines, it reflected a woman with sea-colored eyes, a mobile mouth, and hazel curls, cropped shorter now than when she was in her twenties. Her skin was tanned by wind and sun. Clad in a flannel shirt layered over several T-shirts and tucked into blue jeans, she still looked slim, as though life in the woods had jettisoned extra baggage from her body as well as her life. Dennis wore a beard now, and his hair, too, was shorter. He seldom smiled, but the brooding look he turned on the camera in his twenties was gone.

Jill Phillips and Dennis Hannan met at community college in Eugene, Oregon. She was twenty, green-eyed and gamine, a physical education major and a crack shortstop on a women's fast-pitch softball team. Dennis was twenty-three, intense and shy, a biology major. After high school, he'd seen his life laid out for him, symmetrical as a quilt and just as square-cornered. He'd enlisted in the navy, then left after a single tour. By the time he met Jill, his hair had grown into a halo of brown curls framing brown eyes.

After a botany lecture, Jill turned to the stranger on her left and asked, "Do you get this stuff?" It was a genuine question—

Jill was no flirt. Dennis *did* get it. He shared his botany notes and, later, his dream of homesteading in the North. Dennis and Jill both issued from rural, middle-class backgrounds that emphasized experience over education. Other, less tangible qualities drew them to one another: a tendency toward romanticism, love of the wilderness, and a yearning for simplicity.

In 1981, they married in a civil ceremony at her parents' home in Elmira, Oregon. He wore a borrowed suit, and she carried wildflowers. The following spring, they packed their meager possessions into a pickup truck and drove north. At the Bureau of Land Management office in Fairbanks, where they went to fill out fire-fighting applications, they learned of federal land near Lake Minchumina (pronounced min-CHEW-mi-na) that had recently been opened to settlement. They would have chartered a plane that same day, except they were broke.

They scrounged up jobs making beds, cleaning bathrooms, and night clerking at fourth-rate inns. To save money, they lived out of the back of their pickup, moving every few days to avoid campground fees. They ate bologna sandwiches and washed up in the restroom at the public library. At night, they curled like nesting spoons into the drawer-sized space between their belongings and the tailgate. Over the course of nearly two years, they were able to save sixteen thousand dollars—all but four thousand dollars of their earnings.

On moving to Deadfish Lake, the Hannans expected to join a community of like-minded settlers. Jill especially yearned for the company of mothers with whom she could swap concerns and advice. Instead, she and Dennis and one-year-old Shaun passed the three-month mark in solitude. By summer's end, their provisions were running low. A week's rations consisted of a jar of bear meat and a cup of flour, plus all the beans and cornmeal they could eat. In no danger of starving, they nevertheless grew heartily sick of bear and beans. On the other hand, the hunger they felt for human conversation surprised them. Loneliness—the darker side of solitude—had never figured into the script of their dream.

One summer morning, they heard droning in the sky. A floatplane swooped low before alighting on a neighboring lake.

Dennis and Jill's spirits rose intoxicatingly. If the plane brought new settlers, then there would be a second and perhaps a third plane. Their own outlay of building supplies, winter clothes, and foodstuffs—roughly six thousand pounds—had required six planeloads.

Dennis slogged three miles in his hip waders and mosquito netting to greet the new arrivals. The airplane had taken off by then, but he forged on. He found a couple huddled under a tarp, swatting bugs. They looked young and wretched. The man shot Dennis a hostile look then strode off. He was part Indian, dressed in tan pants with tiger stripes painted on them. The woman stayed where she was, greeting Dennis skittishly. She was obviously pregnant. The two men spoke for a few strained minutes. Feeling like an interloper, Dennis stayed only long enough to glean that the pilot wasn't returning. According to the woman, she and her partner had brought with them everything they needed to live off the land. "I decided there and then to leave them to their wilderness," Dennis said, and he turned toward home.

"You can't live off the land here," Jill remarked. "We didn't plan on it."

In the woods, the capacity for change counts for everything. One cannot react rigidly to elements beyond one's control. The Hannans long ago lost count of the number of times they felt disillusioned. Life in the subarctic wilderness was rugged; not only that, it was impossible without a source of income and, once or twice a year, an infusion of fresh supplies. Four out of five of the Minchumina-area settlers failed to "prove up" (an expression referring to the federal guidelines for gaining title to their land), a consequence that can, by and large, be traced to unrelenting idealism and inflexibility. Whenever the dream of what Dennis and Jill wanted collided with the reality of what was within reach, they revised the dream rather than ignore the reality. Once, Dennis showed me an unpublished article on trapping in which he wrote that, for him, "the hardest thing was separating fantasy from reality...without that distinction, my only mark on the land...would probably [be] just another moldering cabin in the wilderness."

As any cartographer or pilot knows, you cannot find true north with a compass. Instead, the needle wobbles toward a place called magnetic north, which, depending on your distance from the equator, may vary by as many as 180 degrees. Like a dream, true north is only a direction, not a destination; like a dream, it is impossible to chart one's life without it. What declination means in practical terms is that, no matter how meticulously you plot a course through the Alaska wilderness, if you fail to calculate for magnetic deviation, you'll never reach your destination. At the latitude of Deadfish Lake, the angle of declination is roughly twenty degrees. This strikes me as a reasonable objective correlative for the gap between some people's dream of the North and its reality.

Several times during berry-picking season, the Hannans drifted near the new settlers' camp while foraging but did not intrude. They kept busy, canning moose meat and garden vegetables for the coming winter. One afternoon, they heard, for the second time, an airplane land and take off. Torn between curiosity and reserve, they bundled Shaun up and hiked over to the neighboring lake.

On the porch of what appeared to be the foundation for a cabin, a vacant rocking chair creaked in the wind. Belongings were strewn everywhere. With a growing sense of a tragedy barely averted, the Hannans sifted through garbage, reconstructing what had happened. There was a two-and-a-half-pound, double-bit axe, unsharpened; an empty case of baby food; the skeletal remains of a raven and a mouse; unbroken ampoules of silver nitrate for a newborn's eyes; kerosene lamps and (incompatible) Coleman fuel; leather clothing, including a set of tiny buckskins; two animal traps; pack boots with rabbit fur glued around the top; machine-gun belts hanging in the trees; fifty pounds of black powder; a brand-new pistol; and a journal composed in a feminine hand.

It was the debris of a dream. Richly detailed and embellished with drawings at the outset, the journal entries degenerated over time into a barely legible sprawl. On the first page, Dennis read an account of his first visit to the couple's camp. After he left,

the man said he "didn't want any white man on his property."
From the remaining entries, Dennis and Jill discovered that the
baby had been due any day. The mother was twenty-one, the
father eighteen. He'd injured his back early on, probably trying
to cut down trees with an axe more suited to a professional
lumberjack and unsharpened to boot. Both suffered from
agonizing stomach cramps and diarrhea, symptoms of *giardia,* a
parasitic protozoan that thrives in beaver feces and is contracted
from unfiltered water. Worst of all, though, hunger haunted
them. They devoured everything in their packs, including the
baby food. Humbled and broken, they even sought but failed to
find the Hannans. Jill wishes fervently they had succeeded: "They
could have lived off beans and cornmeal like we did. And sugar—
we had plenty of sugar," she said.

In a last-ditch effort, the pseudo-Indians (as Dennis dubbed
them) built fires and waved a red towel to signal their distress to
passing planes. By then, the journal entries were veering between
desperation and despair. Jill speculates that the woman, if not the
man, was failing rapidly and might have died within a few days
had not a pilot spotted the distress signal. What became of them
after they reached safety is anyone's guess. Their cabin, however,
is now moldering in the wilderness.

In 1893, the historian Frederick Jackson Turner confidently
if prematurely declared that the American frontier was closed. In
fact, the Homestead Act remained in effect for forty more years
in the contiguous United States and nearly another century in
Alaska. By the first half of the twentieth century, missionaries, fur
traders, gold miners, and whalers had plundered the North's resources, but the prevailing view, in one anthropologist's words,
was of "a region beyond the margins of civilization, where
human beings do not belong and cannot flourish." A clause in the
Federal Land Policy and Management Act of 1976 imposed that
year as a deadline for the expiration of nearly all settlement laws
in the contiguous United States. Alaska was granted a reprieve
until 1986. Following the opening of thirty thousand acres near
Lake Minchumina (and, later, more than ten thousand acres near
Slana, in eastern Alaska), would-be settlers besieged the Fairbanks

office of the Bureau of Land Management with letters and phone calls. In time, however, the hype has faded; now, more than a decade later, fewer than one hundred people make their home on what is truly the Last Frontier.

History, geography, and imagination all converge at the frontier, which continues to speak to our distinctly American fascination with what lies on the other side of civilization—to our New World temptation to re-create ourselves in unknown territory. In some ways, the imperatives of the frontier haven't changed since the California gold rush or, for that matter, since Plymouth Rock. A degree of purposefulness, of self-reflection, arises from the choice to live outside the margins of civilization. For the last settlers, the frontier in the 1980s meant freedom, a fresh start, solitude, independence, community, peace, prosperity, happiness. These are lofty concepts, but the vastness of the Alaska wilderness demands a corresponding breadth of spirit from those who would make their home within it.

Yet the frontier as geography is fast becoming an anachronism: it refers more often to a concept than to a place, and its frequent enclosure in quotation marks indicates ironic distance. Now that advertising executives and presidential speech writers have latched onto the term, the frontier's most frequent application is to economics or medicine or Cadillacs or outer space, not geography. What the Wild West, interplanetary shuttles, and settlements in the Alaska wilderness have in common is a place at the edge of what is known. And known to whom? As revisionist historians aptly point out, the world's remaining frontiers are not clean slates but palimpsests on which indigenous peoples have trod for millennia. The Athabaskan Indians, to name but one group, have no equivalent in their languages for our word "wilderness." "Wherever they traveled," wrote S. D. Grant, "it was simply 'home.'"

Formal schooling at Deadfish Lake happens from eight to one, Monday through Friday: three heads bent over a folding table, books and papers pushed into the pool of light. This schooling is Jill's undisputed domain; she associates it with the smell of hair singed by lantern flame.

Eleven-year-old Shaun Hannan takes after his mother, nine-year-old Stormy after his father. The older boy has Jill's aquamarine eyes, toothy grin, irrepressible giggle. Stormy is small-boned and dark-haired, with eyes like the velvet on caribou antlers. Both boys wear their hair cropped close to the scalp, like marten fur.

The boys work from textbooks prepared by Lower 48 publishers. The books pose questions such as "Which animal are you more likely to see at the zoo, a cow or a bear?" and "How much does a bicycle cost—six dollars, sixty dollars, or six hundred dollars?" Neither Shaun nor Stormy has ever been to the zoo. I wonder what they would think of barbed-wire fences and cement walls protecting humans from animals, cutting off nature from civilization. At Deadfish Lake, bears shamble myopically across the Hannans's path from time to time. As a rule, though, they give the humans a wide berth. Several years ago, the family was out walking when a pair of cubs meandered into view. A few seconds later, the sow charged out of the woods. The Hannans never carry guns. Jill dove off the trail with Stormy in her arms, bracing for the sensation of claws troughing down her back. But the bear was only bluffing. After making her point, she huffily gathered up her young and shuffled off. Bears are a dime a dozen at Deadfish Lake. To see a Hereford cow—now, that would be something.

Neither Shaun nor Stormy has ever shopped for a bike. Jill says Stormy was exasperated by the question about how much one costs. "It depends on what kind of bike," he said. "I mean, you can get a used one at a garage sale for six dollars. And those really fancy mountain bikes cost six hundred."

Stormy guessed sixty dollars, though, because he thought it was the correct answer, and he was right. The textbook presents a tempting target here, yet criticizing it ignores the larger question of whether a public-school education is at all relevant to a couple of boys growing up in the woods. "These boys have terrible times with baseball questions," Jill says.

Shaun and Stormy's parents have decided for the time being to divide the academic year between correspondence lessons at Deadfish Lake and the one-room school at the tiny community of

Minchumina, thirty-five miles west of here. Knowledgeable beyond their years, the boys get bored in the classroom, but the company of other children compensates somewhat. I once asked Jill what values she wanted to impart to her sons.

"Common sense. Decency. Courtesy. I think they're important values no matter where you live," she said.

"You don't get something for nothing.

"If you don't learn and grow, there's no reason to live.

"Don't run twenty gallons of water down the sink while you brush your teeth."

Presently, Jill was sprawled on her bedroom floor, groping for something under the bed. She emerged with a dusty, unopened box of white zinfandel. Dennis and Charles shook their heads, so she poured one cup for me and one for her. After a second cup, Jill began to giggle. "I better stop or I'm not going to be able to go for a walk."

"You're going to have to," Dennis replied, deadpan, "because I'm taking away the car keys."

By the time the six of us had consumed moose Stroganoff and washed the dishes, a hush had fallen. High clouds raked the sky which, until that hour, had been fat with rain. A solitary loon sliced the surface of Deadfish Lake. In the faint moonlight, we followed a narrow trail along the shoreline. Half a mile south of the cabin, a jawbone of ridge trails off into tundra. Here is a flowing creek transformed by the labor of beavers into a motionless marsh. Swamp grass impales the setting sun, which oozes like broken egg yolk into still water. As far as the eye can see, there's no sign of human habitation.

Interpreting Ezra Pound's translation of an archaic Chinese text, Guy Davenport wrote that "poetry is a voice out of nature which must be rendered humanly intelligible so that people can know how to live." At this time of night, in the wind, nature's voice becomes audible. Fifteen miles away, the Kuskokwim Mountains fade into the darkening sky; they are invisible now except for strands of snow streaking their crowns. Too late, Dennis pointed out a fox den not twenty feet in front of us. Had we been more decorous in our approach, we might have seen kits scuffling and tumbling in the grass. Even so, this is a profoundly peaceful place.

I ask the question uppermost in my mind: "Why stay?" I think I understand why people go into the woods to pursue a dream. And, having spent most of my life in Alaska, I've felt what Thoreau called "the tonic of wildness." What happens, though, when the cure is complete, the dream fulfilled?

"Why do I stay?" Jill echoed pensively. "The sun shining through birches glazed with ice crystals can still take my breath away. It's so quiet, you can hear the wing beats of birds. And you're always learning something new. One day we saw a mink in a larch tree. Up 'til then, we didn't know mink climbed trees."

Scab on the Chugach

Sheryl Clough

Early on Thursday, October 13, 1994, I gaze out my kitchen window at the Chugach Mountains, the peaks forming a steep spine that marks the eastern limit of Anchorage, Alaska's geologic body. The summit vertebrae, sparkled by fresh icy dust, glow deep indigo in the still dark morning. As the snow cover deepens in the coming weeks, moose will descend to forage, strolling through city parks and down the streets to graze on brush growing in vacant lots and falling over fencetops. Some people regard the moose as a nuisance, but seeing one always makes me feel blessed, marked as a resident on a planet of large animals roaming. I look forward to seeing the moose at close range almost as much as I dread my task for the day: to cross the striking teachers' picket line at West High School and apply for work as a substitute teacher.

The Anchorage School District has called for substitutes, no secondary certification required, at a pay rate of $200 per day. As I drive up, mine is one of many cars attempting to enter the parking lot. The strikers carry the requisite placards, which I don't read; I'm too nervous trying not to hit the marchers, who crowd the pavement like microbes squirming in an open wound. They obstruct entry of job seekers, standing in the way of incoming cars and banging their fists on the hoods. Yesterday an applicant's car clipped one of the striking teachers in this lot; the incident made the evening TV news.

I roll down the window to accept a flyer telling me why I should not cross the line. A woman yells through the opening, "Please don't cross it." I yell back, "I haven't worked in over two months." Her open mouth half-deflates.

Bile churns in my stomach at the thought of entering the building. I'm not a member of any union, but still feel queasy at undertaking this action which, to the strikers, looks pro-management. I walk slowly down a long linoleum hallway, at the end of which other hopefuls form a line: 10 a.m. and there are more than a hundred people applying for work already.

The woman next to me in line, Marcy, reveals that she has a teaching certificate and conducts home schooling for her daughter. "I worked at an alternative high school, but that ended quick when I was attacked," Marcy says. *Physically attacked;* that takes a while to sink in, and I consider that so far I've been pretty lucky in the classroom. I think of my friend Carla, accused of racial prejudice by a physically intimidating black athlete when she wouldn't let him slide through her composition course on the basis of his substandard work. Marcy's exit from a violent classroom is the act of a survivor, I think.

"What about socializing with other children?" I ask Marcy.

"Ah, the standard question," she says, but we agree it is a legitimate one. To address this, she conducts an after-school arts and crafts session for neighborhood children, to give her daughter the opportunity to interact with other kids. As we get closer to the door and our turn at the application table, we extract our diplomas from our·shoulder bags at the same time. I note that Marcy has brought along a neatly prepared resume; this makes me feel less compulsive about bringing my own freshly printed curriculum vitae. The two women behind us express surprise that diplomas will be expected, although last night's TV news story specifically mentioned the degree requirement.

At the first table, a woman asks whether we are present employees of the Anchorage School District. The answers split us into two groups, and we look for empty chairs to sit in while filling out the stacks of application papers we've been handed. Another long line, another stack of forms…sometimes it seems that this is what modern life is composed of, but the $200-per-day carrot dangles. Dutifully I bend my donkey head and grip the pen.

Back in line for the second table, my forms complete, I chat with a woman named Patricia who hopes to get one of the $25-per-hour classroom aide jobs. "Do you have experience with high school students?" I ask. She says, "Yep. And kindergarten, first, second, I've done 'em all." In fact, Patricia reveals, she had just been hired by the district full-time and was going through the preliminary paperwork when the strike was called. "You're a shoo-in for this job," I assure her.

At the second table, a woman wants to see my UAF diploma. This is the first time since finishing graduate school at the University of Alaska Fairbanks that the piece of paper has borne any relevance, and I brandish it as though I'm trying to sneak into a ritzy party with a forged invitation. The third-table personnel check it again and ask for ID proving the right to work in this country; at this point my passport speeds things along. I notice that as I get further into the process, the lines get shorter. I'm in line for the fourth table, "interviews," when a woman sidles blatantly into the line, directly in front of me. I've tolerated this queue-crashing too many times in my life, and the grim determination required to get through scabhood rules out tolerance for it today. "You'd better go to the back of the line like everyone else," I say.

Her shoulders rise. "I got in line the same time they did," she says, gesturing toward a group that includes Patricia.

"I have no control over how fast these lines move." I turn around and say to the people behind me in line, "If I were you, I wouldn't stand for this."

"I've got my kids out in the car. I'm not going to the back of this line." Her lower lip juts forward.

My voice rises along with my chin. "I can guarantee you're not going to interview before I do."

She grumbles some more and gets behind me, but still ahead of the rest of the line, which by now holds twenty-five more applicants. They not only fail to protest, but engage her in friendly conversation. I turn my back on them all and grumble something about the obsequiousness of the oppressed. The man ahead of me in line hears. "It's people like her that create the problem," he says, pointing to the wall where a large banner hangs, proclaiming a "positive attitude" message. Her attitude is fairly unusual in Alaska, where most folks will go out of their way to help change a tire, give a ride, or share a meal. But Alaska's distance from the Lower 48 cannot render it immune from the hundreds of people moving in every year, and some of them are bound to display less-than-desirable attitudes. The perspective and manners considered uniquely Alaskan may soon tread the endangered path, alongside the last grizzlies.

"My name's Sheryl," I say, and we both extend our hands. "Steve," he responds. Steve tells me he hopes for a classroom aide position and relates his diverse work experience, including painting murals on buildings for a company in California. He liked that job, but eventually the company crumbled and he moved north. Like me, he's been out of work for several months. "It's a good thing I got the dividend; that'll keep me going a little while." To read and hear the advertising in newspapers and on radio and TV every October, one would think all Alaskans rush out to buy airfare vouchers or new hot tubs with their Permanent Fund Dividends. I am grateful to Steve for partially restoring my perspective, and we chat about our children. He has two, a boy and girl who live in Oregon with their mother. I brag, thankful for an opportunity, about my smart, beautiful daughter, a paralegal in Seattle.

"Good luck," I say, as Steve sits down at an open table for his interview. There are three interviewers at work. I hope to get the woman who has written her name in felt pen on her cardboard table placard. It reads, "Hi, I'm Kate."

Marcy, Patricia, Steve, and I are all here for the same reason: we want more. More work, more respect, more self-esteem, and, like the striking teachers, more money. It is possible that some of us want more of things we cannot even identify, like Rocco, the character Edward G. Robinson plays in the film *Key Largo*. Rocco wears expensive suits, drives luxury cars, and smokes only the best Havana cigars. Yet, when Bogart asks the gangster what he wants, Rocco looks blank. Bogart helps him out: "You want more, doncha, Rocco?"

Light dawns in Rocco's eyes. "Yeah, that's right; I want more!"

Bogart asks him if he thinks he'll ever get enough.

"Well, I never have," Rocco answers. "No, I guess I won't." He sneers at the very notion that it's possible to have enough of anything.

The October 14, 1994, issue of the *Anchorage Daily News* quotes a senior teacher at West High School who, like Rocco, wants more. He is "resentful that he no longer qualifies for raises" at his top salary level of "about $57,000" per year. "I'd like to be able to buy my wife a new car," he says, "see my kids be able to do the same sorts of things other people do." What are these things they cannot do at $57,000 per, I wonder while reading that article. Buy a Lear jet? Live on the Riviera? And why can't his wife get out there and earn her own new car? For that matter, shouldn't this husband and wife reevaluate their allegiance to the value so many Americans have traditionally placed on driving a new car? I'm resentful that he's resentful. After all, what I want more than is zero: zero income, zero health coverage, zero pension plan, although I've worked all my life, ever since I was old enough to pick strawberries in the fields outlying Monroe, Washington. Having spent the past three years as a graduate student working hard for $7,800 a year and no benefits makes me more vulnerable to complaints, I admit. And yet, to the graduate students in my program who were not awarded teaching stipends, that $7,800 plus tuition waiver looked good; it was more than what they had.

The poverty notorious among grad students takes an even more severe twist in Fairbanks, Alaska, where high rents and the paucity of decent jobs drive many to live in cabins in the woods, without running water or indoor plumbing. These folks haul their water from town in five-gallon plastic jugs, which must be kept indoors to prevent freezing. Even to those accustomed to living without plumbing, the outhouse experience takes on new ramifications at minus sixty degrees. One key to survival here, as in so many parts of Alaska, is humor: paper the walls with "Far Side" cartoons; line the shitter seat with beaver fur; tape a cardboard thermometer that reads "+80°F." to the inside door and surround it with pictures of Tahiti.

Of course, not all Alaskans live with outhouses, and not all Anchorage teachers earn $57,000 a year. The district well knows that it's in its own best interest to portray the striking teachers to the public as a bunch of insatiable malcontents who put their own comfort ahead of children's education. It seems that the district wants more, too: more control, more power to make its employees jump through arbitrary hoops, and a diminution of the union's influence in bargaining. It sometimes seems that the physical remoteness of Alaska contributes to an attitude of arrogance, even nonaccountability, on the part of those in power. When my friend Shirley taught in the village of Shungnak, her frustration in the face of arbitrary administrative dictates found an outlet in her songwriting, and we laughed over the lyrics to her tune "Administration":

> There's something that keeps me from continuing on
> And that's why I'm writing this song.
> Watch out for the gun of Administration
> They'll shoot down your job and close down your home.

I remember Shirley's letters from Shungnak, describing how it felt to be the only white woman in town, to keep her snow shovel indoors for the times when the drifts grew higher than her front door, and to grow tired of eating caribou week after week but that's all there was. Two house trailers, the only plumbed housing units provided by the district, were in danger of being closed, to save money. Yet Shirley reaped a rich payback from the landscape where she taught: other letters described cross-country skiing along the frozen Kobuk River, beneath the swirling electric green and pink aurora borealis, dozens of caribou running alongside. And the money was good in the bush: she traveled to South America one year, Hawaii another.

Back when the Anchorage discord began, the teachers' union claimed that there were issues other than money involved, that its members were being forced to accept new contract terms without good-faith negotiations. Some grumbling about "respect" was heard. Posters that read "Support Our Teachers" could be seen around town, stapled to utility poles. Those Anchorage citizens who saw the strike as a money grab, pure and simple, added vertical lines to the posters in strategic places: "$upport Our Teacher$." Judging from the hundreds of people applying as scabs, the teachers may have miscalculated public sentiment when deciding to strike; they may not have taken into account the large numbers of Alaskan workers who enjoy fewer benefits and less money than teachers, or are unemployed.

Unemployment is perhaps a more common status in Alaska than in other places, because of the seasonal nature of so many jobs here. Fishing and its related jobs on processors and in canneries is not as viable an income source in winter. Construction work is seriously limited by temperatures and location, and in the permafrost regions may be altogether unfeasible. Logging in winter—no way. The thousands of jobs related to tourism are good maybe April through August, except for the few dog mushers who offer winter sled rides. Teaching lasts through the winter, but as the budget scalpel cuts ever deeper, there are more teachers competing for fewer jobs. At the university level, the budget cutters increasingly employ part-time lecturers instead of tenure-track professors, saving a great deal of money in salaries and benefits. An adjunct faculty member is worse off than a grad student, factoring in the value of the latter's tuition waiver. An English lecturer in the University of Alaska system earns slightly less than $2,000 for teaching one semester-long course, with no benefits whatsoever. And yet the employment prospects in Fairbanks are so poor that the competition for these jobs is heated; one department head, in an effort to give jobs to more people, imposed a limit of two courses per semester, per lecturer. "Adjunct" here mutates toward synonymity with "exploited."

Some of the pro-strike sympathizers grumbling about the school district say, Can you imagine, they think we should be *grateful* for all we've got. Their verbal emphasis hits that word "grateful" like an ice pick hammering a crystal's cleavage plane. I think of feudal estates: the well-fed lord galloping through the grounds on a sleek steed and tossing meat scraps toward grateful serfs who scrabble frantically in the dirt to find the morsels first, before their neighbors can get them. The modern version: out-of-work teachers anxiously scanning electronic job postings via computers and modems, to apply for available jobs before the hundreds of other applicants who will inevitably follow, not grateful for the data but driven to be the first to act on it.

I don't know that gratitude is an appropriate concept here. It seems to me an employee has the right and even a moral obligation to self, to seek the best conditions and recompense possible for his or her labor. One of my favorite poets once wrote that a worker must be better off at the end of a workday than at its beginning. It seems to me that this train leaves the tracks where grateful ends and Rocco's vague, uncomprehending, uncompromising greed begins, somewhere in the vast borderless country inhabited by millions of people who cope, not grateful and not resentful, on fifty-seven grand a year, or less.

Writers and other activists who pursue the idea of deliberately consuming less, wasting less, and learning to live with less are often labeled kooks, Communists, and worse. The environmental movement in particular, with its emphases on reducing wasteful packaging, recycling, and reusing waste or "gray" water, has been a target of producers who want more, and who are willing to pollute, injure, maim, and deform in order to get it. Teachers pounding on scabs' cars and sign defacers turning letters into dollar signs are pretty tame terrorists next to those riled up by eco-issues. I've seen logging families in Darrington,

Washington, hang spotted owl effigies in their front yards, right in town. These behaviors are all part of the same struggle: the struggle for more than what we have, at whatever cost, and regardless of whether there is enough of that ephemeral "more" to spread around to everybody who wants it. Alaska's sheer physical size seems to encourage the impression of endless resources. How will Alaska be different from anywhere else, though, after the last oil patch is drained, the last tree cut, the last salmon netted, the last caribou driven from her habitat?

I see that Steve's interview is finished; he smiles and gets up to join the short line of people waiting for their tuberculin skin-patch tests. Marcy beckons to me to sit down. Five minutes later, I've been hired as a substitute teacher. TB test from an efficient needle-jabber, photo for an ID card, orientation sheet, and I'm out the door. I stare at the site on my arm where the needle has so recently invaded, the patch of pink disrupted skin, the community of cells that will need time to heal.

Outside the crowd has grown larger and noisier, with more placards waving. Some strikers beat their palms against the hoods of the job applicants' vehicles. This strike cleaves people into factions the way surgical tools pull skin and ribs away from a beating heart. Mine pumps faster as I walk through this disgruntled crowd toward the relative safety of the truck. I'm almost there when a reporter steps in front of me and asks why I'm here. The pace of the day propels an unmeditated answer.

"Politically, I've been pro-labor most of my life, but when you're unemployed for any length of time, it's kind of a luxury to hold that position. I haven't worked in over two months. I need the money." He scribbles in his notebook and turns. Immediately I wish I'd declined to answer, but the reporter is already out of range. I get into the truck, sigh, and drive carefully through the throng, rolling the window down to shout to the milling strikers, "Good luck." I'm a teacher, after all, one of them, and one who has known the absurdities promulgated by power-hungry administrators, but above all one who needs to work. And I want to do that work in Alaska, the wildest, the biggest, the most beautiful place I know.

Why I am here... has less to do with money than with the love of teaching and of wild landscape. It has a lot to do with the desire to resist mega-consumerism, to resist living on a landscape paved with nearly contiguous shopping malls, and to embrace living among people who are sometimes belligerent ("Secede or Succumb!"), occasionally irrational, but always creatively independent.

My quote is reproduced accurately in the next day's *Anchorage Daily News,* and I see some heads turning and mouths moving when I play bridge at the local club. Many members are current teachers and retired teachers; few are neutral about the strike issues. One elementary teacher in particular makes no effort to disguise her hostility. I think of those swirling toxic microbes invading the body politic. Neutral response or no response equals passive and certain death, whether you're fighting clear-cuts, unemployment, or an overcontrolling administration.

My friend Chris, a retired teacher, takes a different attitude than most toward the strikers. "What are they teaching our children," she says, "when it's okay to yell at people who don't agree with you, to beat on their cars and call them names?" Chris's daughter is a teacher, too, one who has refused to join the strike and who is now ostracized because of that. The double bind: strike and earn the enmity of the administration; refuse to strike and suffer the hostility of peers.

Much of the hostility toward scab workers apparently springs from the strikers' notion that "their" jobs are being taken away from them. Walter Block in *Defending the Undefendable* writes, "The first point to establish is that a job is not a thing which can be owned by a worker—or anyone else" (p. 237). Writes Block:

> *One wonders how the workers would react if the principle upon which their anti-scab feeling is based were adopted by the employer. How would they feel if employers assumed the right to forbid long-term workers from leaving their employment? What if he accused another employer who dared to hire "his" worker of being a scab! Yet the situation is entirely symmetrical.* (p. 238)

In Alaska especially, an attempt to deny anything to the people is to wave the proverbial red flag before the bull. Alaska tends to attract those who feel overregulated by life in the Lower 48. I don't know how unionized workers in Alaska walk their own fine line between union regulations and the need for independent lives that drew them here.

"Becoming a scab is a dishonorable thing!" shouts a striking teacher in the West High parking lot. My day as a scab pushes me to reevaluate my own thinking. As a member of a union, I hope I would honor its objectives in exchange for having enjoyed its protection and benefits. But I can't get past the fact that I don't belong to any union and therefore owe no loyalty. And what of the loyalty I owe to my husband and our marriage, to be a partner, to bring in some of the income? Musing, I watch the strike news on TV and hear a male teacher refer to himself as a modern-day Joe Hill. Hearing the name jolts a memory of Joan Baez singing the ballad in the sixties: *From San Diego up to Maine / In every mine and mill / where working men defend their rights / It's there you'll find Joe Hill.* I realize that song is all I know about Hill, and next day I visit the Loussac Library to find out more.

Hill was a Swedish immigrant, songwriter, and organizer who hooked up with the IWW (Industrial Workers of the World) in the early part of this century. His activism in labor matters became notorious, to the point that employers blacklisted him and he eventually turned to armed robbery to survive. Executed by firing squad at the Utah State Penitentiary in 1915, Hill's last words were "Don't waste time in mourning. Organize." Hill's eloquent brevity persists in the first two lines of his last will and testament: "My will is easy to decide / For there is nothing to divide."

The gall of a well-educated, well-paid modern teacher with generous health and pension benefits comparing himself to a penniless immigrant desperado leaves a bitter taste in my mouth, along with fair certainty that the comparer knows nothing about the life of Joe Hill. And so our language mutates: the suffering and desperation behind a Swedish criminal's name becomes an easy, fiery catchword tossed about by people who cannot appreciate the allusion, and certainly not the extent of deprivation endured by an early pioneer of the labor movement.

I think Joe Hill would have loved Alaska. His brand of independence and radicalism draws so many people here. "Independent union organizer" strikes me as oxymoronic, and yet sometimes survival requires unity, the way the early Alaskan pioneers kept up a bush telegraph so that they would know who needed what help, transportation, or supplies in far-flung locations. The striking teachers are not underpaid and are not in any danger for their survival. In their quest for more, they are buying into the advertising-mandated mind-set that pushes us all toward ever-increasing levels of consumption.

I have no easy answer for how to supply our consumptive lifestyles, or how to maintain Alaska-style independence indefinitely in the face of an influxing population that does not uphold that value, or how to give jobs to all the teachers who need them. I seek not answers but comfort, and maybe clarification, in language. Language, like the cells of our bodies, mutates, evolves, and divides; it can also help us to heal, to reconvene the social community so necessary to human progress. I reach up to my poetry shelf and pull down Neruda, flipping the volume open to "The United Fruit Co." *When the trumpet sounded, it was / all prepared on the earth, / and Jehovah parceled out the earth / to Coca-Cola, Inc., Anaconda, /....* The beautiful anger in the familiar words soothes, the clarity of Neruda's crystal vision restoring equilibrium to my little universe. What would he have written about the Anchorage teachers' strike? *When the moose bellowed....* It is hardly imaginable that Neruda would equate the struggling, malnourished South American United Fruit Co. workers with the well-pensioned secondary teachers in today's Alaska.

Alaska. The magnificence, the cold, the individuality; they can hardly be carried by the vessels we call words. I recall Shirley's story of the Shungnak outhouse where she sat in a subzero windstorm. When she tried to stuff the toilet paper down the hole, the backdraft kept blowing it back up at her. She finally gave up and went into her cabin to describe the scene to her friends. They promptly grabbed cameras and raced back to reenact and photograph the untamed T.P. Today the picture hangs on her Wasilla wall, conveying what words cannot.

The last thing I hear driving out of the parking lot at West High School: "Good luck to you." In those words of a striking teacher, I find the implicit wish that the healing of all our wounds may begin. I turn the steering wheel toward home, luxuriating in this night's first stars rising above the ever-present Chugach. I drive conscious of the jabbed spot on my skin, where underneath an angry surface, the insulted cells have not commenced reunion.

Rosie and the Cache Economy

Mary Lockwood

An arctic Native cache is dark and full of smells. Its roof covers rolled-up hides, coats that were once worn over treasures of strong meat. Brushing against a particular kind of fur in the cache, one may recall how a hunter brought it home and how stories of the hunt unwound as the skin was harvested. Remembrance of the feast that followed may cause one to acknowledge how the animal brought friends and family together one more time, and how the meat was consumed far more quickly than the patient, generous hide asleep in a cache set on tall driftwood legs, safe from marauders. Darkness is suitable for this slumber; even the curing time allows one to plan out a special use for the hides.

The old people of Unalakleet, Alaska, grew up with these caches, and by the time I was born, in 1952, the incoming white people brought with them the American version of a Russian trading post called "stores," which bartered with paper and bits of metal called "money" instead of furs. Native families, like the one

I grew up in, still kept caches, but used cash to get things outside our landscape. Since everything in the village is within walking distance, I was given the chore of going to the store when we were low on provisions. I was too young to be trusted with cash. My parents had opened a charge account with the Alaska Commercial Company store, where I brought notes and lists of things to bring back home.

Early one summer day, I stood waiting with a note from Momma in my little hand. It was torn off a letter, her graceful handwriting requesting the store manager to place some items on our account. The note was folded over several times, as if to hide her request in greater secrecy. I ran my fingers across the folded edges and watched the laborious purchase and packaging of the customer ahead of me.

A tiny lady leaned against the high counter, her elbows gripping the top. Above her head to the left, the ornate cash register showed $0004.42¢. A cane was hooked over her right arm. I followed the line of the cane down her calico cloth–covered *parki* with its wide ruffle above reindeer shoes we call *kamiluks*. It jittered as she fumbled with bills and loose change in her large black purse. A self-conscious smile played on her brown face. It wasn't the dim light from the small high windows that didn't allow for swift counting. Old Rosie was blind.

She couldn't see the wood-floored building or the patient cashier or the chaotic merchandise shelved behind the purchasing place or the animal traps of every size bunched alongside a supporting beam. She knew that a wood-burning stove was behind her and that during the cold winter days, one could sit on an empty wooden case to warm up before shopping.

As Rosie looked for payment, the cashier placed her few articles in a brown paper sack.

"Is this five dollars?" She lifted her unseeing eyes and held a folded bill in the general direction of the clerk.

"Yeah, it is, Rosie." He took the bill and rang up the tally. The register rang brashly, then spun gears to spit out the till.

"Here, you have some change coming." He spoke loudly and

made sure she heard the amount scraping the register. Clearing his throat to further get her attention, he said, "Fifty-two cents."

He put the coins in her open thin hand. Rosie lowered her head, following the change as she put it away in a small purse. Snapping away the bits of change in their hiding place, she murmured her thanks.

Finding the payment was just one ordeal. A greater challenge was before her now, for she had to navigate her way back home. She rumpled the paper bag under her elbow, gathering her resources near.

Noticing that she was distraught, the cashier said, "Rosie, there's a Lockwood girl right behind you. She can help you get home. Couldn't you?" He nodded emphatically at me.

What? I thought, Another thing to do? Aw, I just came here to get some crackers.... The clerk was now glaring at me, for I had taken too long to answer.

"Ahem, uhm, uhm, uhm...," I balked.

"*Quin na un na?*" Rosie turned to ask who was behind her.

"Are you Lorena?" the cashier asked.

"No, I'm not!" I retorted.

"*Quin na nun na? Ka ka ruk?*" Rosie delighted in guessing correctly.

"Ah-huh." I nodded out of habit.

"Hi, Mary Jane." Rosie said loudly in English. "How are you?"

"I'm fine. Momma wants these things." I rushed forward to the counter and shoved her note to the clerk. I had to tilt my head to look up at him, for I was far smaller than old Rosie.

The clerk frowned as he read, then brightened up and said, "Okay!"

Reaching for a pad of forms, he wrote down Momma's order, picked up a box of Pilot bread crackers behind him, put it in a brown paper sack, then handed the sack over the counter as he dropped the charge slip in.

"Mary *Jane!*" he said pleasantly, emphasizing my middle name the way older folks of Unalakleet like to do. "Make sure

Rosie gets home, okay?" He gave me a wink and said to us, "See you!"

"*Qu ya na.*" We both thanked him and turned toward the door. I held Rosie's package while she adjusted her cane for action, then gave her purchase back so that I could guide her with a free hand. My roomy rubber boots thundered along the wooden floor, contrasting with Rosie's silent footsteps. I stopped in front of the wooden threshold and told her to pick up her feet so she wouldn't trip. Then we went slowly out of the building, down the two wooden stairs, and began the short walk to her home.

Three-year-old Carol saw us coming, moving like cold molasses, and ran with her hands extended to take the bag out of my hand. "Oh, boy!" she waved her arms and hopped, "Crackers!"

"Take them over to Momma," I directed. The paper sack flew out of my hands as Carol snatched it. "And tell her I have to take Rosie home!" I motioned an ineffective wave to her receding back.

"DON'T FORGET!" I yelled as she disappeared into the house.

We labored over the small knoll past our house. Rosie asked about Momma's potato garden, a remnant of the huge plot of Grandpa Nashalook's that once supplied the gold-rush town of Nome with its tubers.

"The potatoes are coming up. They're pretty small now but seem to be growing fast." I said. "Me and Ler have to weed it." I frowned, thinking of my bossy older sister. "I don't mind, though, because, you know what? Sometime we find beads in the ground!" Grandpa's potato garden once surrounded an old Russian trading post. It had rotted down to a heap, but we still could find trading beads that fell into the rich soil. I always thought beads grew in the ground.

A woman yelled, "Sunshine!" and I followed the voice to see Grandma Selma emerging from her cache. Her happy face poked out of the little door of a miniature log house set on driftwood poles. She waved and said, "Hi, Rosie!"

"Hi, Grandma!" I yelled. Rosie sent her salutations with a smile and a wave. But as we walked farther on, Rosie became sad because she didn't have a cache like Grandma's of her own to go to. After a few more steps, she said roughly, "*Arah*" ("Here," in our expression of agitation), as she pushed her package onto me. "I know where my house is now. I got to find the key." Rosie and Grandma were neighbors of sorts, if you counted a house or two in between, and then at an angle, not just right across, like the white people prefer to arrange things.

On the wide brown road, where it was level, Rosie dug in her purse again. She was muttering how someone had taken some cookware from her house, and now she had to lock the house.

"*Tuh-ruh!* Good, I found it!" She moved purposefully to her tiny log cabin, just big enough for a door, window, bed, stove, and table. It didn't seem much larger than Grandma's cache. In the small storm porch with just enough room to stand, she reached beside the doorknob and found the lock. Jostling the key, she shook the lock and wrestled the door open.

"*A re ga.* It's beautiful to be home again." She laughed tiredly and with an ironic amusement at her impairment that made her dependent on a small child.

"*Ka ka ruk,*" she addressed me. "Put the stuff on the table, okay?" She navigated her way across her small house and put her purse underneath the bed, then pushed the purse against the wall. Sighing in relief that all was in place, she sat down heavily on the bed.

"*Qu ya na,* you helped me today." Her tired, sightless eyes looked down at the floor. "Next time, I will buy you gum, but I don't have any here now. Anyway, God will bless you, and remember that Jesus loves you."

"I know." I recalled the Sunday school song.

I stood still for a while to let her know that I was thinking of her advice, then said, "I'm gonna go home now, Rosie." I said it loudly to announce my intent. I put the package square upon her table, now soft and rumpled from handling. I turned to face her.

"See you," I said.

"See you," Rosie said quietly from the comfort of her dark home.

Portage into the Wild

Steve Chamberlain

It was two o'clock in the morning. There was just the slightest breath of wind as the cold air fell down out of the mountains, flowed down the creeks, and settled onto the frozen river like a dead weight. The cold penetrated; it attacked, regardless of my parka. I danced on the sled runners to keep warm. The cutbank on my left rose and grew into a huge specter—the bluffs—against the vague white snow all around me in the half moon. A sense of unease registered inside me at the looming black enormity of the bluffs. I called the feeling fear and fought against it. Plastic runners squawked against the sharp frozen crystals of snow on the trail like chalkboards under fingernails. The breath from the dogs streamed back and froze on the guard hairs of their coats as they ran. They were white-tipped with frost and their eyes glowed yellow when they looked back into the beam of my headlamp.

Kalskag was twenty-five miles behind me on the Kuskokwim River—more than three hours. The dogs were plodding at less than eight miles an hour, more than 215 miles into the Kuskokwim 300 dogsled race in western Alaska. The next village, Tuluksak, below the dark, high bluffs and past the portage, was thirty-five miles ahead, another four hours, with luck, but probably five. Five hours could be forever. My beard was glaciating with frost from my breath and my constantly running nose. My mouth was encapsulated in ice, locked shut between frozen mustache and beard. There was not even enough room to fit a broken piece of hard candy between my lips. And no way to drink. The greatest irony: running on the frozen river, through a field of snow, ice at my very lips, and I was suffering from dehydration. The cold sucked the moisture from my body, drained me, dried me up in a cage of ice. My lips were numb and burning at the edges. I knew they were freezing.

Even so, it was not fear of the cold that bothered me. My body, being constantly sensitive to pain, had gradually accepted it. My mind no longer fought against hardship and was quite at ease solving the physical problems of life, visualizing, for instance, how I would use pliers to crush the ice from my beard and mustache. By the resistance and squawk of the runners on the trail, I judged it to be thirty degrees below zero. Not that cold. If it were colder I would be driven to stop to build a fire, but now there was only pride, determination, the race. Go. Only the core of life was afire deep in my guts. I clenched my teeth, making the air hole—like a seal under ice—to my mouth even smaller. I could take any-thing for four or five hours. What I did not understand yet was this premonition I could not name, that if I went into the material world hard enough—I hesitate to form an axiom—I would arrive at its opposite.

It was the gloom of the bluffs that bothered me—the way they rose up, monstrous at my side, disappearing in blackness above me. The bluffs were formed by a high tundra ridge running down from the Kilbuck Mountains into the Kuskokwim River in the sixty-mile-long, uninhabited no-man's-land between Kalskag and Tuluksak. A dog team was parked by the side of the trail under the bluffs. This was the same team I had been running with almost twenty-four hours before, just past Whitefish Lake, on the other side of Kalskag. The opposing team had gone on, while my leader, Junior, peremptorily dove off the trail and into the brush.

This other musher was "dead on the trail." No fight left in him. He was feeding raw frozen salmon to his dogs; his movements were slow, confused, almost aimless. His dogs were too tired to chew the frozen fish. No one would want to stop here under the bluffs intentionally after three nights without sleep, fighting cold, standing on two-inch runners; trying to care for the dogs, care for their feet; freezing the tips of fingers while putting on foot salve to keep the dogs' pads from cracking on the abrasive snow; watering—for dehydration was as bad for them as for the drivers; watching for tangles in the thin, almost unseeable lines. My headlamp was dim, the batteries sucked dry by cold. At this point almost anything could cause a tangle, the dogs as tired as the man. They dipped for snow to feed their thirst, put a foot over the neckline—ordinarily no problem—but sixty hours on the trail, a major problem, a tangle, a stop. Some dogs—the cunning ones like Junior—would tangle themselves just to quit. And lately, one of the front-runners in the race had been throwing generous chunks of sausage off to the side of the trail every few miles. The younger dogs lunged for every piece as we passed, breaking our rhythm, our team stride, our concentration, our will.

The "dead man" on the side of the trail was an antidote; I came alive. Junior, having slept in the heat of the day before (while I stayed awake and pampered him), had regained his stamina. I pushed my luck. I snarled incomprehensible syllables of exultation as my dogs trudged past his team. The driver did not look at me. I did not look at him. He might infect us with his weakness.

A mile farther, another musher was stopped in the shadow of the bluffs. At first he was just a black dot in the darkness. I was uneasy. My headlamp was shining, but no stronger than the moon on the edge of snow. Then I made out the huddle of his dogs, the basket of his sled. This team wasn't dead. He had seen me coming; my light told him we were a team and not an illusion. He packed up his sled as I approached, pulled his team on the trail as we passed, and ran his team right up to my runners. It was a lawyer from the town of Bethel.

This was an old Bethel sprint-racing trick. When all else fails, when dogs no longer respond to voice commands, they will still chase another team. Drafting. It is as if the team in front is pulling that extra team along with their own load.

So I stopped. He stopped.

I went. He was right there.

I stopped again. He stopped. I walked back to him. "Say, if you follow a little farther back we can both make good time." I tried to sound amiable. "But if you stay right behind me we aren't going to make any time at all. I can't drag you to Bethel." The tangles, the sausage on the trail, and now this: My team would wither in minutes.

He looked hurt that I'd scold him, mumbled something that might have been agreement. But as soon as I turned the dogs loose he was right there again, right behind me.

I stopped; he stopped. I unpacked my sled, getting out dog pans and the foam-lined box I kept warm water in. I got out a bag of frozen snacks. I would feed and water the dogs, rest them. I couldn't drag him to Tuluksak. There was no going on. I stumbled around, listless, confused like the first man I had passed a short while ago on the trail behind me. I looked down, defeated. And I was only half acting.

Finally, he plodded down the trail. I looked at my watch. I unpacked everything from the sled, as if what I wanted was on the very bottom. I swore because I couldn't find it. The dogs cocked their ears.

Fifteen minutes. Twenty minutes. Just about right. As soon as he was out of sight, I packed everything back in the sled, without snacking. Snacking would slow the team down, make them restive. It was a gamble of time. If I stayed too long my team would cool down and stiffen up. If I went too soon he might be waiting on the trail to ambush me. I pulled onto the trail without my headlamp on. I crouched down behind the sled to make myself—to make the black dot I would appear to be—as small as possible.

He was just five minutes down the trail. He had been lurking for me like a Bethel shark. But I had outwaited him. He thought I had made an honest stop and was snacking his own dogs. With any luck, he had already put something on their stomachs. He would have been stopped for twenty minutes. It is hard to be patient, to do nothing for twenty minutes, at three in the morning at thirty below.

I called quietly to my dogs. They needed one burst. They edged up on their speed. I hissed. They neared a slow lope. I snarled as I saw him look up at the black spot coming toward him out of the darkness. I pushed the sled with one foot like a scooter. The dogs loped. He tried to pull his leader out onto the trail directly in our path to block me and to throw my dogs into confusion. But his leader balked. I whooped past. He threw his gear into the sled and tried to get his dogs on the trail. They didn't want to move.

I drove my dogs into the darkness for three minutes, for five, for seven, right up to the edge of collapse, myself at the edge of collapse, then let them slow down to their normal pace again. There was nothing in sight behind me. He was probably back there, maybe only three or five minutes behind, but had lost essential contact; we did not have to drag him down the trail.

The trail turned off the river, onto the Tuluksak portage, into the dark woods where the winter moon did not illuminate, the last twenty-five miles to Tuluksak. My headlamp whimpered and died. It was like a candle, the half moon much brighter, but in the trees shadows covered the trail. I strained my eyes, trying to pick out the branches that would slap or club me, more feeling the trail than seeing it, my eyes dilated like cats' to see in the dark. I realized my tiredness now. A hypothermic haze settled over me like ice fog on the river.

I considered lashing myself to the sled, like they did to the drunk in the village sprint race on the Yukon. But it wasn't funny now. My eyes were wide open, yet I seemed to be sleeping. All of my will was focused on keeping those eyes open.

Then a terrifying phenomenon overcame me. Little men appeared along the trail, threatening me. Little men. At first I denied it. As soon as my head nodded forward in sleep, they darted out from hiding behind the clumps of willows by the side of the trail and ran at the dogs, causing the team to spook and dive sideways. I almost lost my grip on the sled.

Again and again, they darted out, little men, until I could not deny them but had to defend myself against them. They looked like the little men who attacked sore muscles in the liniment ads in magazines when I was a child. They knew I couldn't do anything about them. I couldn't stop, for the enemy that I had left at such dear cost was behind me; to stop was to collapse. I prodded myself, danced double time on the back of the runners, sang "swing low, sweet chariot" to the dogs. I told myself the demons couldn't exist. But as soon as I let down my guard one of those mischievous little men darted out to run at my team. The little men were getting bolder and bolder, just waiting for my head to stay down asleep, and then only God knew what they would do. They were teasing. As soon as I looked at them they turned and ran back into the bushes. I yelled at them once but stopped. Yelling spooked the dogs; now was not the time for Junior to dive off the trail. I went on, dazed, sacked, razed.

The trail opened up and the little men disappeared. I came onto an ancient oxbow lake left by some stream now long moved somewhere else. A gray New England church steeple rose from behind the spruce trees in the darkness, as if there really was a church there. I stared. I knew it couldn't be there, but there it was, plain as day.

My eyes were open but whether I was asleep or awake after that I do not know. I was deathly afraid of waking up and finding the sled and team gone. If I was dreaming the little men and the church steeple, I might be dreaming that I was still on the back of the sled. The race was irrelevant.

The dogs jumped up out of the last creek in the portage and went up on the frozen meadows. It was the last stretch before the trail entered the frozen Tuluksak River, where the sign hanging in the wilderness read, "7 Miles to Tuluksak, 75 to Bethel," courtesy of the Kuskokwim 300 race committee. I stopped the team like a roosting willow grouse that has stayed out past dark, threw myself on top of the sled, and fell asleep almost immediately.

I don't know whether I slept for an hour or for five minutes. I returned to consciousness fearing that the Bethel lawyer would be at my back any moment. Paranoid and cold. Impossible really to sleep. I got up and ran the team on into Tuluksak. The lawyer must have suffered a worse fate than I because I never saw him again until after the race in Bethel two days later—and we weren't talking then.

I decided to keep the little people and the church steeple to myself. Hallucinations are common in long-distance dog racing, when mushers push themselves to the limit and a little past, but this wasn't a story I felt comfortable talking about at the banquet after the race. I knew I had traveled somewhere where the inner and outer landscape converged during that wild stretch of forest and lake and creek in the Tuluksak portage, but I steadfastly maintained my anchor in the material world.

Several years later I moved downriver to Bethel for work when the Alaska oil boom faded. I came in contact with a man I'll call Melvin; he was a Bethel neighbor's grown son. He lived in a village a short ways upriver from Bethel. Sometimes, Melvin came to Bethel on his snow machine or in his boat (there are no roads between Bethel and the "villages," only the river and ancient dogsled trails turned snow machine trails) to visit his father. When his father was not home, Melvin would visit me.

As soon as he saw my wife he recognized her, or rather, his relationship to her. For a time he had been my sister-in-law's boyfriend, when they were on the track team together at Mount Edgecumbe High School (a boarding school for Native students) in Sitka. Native people of Alaska have for millennia recognized the need for networking, or "trading partners." Although I am Kass'aq (Caucasian), this was enough to establish a connection between us.

Melvin carried a "traveler," a plastic flask of Canadian whiskey under his parka. And this, my own weakness, was cause enough to establish acquaintance with him when he politely asked me if I cared to share a drink. We stood and later knelt and finally sat on the floor of my inside porch. (There are no bars in Bethel.) By the time the "traveler" was empty we had established a sort of friendship. We never talked about my sister-in-law or Edgecumbe or my current profession, as a college English teacher. We talked about track, although his running days were over, and feats of strength, and dog mushing.

In return for the evening of conversation, of bragging stories about hunting, fishing, and dogsled racing, and of whiskey, I gave Melvin one of the young females out of my dog yard.

But as our acquaintance progressed, I began to wish that his father stayed home more often in Bethel or that he gave Melvin the key to his house. There is nothing that I like more, myself, than a jug of whiskey. But I like fresh drinking stories. I gradually became bored with tales of the great track star. His broken nose began to belie his tales of prowess.

It was late fall, night falling sooner, the air becoming colder. I'm not given to subtlety, and Melvin, for any of his faults, was not dull, so he must have perceived that I was tiring of his company. It was then that he tried the baited hook and told me about the Ircinraat. With great awe in his voice, he let me into the spirit world of the Yup'ik Eskimo, telling me that which he did not think I would believe. It was natural—we lived near the Russian Orthodox graveyard—to begin to talk of the supernatural.

He knelt on the floor, put the whiskey jug between us, and swung his fists to the right and to the left. Had he had his hands unclenched he would have looked like the lead dancer in an Eskimo dance, or *yurraq*. As it was, he looked as if he were performing a tae kwon do move in a *yurraq* form, which, as I reflected, looking at the jug between us, must have been just about the way he felt. He was feeling the whiskey spirit and the Eskimo spirit at the same time.

"My grandpa told me about the Ircinraat."

It was a puzzling word I did not recognize. The word danced on my tongue as I repeated it to myself. I sat down on the floor a gauged distance in front of him, within reach of the "traveler," but out of reach of the fists if they should opt for tae kwon do.

"He warned me," Melvin continued. "Up by the bluffs between Tuluksak and Kalskag, the portage. They are mischief. They come to you when you are tired."

I leaned forward. A strange feeling ran up the back of my neck from the base of my shoulders.

"Do you know what they are?"

"I don't know the Yup'ik name," I said. "Ixinghauks?" I tried to pronounce it in Whiteman.

"Yes. The little people."

Right then my hackles stood up at full attention. I could feel the guard hairs on the tips of my ears quiver. "The portage below the bluffs?" I asked. I was familiar with the upriver stories of the little people. My mother-in-law had told me about them at the upriver fish camp, early in the morning when we got up to light the smokehouse fires. But she had always spoken to me in English, not using their Yup'ik name. I didn't consider her a foolish old woman, but the little people were hard to accept. She had told me once about little people coming by in a sled and then disappearing. The next day someone came with a real sled and dog team in the same manner. But I had never put that information in any category. Her daughters' eyes tended to twinkle when she talked about little people.

All of these thoughts passed through my mind as Melvin spoke to me. He must have read it in my face with the cunning of a whiskey drinker.

"You don't believe me?" he demanded.

I perceived his next move. If I laughed at him, he would denounce me as a spiritless Kass'aq, a white man without a soul.

But I told him what I had never told anyone. "I believe you," I said. "In fact, I've seen them myself—exactly where your grandpa told you about them. The exact circumstances, too," I said cautiously. I watched his reaction. How much Kass'aq was he beneath the Yup'ik veneer? The missionaries had been on the Delta a hundred years and had done their job well, downriver.

Now it was Melvin's turn to show surprise. He looked at me in disbelief.

"It was the first time I ran the Kusko 300," I told him before he could denounce what I had said.

I saw it in his face then: He did not believe.

"I called it a hallucination at the time. You know, all mushers have hallucinations when we go without sleep for a couple days." This was partially true. But when different people have the same hallucination at the same place under the same conditions at different times, the rational mind begins to waver. The phenomenon of the little people, hallucination or no, took on a psychic reality for me then, just as it had for Melvin's grandfather. I knew I was treading on dangerous ground. When a man throws away Christian dogma and begins to rely on the reality of his own experience, he is in trouble in this country.

And how could I prove this? Unless a man has hunted with you and traveled with you, he does not believe the stories you bring back. This is why men keep trophies. How could Melvin believe me? He is an Eskimo, one of the race of supreme hunters on the face of the earth, and I a Kass'aq, a race not known for its affinity with nature, and a schoolteacher on top of that, once more removed from the natural world. I'm afraid I failed.

Melvin came only once more that winter. He told me again about the Ircinraat, perhaps testing me. I told him again that I believed what his grandfather told him, that I too had seen them. We were close to becoming enemies then. Had I usurped the spirit world he could not believe in? And how came I, sensualist and materialist, to advocate a spirit world?

I reaffirmed that it was one of those things you keep to yourself. I mentioned it to my wife briefly. She just looked at me, Yup'ik herself. I was intruding on sacred ground. I couldn't wax eloquent on Yup'ik spirituality.

So much has been taken away from Native people. This, maybe, is the greatest thing taken away. The stories, the legends, the teachings are still told, and the people cherish the telling. But few understand them; fewer believe or have experienced them. And when they have, often their modern education has persuaded them to deny their own experience.

The longer I stayed in Bethel, the heartland of Yup'ik culture, the more pressure I felt to deny my experiences with the people upriver in Aniak. I was for some years a hunter and trapper myself, before the obligations of raising a family bore down on me and forced me to join the middle class and "make something of myself." But what I had learned in the wilderness, in the natural world, was more powerful to me than the institutions I became involved in. The little people were more vivid and real to me, more honest, than a tenure-track vita. I became restless and enrolled in classes to reinstate my secondary teaching certificate so that I could move back into "the bush" and earn a living.

I was taking a course in Alaska Native studies with other teachers seeking recertification. Our professor was Clara Antolik, an anthropologist and herself a Cup'ik, a people on the Bering coast who maintain their own cultural identity within the context of the larger Yup'ik culture, though they speak a Yup'ik dialect.

During one of the class sessions the word *Ircinraq* (Ircinraq is the singular form of Ircinraat) occurred. The hypothesis for the discussion that evening was that Native people, people in nature, are more susceptible to meeting this natural (not supernatural) phenomenon than non-Native people. Clara was talking about Ircinraat.

I recalled reading how Japanese and Chinese poetry, steeped in nature, often fell on deaf ears in the West because Westerners were so alienated from nature that they could not understand what the Easterner was talking about. How many people in New York, the argument went, could differentiate the smell of a cottonwood tree from the smell of a birch tree, for instance? How much further removed were Ircinraat? Clara's explanation was similar. How could a person not immediately caught up in the natural world of the Eskimo ever understand, let alone see, little people or Ircinraat?

This is Clara's story. During the 1950s, she and her girl-friends were playing at a fish camp near a spit of mud that ran out into the Aprun River, when they saw a man in a kayak coming down the river. Since one of the girls' fathers was out hunting and was expected back, they thought it must be him. They were going to run up and tell the girl's mother to start cooking for her father, as was the custom when the man came back from hunting.

They ran down to the spit of land, but when they did, the man did not come around to the other side. He never appeared—he just disappeared. There was nowhere he could have gone.

Clara went up and told her father. He said, as if it were nothing special, "That was an Ircinraq." Clara said she and her girlfriends did not believe it. They were Catholic children and did not believe in that sort of thing. They could not explain what had happened.

The next day the girls were playing on the beach and a man appeared again at the same time of day and in the same manner on the river in a kayak. But they weren't going to be fooled this time, so the girls waited and didn't run up to tell their mothers. This time the man came around the spit and landed in front of the village; it was the girl's father, returned from his hunting trip.

Clara's father explained that Ircinraat could foretell what would happen in the future by demonstration or presentation, as this one did (and just as the one my mother-in-law had seen did).

A woman in class asked Clara if she really believed she had seen that.

"Yes, I really saw it."

"Oh, it's funny how people cling to their beliefs."

"Yes, we said that," Clara replied. "I went home. I told myself, *I'm a Catholic; I don't believe in that sort of thing.* But it didn't go away. I saw it. All of us girls saw it.

"They're part of the natural world. Native people have an easier time seeing these natural phenomena because they are more in tune with nature. They live with it. The Ircinraat can be either mischievous or they can foretell the future. The one we saw was foretelling the girl's father coming home the next day."

"Do you really believe that?" the other woman persisted. She wouldn't be convinced. She was a Christian fundamentalist.

"There are lots of miraculous things happening in the Bible," Clara answered. "Virgin births, men raised from the dead. Do you believe those things? I don't think Ircinraat are any harder to believe."

I saw then it wasn't a matter of belief—it was only a matter of meeting them. For me.

Site Visit

Melissa S. Green

Around 10:30 a.m. the fog finally begins to lift. Trooper Dekreon seems as relieved as I to escape the confines of his tiny office. Next door at the MarkAir terminal he introduces me to the charter pilot, a young white guy named Greg Mickelson who arrived in Alaska bare weeks ago. Mickelson leads us out to his plane, a little four-seat Cessna, and we strap my green pack under the cargo net. I take one of the back seats; Dekreon sits up front with the pilot. I'm glad not to sit there—you can see fine out the side window, but in front all you get is sky and instrument panel, at least if you're as short as I am.

Soon we're aloft. Below us, as we tilt to the right in a long turn, I see the houses of St. Marys tucked in the crook of a big hill—Andreafsky Mountain, according to the maps I picked up yesterday before flying out of Anchorage.

I have studied the maps carefully out of no greater need than simply to know where I am. It's a strong need for me. I'd make a lousy voyager on the starship *Enterprise* because I'd be unable to tolerate materializing here, materializing there, with no physical sense of where one planet was in relation to another. I felt like that when I first flew to Alaska from Montana. It took one trip by state ferry and another by road between Alaska and the Lower 48 before I felt how the earth beneath my feet connected with the earth beneath my parents' feet, how one clod of dirt held to another, to another, to another, all the way back to my birthplace.

There is no road between Anchorage and St. Marys, nor could I walk that distance. But the maps help. I can look at them, run my fingers across the smooth flat blue of Cook Inlet, up the thin blue wavy lines of rivers and creeks on the other side, through the light green of streamside willow and alder, through birch and spruce forest. I can imagine that closely spaced brown contour lines are the steep rocky slopes and high peaks of the Alaska Range, that wide white worm shapes are the icy masses of glaciers grinding at the rock beneath them, that blue meltwater lines carry rock dust and grit into thicker blue rivers—the Big, the Swift, the Stony—that add their silty waters to the muddy Kuskokwim as it winds through the Kuskokwim and Russian Mountains and flows past the villages of Aniak and Kalskag. But while the Kuskokwim continues southwestward past Akiachak and Bethel to dump itself into Kuskokwim Bay, my finger veers northwest to portage through a wilderness of tiny blue-dot lakes to Russian Mission on the Yukon River; and now south, now west, now north, my finger traces the winding river till, at the Andreafsky River, it leaves the Yukon to travel a final three miles to St. Marys.

In reality, my flight from Anchorage yesterday landed me in Bethel, where I spent my three-hour layover nosing around the Alaska Commercial Company store, wandering around with my camcorder on the waterfront where fish tenders and freight boats further the commerce of the Kuskokwim River, and eating at the same Chinese-Mexican restaurant where my colleague Nancy and I shared a meal two years ago, on my only other trip to bush Alaska.

By the time I returned last night to the Bethel airport, it was drizzling. It was drizzling also when I touched down in St. Marys.

Drizzle turned into a cold heavy rain, which overnight was supplanted by the thick fog I woke to this morning. Socked in by the fog, Mike Dekreon and I have spent the last two and a half hours in the cramped office that serves as the St. Marys Post of the Alaska State Troopers, going over the 1993 jail records for Emmonak, the second of five Alaska Native villages I will visit today with Dekreon as my guide.

We level out, heading north-northwest. To our right the Andreafsky Hills roll northeastward, where they melt into the Nulato Hills, running almost to the coast east of St. Michael, northernmost of the settlements of Russian America. Russian influence is more pervasive on the Kuskokwim River than here, on the lower Yukon, but occasional reminders of it can still be found in place names like Russian Mission and Andreafsky or personal names like Kameroff and Alexie—both very common on the Yukon-Kuskokwim Delta. The Yup'ik Eskimo word for white person, *kass'aq*, is borrowed from the Russian *kazak*, cossack.

Now that we are out of the hills I would be hard put to tell which direction we're flying if I didn't already know from the maps where Kotlik, my first destination, lies in relation to St. Marys. The sun is high and the only shadow below belongs to the plane. The land is as much water as ground—tiny ponds, large lakes, long sinuous sloughs snaking among them. It's difficult to determine whether a river is a tributary or a channel of the Yukon because the Yukon this close to the Bering Sea coast splits up into so many "sub"-Yukons, almost an indeterminate number of them, depending on whether you consider a particular stream part of the Yukon or a river in itself. The Yukon dumps about eighty-eight million tons of silt annually into the Bering Sea; plenty is also dropped at its flanks, causing continual shifting of channels and sloughs in land that is itself largely marsh. St. Marys owes its present location to the river's shifts. It was founded in 1948 when the Jesuit mission of Akulurak, far downriver, was forced to relocate because the slough it was on silted up so severely that supplies couldn't be boated in.

In front of me Dekreon looks downward, seemingly as intent as I on studying the land below us. I talked with him several times over the past week, setting this trip up, but it wasn't until this morning that I first saw him, unmistakable in the light blue uniform shirt with navy blue pockets of the Alaska State Troopers. He's a tall man, big, with graying hair under his navy blue Mountie hat. Somehow I'd decided from his voice that he was younger, black-haired, gung ho. Maybe I'd imagined him as he might have been a few years ago, before experience granted him gray and the wisdom of knowing his work.

Suddenly he half-turns his head so I can hear him shout above the engine noise, "Look there! There's some swans!" I follow his pointing finger but I see nothing but water, land, more water. Dekreon is staring downward again, looking for more swans. After however many years he has lived and worked out here, flying over this same drowned world, it still holds his attention. I like him for it.

The place at which the Yukon River begins to divide itself into its several "passes" to the sea is known on the map as Head of Passes. Downriver from there, the northern branch of the river is named Kwikpak Pass, after the river's original Yup'ik name—Kwikpak means "big river"—and the southern is called Kwikluak Pass. Some of Kwikluak Pass's waters thread though a maze of marsh and pothole lakes as Kanelik and Akularak Passes, both of which eventually run into Kwemeluk Pass, where the village of Sheldon Point, another village I am to visit, lies. There's Kwiguk Pass, where Emmonak is, and Alakanuk Pass, where Alakanuk, another of today's villages, is found. We've already flown past Mountain Village, which is just ten miles from where we set off—we will catch it on our way back to St. Marys, as the last stop on today's whirlwind tour.

Kwikpak Pass, to the north, also splits its waters—Kawanak Pass, Little Apoon Pass, Apoon Pass, where the Kotlik River and the village of Kotlik lie. These are not all the passes, nor do these include the sloughs, the channels, the short rivers, and the creeks, some of whose sources are waterlogged ground, if they can be said to have identifiable sources at all.

Looking down at this vast watery labyrinth, I wonder, *How can anyone live here?* I used to ask the same question riding

Greyhound buses through the flat monotony of North Dakota on my trips between home and college. *How can anyone live here?* I've lived all my life near mountains—the northern Rockies, the Cascades, the Chugach Mountains near Anchorage—and there have always been hills, trees, unevenness to the horizon. The patterns of water and land below fascinate me with their peculiar beauty, but to live here? It's so flat, so wet. Then below us I see the silvery glint of a skiff motoring along some stretch of the river, and I think, *If the people driving that boat knew what I'm thinking, they'd say I don't have a clue.* There is more to this land than I can see now. Of course it can be lived upon. It's rich, replete with king salmon, silvers, chum, grayling, char, and blackfish, bearded seals and walrus, black brants, cackling Canada geese, emperor geese, scoters and eiders, swans. It's a land full of life. If the horizon is monotonously even all around, still it is flush with the sky. In my mind I hear my partner Rozz again tell me what she learned on a three-month walk she once took. "Sky is everywhere," she said, "but people hide from it. They hide from it inside their houses." The people here, I think, do not hide from the sky.

It is to see this land and to understand these things that I eagerly took on the tasks of this trip and the one before, the one I took in 1992. For people like me, who don't own their own airplanes, boats, snow machines, or dogsleds, it costs too much to get out to the vast areas of the state that can't be reached by road. We get out, if we get out at all, by finding work that will take us there. In my case, I work in an office—the Justice Center at the University of Alaska Anchorage—that contracts each year with the state Division of Family and Youth Services (DFYS) to monitor Alaska's compliance with the federal Juvenile Justice and Delinquency Prevention Act (JJDPA). The project includes making visits each year to one-third of the sites in the "monitoring universe" of jails, lockups, and juvenile detention facilities. This is the second time the regulars on the project, Nancy and Richard and Cassie, have invited me to take time out from my normal duties as a publication specialist to make one of the trips.

JJDPA requires three things of states in regard to the detention of juveniles. The first, "deinstitutionalization of status offenders," means that kids accused of status offenses—offenses like drinking alcohol, truancy, curfew violation, or running away from home, which wouldn't be crimes if they were adults—aren't to be locked up or held in any sort of secure confinement at all. The second requirement, "sight and sound separation," means that juvenile offenders must be kept out of any kind of sight and sound contact with adult offenders. The third goal of JJDPA is "jail removal"—the complete removal of juveniles from adult correctional facilities. The law provides some leeway: There's a six-hour "grace period" to permit juveniles accused of criminal offenses to be transferred from adult facilities to juvenile facilities; and under Title 47, Alaska's "protective custody" statute, both juvenile and adult inebriates can be incarcerated for their own protection for up to twelve hours or until they're sober—an important provision, given weather extremes in much of the state that can freeze people to death.

All of this seems to make sense. In high school I saw a TV movie starring Linda Blair about a nice girl whose father beat her. She ran away, got caught, and was sent to a reform school, where bad treatment and bad influences soon turned her into a real delinquent. That movie could've been a propaganda piece for the "status offender" portion of JJDPA, but its premise seems true: If kids who get into minor trouble are institutionalized with serious delinquents and criminals, they might become serious criminals themselves.

The Linda Blair movie notwithstanding, things change once you move out into bush Alaska. For one thing, villages of two hundred to five hundred people with economies based primarily on subsistence hunting and fishing don't have the tax base to build jails large enough to hold kids out of sight and sound from whatever adult might be locked up at the same time. I think about the members of Congress who sat in their Washington, D.C., offices drafting out the Juvenile Justice and Delinquency Prevention Act of 1974. Did they consider how things work in a tiny remote village in Alaska hundreds of miles from the nearest juvenile detention facility? I think about what the troopers in Aniak told me two years ago about a training video they'd just seen on handling juvenile offenders. "We just laughed at it," one of them said. "It was California—it just totally didn't apply."

Kotlik comes into view, a thin string of tiny buildings stretching along one bank of the Kotlik River. All the Yup'ik villages I've seen are like that—thin and long, extending along rivers and sloughs, oriented to the water that is at once foodstore and highway. The houses grow as we get closer, and Mickelson gets on the radio with someone in the village to alert them to our arrival. As we descend, a patch of empty ground to our right suddenly sprouts white crosses—a graveyard. We touch down at the little dirt strip at the village's edge just as a middle-aged Yup'ik man pulls up on a three-wheel all-terrain vehicle. Behind the ATV is a small trailer bearing two shy, giggling youngsters in baseball caps. Dekreon helps Mickelson turn the plane while I point my camcorder at the boys—"You're on *Candid Camera!*"

I sit in the trailer with the boys; Dekreon rides on the back of the ATV. Mickelson stays behind with the plane as we drive into Kotlik on its main street, a boardwalk barely wide enough for two ATVs. Other, narrower boardwalks run off from it to people's homes. Every house we pass is raised up from the ground on stilts, a precaution against flooding. On the outskirts of the village many houses are unpainted, their plywood exteriors darkened by rain and cold and age. Others are weathered a dull silver. Farther in we encounter red or dark brown homes with shallow-pitched blue roofs, all a standard design, square and blocky. Probably they were built by the state as part of a housing project, or perhaps by the village government.

It's apparent most residents here can't afford to be as house-proud as suburbanites or my Anchorage neighbors. Every piece of wood that goes into building these houses is shipped in, because no trees grow on this soggy plain. There are no yards per se, no fences, but the liberal spaces between houses are scattered with barrels, buckets, pieces of plywood, small sheds and outhouses, old motors, and junk, some of it the common detritus of a place that has no landfill, some of it destined to be recycled, repaired, reused.

A system of heavy piping, several feet above the ground, is undoubtedly for the village water supply. Many such insulated systems in the bush are built above ground. Below the ground, they'd quickly be damaged by frost heave, as happened to a brand-new water and sewer system in a state housing project in Bethel a few years back. Where the pipes cross above the boardwalk at one point, a sign is attached: "Speed Limit 10." The sign is directed at ATV drivers: there are no cars here, no trucks, just ATVs, boats, snow machines, and perhaps a few dogsleds to go with the animals in the two dog lots we've passed.

We reach the Kotlik Public Safety Building. On the opposite side of Kotlik from the airstrip, it is a small red building with a blue roof and a ramp leading up from the boardwalk to the doorway. There is no sign to identify it. Looking around, I see no signs anywhere to distinguish "public" buildings from people's homes, nor are there any characteristic architectural features to help you tell the washeteria from the school, the Catholic or Assembly of God churches from the village offices or store. As in Akiachak, Aniak, and Upper Kalskag, the Kuskokwim River villages I visited two years ago, if you want to go somewhere you either know where it is already or you ask.

We are greeted by VPSO Thomas Prince, a good-looking young man in white sweats with a complexion darkened by the long hours of summer sun. VPSOs—Village Public Safety Officers—are village residents, usually Alaska Natives, who train for six weeks at the trooper academy in Sitka in law enforcement, fire suppression, search and rescue, and other public safety duties. Many are assisted by Village Police Officers, or VPOs. VPSOs are paid by their regional nonprofit Native associations, but each VPSO is supervised in the field by an "oversight trooper," an Alaska State Trooper posted in a nearby village—in Prince's case, Mike Dekreon.

I hand VPSO Prince the standard letter of introduction— "The Justice Center at the University of Alaska Anchorage has again contracted with the Alaska Division of Family and Youth Services to monitor...." Dekreon jokes with Prince about his "uniform." The standard VPSO uniform is similar to that of the troopers except that it's in shades of brown rather than blue. It is not a pair of white sweats.

Dekreon puts his arm over Prince's shoulder and walks off with him, talking. Dekreon is accompanying me not only for my benefit but also for his own: because my office is paying for the charter, using project funds the Justice Center received from DFYS, he's getting a free ride. Smoothing the way for me is a small price to pay for an extra chance at touching base with the VPSOs he oversees and to help them clear up any problems they might be having with their work.

Prince's assistant, a VPO whose name I've already forgotten, leads me into the public safety building. At the end of the building's short hallway, painted white, is the lockup: two cells with red wooden doors and small barred windows. The cells are small, empty rooms with linoleum floors and no external windows. There are no cots or locks on the doors, although I don't think to ask why. I take pictures of the cells with the inexpensive plastic camera Rozz lent me, then videotape them. "No possibility of sight or sound separation," I tell my camcorder. I try to photograph the VPSO office, but Rozz's camera refuses to work. I fiddle with it for a few moments, then give up and tape the office instead—desks with neatly stacked papers, file cabinets, a map on the wall next to the partly open window. The sun is shining through.

Dekreon and Prince rejoin us. After I explain briefly what I'm looking for, Prince shows me a handwritten "Kotlik Public Safety Custody Roster." Its existence takes Dekreon by surprise—the folks here seem to be doing better recordkeeping than he expected. The roster is not quite perfect for my purposes, however. It lists date (presumably of arrest), offense, name, date of birth, and social security number, but the time in and the date and time out are missing. This means Richard and Cassie will be unable to determine how many hours each person was held, and therefore whether or not any juvenile detentions violated the time limits imposed by JJDPA.

Prince sends the VPO off to another building to photocopy the 1993 portions of the log for me. Then he shows me a "Juvenile

Confinement Admission and Release Log." This is a standard DFYS multipart form, which is obviously not being sent to DFYS, because both copies are still in Prince's hand—until, that is, he separates them, giving the white copy to me and keeping the canary yellow for himself. Three years of juvenile cases are listed on the form—a total of about eight cases altogether, three from 1993. Prince, new to his job, has personal knowledge of only the last case, from December 1993, which he believes involved a youth who was joyriding—on an ATV, I assume, or a boat—and was held, but not locked up, until his father came to get him. These may not be the only juvenile cases Kotlik had in those three years. Arrestees are sometimes flown out of a village immediately after arrest, with no time held in the village. Other youths are released immediately to their parents or some other adult relative. Sometimes, when a family doesn't want a kid at home because he or she is drunk, maybe violent, release to the family is not possible and the kid is placed in protective custody.

There is nothing else from which to attempt record verification. Prior VPSOs might have kept informal notebooks, but, as Dekreon comments wryly, "If you try to verify that way, you'll be here five hours." I have to agree. Personally, I've just now decided I don't give a damn. I'm being picky because I'm out here to do a job—the job that gives me a chance to come out here in the first place. But as I begin to pull myself out of the job and to perform it automatically, without involvement, the whole exercise becomes in my mind more and more farcical. I'll grant that JJDPA makes some sense in Washington, D.C., and in Los Angeles and in Anchorage and Fairbanks and Juneau. But in a village of less than five hundred people, in which virtually everyone knows everyone, in which most people are related by ties of blood and marriage and common hardships and common joys, what possible sense does it make to worry about whether a male of nineteen years (hence an adult) and a male of seventeen years (hence a juvenile)—who may even be brothers or cousins— just who exactly cares if they can hear and see each other in a lockup? Make it any set of ages, fifteen and seventy, twelve and fifty—it all comes down to the same thing. Don't the two of them see and hear each other most days of the week, anyway? If VPSOs and VPOs don't have a reputation for superscrupulous recordkeeping, who can blame them? It probably doesn't make a damn bit of sense to them, either.

Dekreon and Prince are talking about alcohol. The village council wants Prince to stop and search people at the airstrip before they come into town in order to prevent them from smuggling in liquor. Kotlik is one of several villages that has opted, under Alaska's local option law, to go dry. Prince's problem is that the public safety building is on the opposite side of the village from the airstrip. Even if he starts for the airstrip immediately upon seeing a plane land, by the time he gets there the passengers have already walked into the village. If they have any booze with them, the booze has walked right in with them.

Strictly speaking, such searches might be questioned under the U.S. or Alaska constitutions, but the legalities are uncertain here, where questions of Native sovereignty are still very much at issue. Certainly such searches are not unknown in Alaska Native villages, whose people are increasingly sensitive to the relation between alcohol and Native deaths, whether homicide, suicide, or accident. Everywhere you go in the bush there is that equation of alcohol and crime, alcohol and death. The 1993 jail records for Emmonak—the only village of those I'm visiting today with a real jail, rather than a simple two-cell lockup—showed a number of kids who were detained on MCAs and PCs—Minors Consuming Alcohol and Protective Custodies. Here in Kotlik a boy went on a joyride—was he drunk when he did it?—and a girl visiting from another village was so messed up from drinking that she had to be flown to Bethel for a mental health evaluation. Faced with all this, I wouldn't be a constitutional purist, either. Airstrip searches and seizures of liquor without warrants are not the final solution to the problem, I agree, but they'll sure help until the solution is found. It's like someone bailing out a boat with a hole in it. The bailing won't stop the leak—only finding and plugging up the hole will stop the leak. But until that hole is plugged, am I going to tie the hands of the person bailing and say, "That's not how to keep your boat from sinking"?

I know something about alcoholism. My mom's dad was a binge drinker, and although neither of my parents is an alcoholic, the effects of my grandfather's alcoholism have filtered down to me, my family, the families of my cousins. Just about everything I've ever read about alcoholism stresses that it's a family disease. But this is the first time I've thought about that when I've thought about the bush. A village: two hundred, three hundred, five hundred people, maybe, a few families related to most other families by blood or marriage, at the very least by common traditions, common trials. If alcoholism is a family disease in a large city like Anchorage, then how much greater its impact must be in a small, relatively isolated village, even if only one person there is an alcoholic—like the difference between the explosive power of a stick of dynamite set off in a open field and that of a stick of dynamite set off in a tiny hole in a rock. And in the rural villages of Alaska there are no detox centers, no treatment centers. The lockups are drunk tanks as much as they are holding cells for accused criminals.

It's easy for some people, walking along Anchorage's Fourth Avenue and seeing inebriated Natives asleep on the pavement, to write them off as just a bunch of pitiful, conquered drunks. But what about the other side of life, away from Fourth Avenue—in Kotlik, in Emmonak, in other villages? A photographer named James Barker put together a book called *Always Getting Ready* about Yup'iks and subsistence on the Yukon-Kuskokwim Delta; there wasn't a speck of booze in it. There were photographs in it of faces serious with the effort of pulling in a net full of herring or hauling a beluga onto shore, faces watching alertly as the meat of a young man's first bearded seal was distributed, faces intent over the repair of an outboard motor or the placement of bright pink fillets of salmon on a fishrack for drying, faces full of drama and laughter at festivals and potlatches, faces rapt and joyful in the midst of dancing. There's a strength to these Yup'ik people—the "real people," their name for themselves means—a fabric that is perhaps frayed and worn, but there are those who are working singleheartedly to mend it, like the man in one Barker photograph sitting on the bank of the Black River methodically mending his salmon net so that it will be strong and will catch food so that he, his family, his people, will live.

These thoughts click away in me as the automatic part of me, the part still on the job, sits at the VPSO's desk jotting a last few notes—"Prince says normal procedure for dealing with juvs is hold them without lockup until parent, relative comes and gets." Dekreon and Prince have left the building again. When I finish my notes I leave the building, too, and the VPO returns with my photocopies from wherever the village copy machine is kept. We stand at the door of the public safety building, enjoying the sun, swiping at occasional mosquitoes, hearing Dekreon and Prince talking nearby in tones too low for us to know their words.

I say, "It's a beautiful day here today. This is a beautiful place." I mean it.

Some moments pass. He says, "Yes, Kotlik's a good place. But we have problems with sanitation. When it floods." Kotlik's sewage system consists of honey buckets and outdoor privies.

We haven't said much. Yet I sense from him, I sense from within me, a desire to continue this, to go beyond it, to know each other. Old Hebrew prophets like Amos and Isaiah considered "justice" more or less as a verb. You *did* justice, you didn't just sit back and wait for someone to hand it to you. You didn't just go and beg a judge for justice, or hire a bunch of lawyers to procure justice for you, or pass a law or call a cop and call it justice. Justice demanded everyone's active participation with one another, in community with one another. And if that's what justice really is, then why do I know this man, not by his name, but by his job title? Why do I concern myself with MCAs and PCs and all the other offense categories and acronyms? Why are the traumatic and ugly events of troubled people's lives pared down into data elements for Richard and Cassie to enter into a data file to perform statistical analysis on? When the analysis is complete, will its results really tell us, or the people in Washington, D.C., who will ultimately read our report, anything about justice in Kotlik, Alaska, or in Juneau or Fairbanks or Anchorage or Los Angeles or Washington, D.C.? If I am to do justice, I should stop here for longer than just an hour and talk with this man, and he with me, because how can we be just with one another if we don't even know each other?

The four of us walk along the boardwalk for a while until we meet up again with the middle-aged man who drove us in. Dekreon and I climb back onto the ATV for our ride back to the airstrip. We must have gotten into a different part of the village now, onto a different boardwalk, because I see the waters of the Kotlik River for the first time from within Kotlik itself. The water flashes between the houses as we move. I hear a motor, I see a skiff. I want right now to stop my job, to step out of it briefly, to stay here for just a little bit. Instead, I get back into the airplane with Trooper Dekreon and we fly to Emmonak.

Color-Blind

Kay Landis

One hot summer day in Idaho during the Great Depression, twelve-year-old Helen Swanson set off from her home, alone. In her pocket was a precious nickel, earned through hard labor, hoarded through months of privations, saved especially for an afternoon such as this.

The family was not starving, but still, nickels were scarce. Her father worked, now and then, at the sawmill; her mother took in laundry. Helen had earned her nickel helping her mother wash and dry and press the cotton cloths used by the mill owner's wife to soak up her monthly blood. She hated this job above all others, but she endured it because of what it would make possible. It was a milkshake she dreamed of as she worked, her favorite treat, and today she would have one at the drugstore in downtown Lewiston. I can almost hear her tuneless hum as she skipped along, anticipating the cool rich sweetness just ahead.

What was she thinking as she made the decision to cut across the vacant lot? Her mother must have warned her never to leave the road, but she knows that this is a shortcut and she can't wait. The quicker she gets to town, the sooner she will taste the creamy vanilla, feel its coldness in contrast to the hot Idaho sun overhead.

There's a man lurking near the field, a stranger, but perhaps she doesn't notice him at first, or perhaps she thinks he's just a hobo. Hobos were a common enough sight in those days, and one didn't immediately fear them. Mostly they were harmless—men just like her father, only a little less lucky.

As she approaches the middle of the field, there where the dry brown grass is tallest and the ground most uneven, she realizes that the stranger is following her. She doesn't think he's a hobo now; his approach is too deliberate, too purposeful, too menacing. He has begun a slow trot and is heading straight for her.

Young Helen has a towhead of Swedish blonde hair and a round, simple face, soft and curvy and earthy and open to the sky. She is tall but spindly for her age; her long white legs and awkwardly long arms are not designed for running. But run she does now, run for her life, stumbling over hard-baked earth—once, perhaps, even falling to her knees.

Well, as we would say today, "nothing happened." She made it to the street, a little flushed and quite out of breath, but otherwise unharmed. By the time she reached the next block and dared, at last, to look back, the man had vanished. She had been, as we say, lucky. Yet later she will realize that somewhere in that field of hot dry dead grass and detritus, she had lost her nickel. She will not get a milkshake this day.

As scary stories go, this one is pretty tame. I can think of far worse things that could have happened, that do happen, every day to little girls. But this story of the little girl was my mother's, and I grew up on it. She told it to explain why I was never to take a shortcut down the old county road to the beach. Why I was never to go to Schmitz Park, where the trees were tall, and the trails muddy in their shade. Why I was always to be careful and never talk to strangers. I remember how her voice would become small and hushed as she talked about "the man," as if to speak any louder might make him come back. And I remember, too, how her voice would turn soft and dreamy when she described the milkshake she never got. The milkshake was the point, of course: not what might have happened to her, but what did. In some ways, I think, she thirsted for that sweet cool milk for the rest of her life.

I consider myself warned. My mother's story, tame as it was, had its effect. I know, too, what happened to Eve, when she wandered off by herself and ran into the snake. I know about the wolf lying in wait for Red Riding Hood. And I vividly remember my first real death: Nancy Liptrap, who had the locker across from mine in junior high. Nancy Liptrap, who was the first of us to wear wire-rimmed glasses and long peasant skirts, who had an easy laugh and a warm heart and was voted Best All-Around Personality in the ninth grade. Nancy Liptrap, whose body was found stabbed and beaten and abused and abandoned in the woods behind the school the very next year.

And I've seen the chilling headlines in my own morning newspaper: "Woman Found Dead in Earthquake Park." I'd be a fool to ignore reality: Sometimes men kill. But I still walk in Earthquake Park regularly, in spite of the warnings. I take my happy little puppy Gus, and we traipse through the woods, off the paved trail because that's where the good smells are. We go once or twice a day, for an hour or more each time. I keep my eyes open—for moose, which are common, and for lynx, which are not. And for men, too, of course. Men lurking in the bushes. Sometimes I even pick up a stick, just in case. But still I go. Every day. Because I learned more than one lesson from my mother. I learned something about fear, but I learned something about sweetness as well. And though I cannot be entirely free of the fear, I have decided that I will not run. I will not stumble and fall to my knees on the hard-baked earth. I will have the sweetness my own mother missed.

And so far I've been lucky. Nothing truly bad has ever happened to me.

⑥

I live now in Anchorage, Alaska. Home to half the state's population, Anchorage sits on a roughly triangular peninsula of land, with the Chugach Mountains bordering the east and the twin arms of Cook Inlet washing the shores on the remaining two sides. The apex is just past the airport at Point Woronzof, at the farthest west end, where Cook Inlet divides into Turnagain Arm running southeast and Knik Arm running northeast.

Along the shoreline of both sides of this triangle is the Tony Knowles Coastal Trail, named after a former mayor of Anchorage, now governor, who oversaw much of its construction. Parts of a bike-trail system were built in the mid-1970s along the Chester Creek greenbelt, which runs east to west and bisects the city of Anchorage for most of its width. Under Mayor Knowles's administration in the 1980s, the trail system was extended along the shore of Cook Inlet, past Earthquake Park and southwest to Woronzof, around the perimeter of the airport, and southeast along Turnagain Arm to Kincaid Park. From downtown to Woronzof is approximately eight miles; from Woronzof to Kincaid another eight miles. The trail is blacktopped, wide enough for three people to walk abreast, or two bicycles to pass each other comfortably. In winter, one side is groomed with the twin tracks of a diagonal stride cross-country ski trail, while the other side is packed for skate skiers. The trail is considered multiuse.

For many of us, the trail is one of the best things about living in Anchorage. It is a place to meet friends on our endless golden summer evenings, to walk together arm in arm in the low but dazzling sunlight, to laugh at our dogs as they romp through the woods. It is a place to ride our bicycles at maximum speeds in the early mornings, through fogs of gnats in the low spots, past profusions of clover that scent the air in June, leaning into the corners and flying over the frost heaves. It is a place to walk silently on a winter afternoon, the snow gently falling, already muffling the streams and the willow forest. It is a place to see moose, nearly every day in winter, and beluga whales, their glistening white bodies rolling in the gray waters in spring, and mallards, pintails, wigeons, and blue-green teal in the ponds of summer, and once, one cool fall morning, a lynx, motionless as stone in a hollow of brown and yellow leaves.

The trial borders the city like a wilderness moat. On the side near downtown it is well used, which is why Gus and I so often walk off the trail into the woods on either side to be alone. But on the stretch between Woronzof and Kincaid, it is much quieter. No neighborhoods come close, only the airport and a detox center run by the Salvation Army. It was here, on the loneliest but also the most beautiful section of the trail, that I had my own encounter with fear.

I have driven out to the end of Northern Lights Boulevard and parked my car at Point Woronzof. My plan is to walk with Gus from Woronzof to Kincaid, arriving at the warm-up shack right around five-thirty, the same time my husband Paul gets out of work. Since his office is only a couple of miles from the trailhead at Kincaid, he can pick us up and take us back to my car. We have coordinated all this by phone and are agreed.

It is late summer, and the sun has already lost so much of its fire that it can no longer burn the clouds away. The afternoon is cool and gray, with a sharp but intermittent breeze. Although I have my warmest pile jacket on, zipped up to my throat, still the wind gets through, making me shiver. I walk fast to keep warm, but as I near the halfway point, three or four miles in, it is already approaching five o'clock. I begin to realize that I will be late.

I have seen no other walkers or bike riders in quite some time. Probably this is a function of the weather and the fact that I'm at the midway point. Walkers from either parking end may stroll a mile or so in, but generally do not come all this way. Bikers do, of course, but this is the end of the trail farthest from town, and there are fewer bikers than near the lagoon, where they can ride easily from their homes in Fairview, downtown, Turnagain, or midtown. Only the serious bikers get this far out.

I hear a rustling coming from the deep alder thicket on my right. It is not the wind. Immediately alert because of moose or even the occasional grizzly making its way into town, I tense and turn toward the sound. When the sounds become a man, I relax instantly, unconsciously, with a sheepish laugh. "Oh!" I exclaim. "You startled me!"

Even as the words come, I am fearful again. The fear is a vivid little stab of lightning behind my eyes. It annoys me, and yet I respect it, too. I'm no fool. I know what can happen.

The man steps through the tall grass deliberately, purpose-fully, his eyes on mine. He's extremely good-looking—not that I should notice such things, being a happily married woman of twelve years or more—and he's carrying a long black package in each hand. He heads straight toward me. Gus springs off the trail and toward him, wagging his happy blond tail and sniffing the air.

"Can you see color?" the man demands. "Red? Can you see red?"

His tone is urgent without being unfriendly. I am even more startled at this unusual greeting than I was by his sudden ap-pearance, but I can think of no immediate danger in telling the truth. It's not like asking, "Are you alone?" to which a lie might serve me better.

"Yeah, I guess so," I reply, hesitantly but truthfully. I think of stoplights and Christmas presents and candy apples at the state fair, red enclosing red. I do not immediately think of blood. "Why?"

He ignores the question, probing further with his own concerns.

"Can you tell red from brown, I mean? Can you distinguish red from colors that come close?"

I think of fall, when the woods are ablaze with the yellows and oranges and reds and browns of dying leaves. It's a tougher question than it first appears. Drawing the line between colors is always somewhat arbitrary. Although some things are clearly red, like the Jeep we rented in Hawaii last year, and some things are clearly brown, like the dirt of my garden, still some things are in fact reddish brown and others brownish red. I am always wary of drawing lines.

Still, I think, I can do it as well as the next person.

"Yeah," I nod my head, "pretty much."

Suddenly, he turns chivalrous. "Would you come with me?" he asks, gesturing with a sweep of his arm toward the bushes from whence he came. "Do you have a minute? I need your eyes."

It is then that I realize the long black cannon in his right hand is actually a spotting scope and the long black truncheon in his left a tripod. A pair of expensive-looking Nikon binoculars hangs from a string around his neck.

"I'm color-blind," he explains. "I don't see red. I think I've spotted a Eurasian wigeon down there," he gestures toward the mudflats two hundred feet below, "but I can't be sure. You could confirm the sighting for me. Will you come?"

His smile is warm and boyish. Gus seems to like him. For a minute I forget that Gus likes everybody. The whole thing seems harmless enough. I follow him into the alders, down a short incline to the head of the bluff. He sets up his tripod and the scope while he talks.

"Do you know your ducks?" he asks me, and I am disarmed. I love ducks and I tell him everything, all the ducks I know: mallards and pintails and shovelers and teals, the ducks I see in town; goldeneyes and buffleheads and scoters and mergansers, the ducks I know from the Kenai River.

"How about wigeons?" he asks.

Wigeons just might be my favorites, I tell him, with their pretty little heads, dainty bills curved upward, the males with their white-streaked foreheads, prominent without being ostentatious, and the females with their mottled gray and brown heads, the picture of subdued good taste. They do not need bright colors or dramatic contrasts to be elegantly beautiful. They are not plain or drab, merely refined.

American wigeons, also sometimes called baldpates, are common summer residents in the Anchorage bowl. Of the estimated three million breeders nationwide in an average year, 9 percent, or

270,000, make their way to Alaska from wintering grounds in Washington, Oregon, the Texas panhandle, and Louisiana. They arrive in April and May, before the ice and snow are completely gone, pairing up into what birders call "seasonally monogamous" family units. I see them paddling along the shores of Lake Hood, the floatplane lake, on a summer morning, and gliding gracefully through the shallows of Westchester Lagoon in a summer evening: two by two, they go. Two by two for the season.

Along with mallards, pintails, shovelers, and teals (all the common in-town ducks we see in local ponds), wigeons belong to the family of "dabbling ducks" or, more commonly, "puddle ducks," so called because they don't dive but feed by tipping themselves over, head down, tail up in the air, to reach pond-weeds just below the surface. "Duck butts!" Paul and I would laugh as we went by, their succulent little tushes winking and wagging in an endless array of mooning that always seems some-how saucy and flirtatious. Gregarious, they hang out in loose flocks with other puddle ducks, often in close proximity to scaups, diving ducks who go deep to tear succulent vegetation from the lake bottoms and whose leavings are of particular inter-est to wigeons, as treats otherwise beyond their reach.

The man is training his scope on a flock of ducks on the mudflats below. From where we stand they appear to me as barely perceptible blurs of motion, brown on brown, as if the mudflats themselves were slightly, tremulously, aquiver. I would not have noticed them on my own, might not even have noticed the snowcone of Denali against the horizon behind them, ghostly but just barely discernible against the haze. At this distance I could distinguish nothing.

"There he is," he says and steps carefully back from the scope. "He should be almost dead center in the field. He's larger than the others, and if he's the Eurasian wigeon his head will be red instead of gray or brown, and the forehead streak will be yellow. That's what I can't tell," he sounds rueful. "If the color is right. He's big enough to be the Eurasian, but I can't confirm the color."

Now it's my turn. I must turn my back to this strange in-toxicated man, bend forward in an awkward, closed-in pose, close one eye and fix the other on a small glass window. I will be completely vulnerable. This man could do anything.

I hesitate. This stepping forward is more complicated than it seems, at once a brave and reckless act. I am trusting a total stranger, in a remote place, off the trail, at the edge of a cliff, with my life. Why am I doing this? My feelings are divided between a desire to help this nice man, the chance to see something rare and wonderful, to add a new bird to my life list, and another need, a need so fierce it consumes me now: a need and a desire for the trust itself, a denial—no, a refusal—of fear. I do not want to live in a world of fear. I want to feel free to go anywhere, speak with anybody, look through any window to see what I can see.

My fear is based on my sex, of course. My gender. My female body, which is weak, and my female mind, which some say is even weaker. My mother would be crazy with fear in such a place with such a man, exotic puddle duck or not. My husband would shake his head in frustrated anger and warn me again to be careful. But I'm not an idiot either. I haven't walked into this blindly, haven't followed just any man, but a bird-watcher, not just any place, but to a lookout perched above a great squabbling mass of ducks. I hate it that I have to feel this fear, but I refuse to allow it to control me. I step forward and put my eye to the glass.

I see him immediately, the Eurasian one. He's nearly a third larger than the others and his head and neck are a ruddy-reddish brown, starkly different from the gray-brown of his fellows. His forehead streak is creamy yellow, warm against the red of his head, as if smeared with a buttercup and kissed by the sun. I can see the colors clearly; I can confirm the sighting.

"Oh, it's red and yellow all right," I say excitedly. "He's beautiful!" In my excitement I knock the scope and it swivels to the right and I lose him. A group of five American wigeons suddenly fills the frame, gray and brown and white. I scan slowly back to the left and suddenly there he is again, unmistakably big, unmistakably red, unmistakably yellow. I hold my breath to keep my face still and watch him bury his head beneath a wing to preen.

When I can tear myself away, I look over at the man. He is staring the same direction as I am, holding his binoculars steadily, a small smile on his face. He's never seen a Eurasian wigeon before, he tells me, so this is an addition to his life list too.

How did you spot him? I want to know. *How did you know where to look?*

Eurasian wigeons, far fewer in numbers than American wigeons, are far more adventurous. Considered widespread stragglers, they breed from Iceland east across Eurasia to the Pacific and may be found in places as far-flung as Spitzbergen to the Azores on the Atlantic flyways and Alaska to Hawaii, Midway, Borneo, and Celebes in the Pacific. Although wigeons have long been suspected of nesting in North America, no actual nests have ever been found, nor has mating behavior been observed on this continent.

The typical sighting of a Eurasian wigeon in Alaska is of a lone male traveling with a flock of his American cousins. He may or may not, in fact, actually be traveling alone; in the field, the female Eurasian is considered indistinguishable from the female American, so no one really knows whether his mate is with him or not. In any case, his cinnamon-red head and yellow forehead are considered nuptial plumage, so even if he is alone, he must be thinking about love. This particular bird was spotted earlier in the day and phoned in to the Audubon hotline from which my male companion got the word. The sighting fit the profile, so he left work early to see for himself.

True or not, the legend of the wigeon lends itself perfectly to romantic notions: the single male bird, bigger and brighter than all his fellows, setting out alone to see the world. "It sounds like a walkabout," I say. "Like one of those aboriginal rites of passage where the young man goes off alone to seek visions and confront the elements and find his manhood."

We laugh. He begins dismantling his scope again. I hang about for another minute, looking off toward the Inlet at the

Alaska Range in the distance. The breeze turns colder. I remember Paul and the time and Gus wagging his tail at my feet.

"Well, I gotta keep moving," I say. "Thanks for sharing your wigeon with me." And we smile at each other, and then I turn to leave. If there had been anyone on the trail just then, they would have been startled to see a woman emerging from the bushes. But there was no one.

It was past five, and Gus and I still had more than four miles to cover. We set off at a brisk pace as the wind picked up. A mile or so later it began to rain. I was not prepared for this; I had no hat. As the rain pelted my face and ran down my glasses, the world became a watery blur of grays and browns and greens, swirls of color without definition. On other days I might have felt cold, or cranky, or miserable, to be so rained on with so far yet to go.

Yet somewhere close by, I knew, dabbled a bright new duck on his walkabout, come all this way just to see what he could see. And what he saw was this: my world, infinite in beauty. Not without danger, to be sure. But not without trust, either.

And leaning my head back, I closed my eyes and opened my mouth, allowing the sweet cool milk of heaven to rain down my wide-open throat.

Old Harbor

Naomi Warren Klouda

Jeff drove us out into Sitkalidak Strait off Kodiak Island, clear blue day, heavy winds chasing us along. Three fishing clients from Kentucky were with us, anxious to catch big halibut and salmon.

"Hey, Indian guide," the elder man called out. "What's that over there?"

"Sea onions," Jeff called out easily. His eyesight is exceptional, the dip-and-bob a football field away. From the way a fish jumps, he can tell whether it's a king, humpy, chum, or silver salmon. He spots sharks, porpoises, whales, and seals before most people notice the dent they make in the water.

"What do people use them for, Naomi?" he asked me.

"Some people eat the sea kelp and onions at the end of their long cord or they use it as mulch for gardening," I said. Interesting that Jeff, a Sugpiak and indigenous to this island, would consult me. Sometimes he does, as if I'm an "Indian woman," which is my nickname, though I am white.

We settled back in the boat, watching glazed blue waters part in the wake, emerald mountains admiring their own reflections, triangular rocky outcrops cut deeper by braided falls, tufts of grass clinging to the top for dear life. For Kodiak, this sunny day is fall's rare gift, air so clean it makes me feel newly bathed. My relationship to these waters, where Jeff taught me to catch fish, is like my feelings for him: instant, foreign, yet oddly familiar. I met him a year before, when he took me from Old Harbor to Sitkalidak Island for an archaeology dig I was covering for a magazine. At that time I was living in Kodiak.

Jeff, standing at the wheel wearing sunglasses, smiled at the day. Clients mean he gets to show off his world, the bays he has explored since he was thirteen years old, when in an act of faith his father gave him his first boat. Unpredictable changes on water and weather make it a hazardous school, but Jeff survived it—and his parents did too. Alert to wind direction, current, and sky, Jeff seems always to be in a state of reading the elements, yet he does it effortlessly, as if those elements are but an extension of himself.

Gunning his engine, Jeff raced us to a known halibut spot, then pulled to a graceful stop.

"Fishing time," he said. The eager clients—the older man, his wife, and son—don't have to be told. They grab their rods and know immediately what to do. More than three thousand dollars each, that's what they had to pay to get here, first on a jet from Kentucky, then a plane from Anchorage, a small bush plane to the Sugpiak village of Old Harbor, and then this four-day charter. I can't help but watch them, hoping like Jeff that they catch. And catch they do. The first halibut weighs more than me.

In Old Harbor, I walked the dusty road leading from the lodge to Jeff's house while he helped the clients clean fish. About 290 people live here, and I'm one of about four white people present during the summer; now it is fall and the white teachers have returned. The road, which begins at a blue-domed Russian Orthodox church surrounded by manicured grasses, leads me past

Walt's Store, the six- or seven-room lodge, the post office, the new school with its gravel playground, and Harold's Store before I hit the harbor and the beach. If I wasn't in a hurry, I generally preferred to take the beach, then cut up the bluff to the road not far from home. And if I was tired, I stayed on the road and whoever passed by automatically picked me up. When a truck cab was full, the habit was to hop in the back.

The path home isn't long, but it's uphill. Today, only Kelsey, six, and Kathleen ("Bean"), five, are home with a sitter. Loren is off playing with friends. Jeff's two other children are visiting in Kodiak.

"We'll go to the lodge and eat with the clients," I told the girls, which made them happily bounce across the linoleum floors and onto the couch. In the village, almost every home has linoleum. It's easier to keep clean than carpet because of the constantly shedding black volcanic rock outside that underlies thin soils forming the island. And I think it invites the kids to dance and jig and glide in a way carpet wouldn't allow.

"We'll get dressed up," I said, which added to their excitement. The girls have long dark hair and dark eyes slanted like Eskimos, though Bean could be my daughter—lighter skin, lighter brown eyes.

"Fix my hair like yours," Kelsey demanded. And I did, for her and Bean, using the curling iron on their bangs, catching the sides up to the top of their heads in barrettes. We smiled at each other in the mirror when I was done.

"Naomi," Kelsey said, taking my face between her hands. "We look like you."

I smiled back. This cuts across cultural barriers. To *them,* we look alike. Yet I fear the day when they notice I'm not much at all like them.

Dinner was steak the Kentuckians had brought across the country, painfully kept frozen, to eat here with Jeff. They had been here once before. Each year they had sent Jeff Christmas cards, fondly remembering that one trip.

Talk whirled around me and over my head, fishing this place, catching that. The men teased Jeff with mock insults, and Jeff fired back. He was relaxed and comfortable with these clients, drinking a gin and tonic. Marty, an avid fisherperson in her own right, told me she had met her husband while playing in a rock band. She said she quit after a few years because her ears couldn't take the noise. She was in her forties, with neatly applied makeup, light brown hair cut to her shoulders and curling. Now she worked for Kentucky Fried Chicken.

That led to the subject of chicken in particular and meat in general.

I said I once paid twelve dollars for a frozen chicken at Harold's Store when Jeff and the kids got the flu. I needed to make them chicken soup.

"Twelve dollars?" Marty's husband laughed. "You paid that? Was it good?" He looked at the others and laughed all the harder.

"Yeah, it was okay."

"Twelve dollars?" He couldn't get over it. We all started laughing. The girls watched us in interest for a moment, then resumed their wanderings around the lodge, in and out, playing at the school across the street, then checking on us.

"Was it good?" he asked again.

"Tyson frozen chicken," I said. "Made two batches of soup."

"Tyson, you say. Twelve dollars."

Everything costs more in the village. It has to be flown in, and freight is expensive. A three-hundred-dollar batch of groceries flown in from Kodiak's coast guard base, where Jeff has shopping privileges because he's in the National Guard, costs an additional seventy-five to one hundred dollars to fly in. Fortunately, Jeff loves to duck-hunt, so there's usually that and fish and deer, sometimes *winaaq*—sea lion—and *isuiq*—seal.

They digested this information with interest, telling us how little this steak cost by comparison. Watching them, I wonder why I feel more like Jeff than I do them, people of my own race. I've never been to Kentucky or more than a few of the states.

Almost all my life has been spent in Alaska—I'm not even comfortable traveling to Seattle. And all but college in Washington and these two years on Kodiak were spent in Anchorage—urban and bleached generic, like my concept of America.

After about the tenth time the older man calls Jeff "Indian guide" or "Indian chief," the atmosphere is comfortable enough for me to say he's not Indian but Sugpiak (pronounced suk-PE-ahk).

Three pairs of eyes turned to him with renewed interest. "That's the name of the original people of these islands, not Aleuts like the Russians called them."

Marty wanted me to spell it on a napkin. Typical shyness on Jeff's part caused him to leave the vocabulary to me, since I knew he was on a campaign to set the record straight in tribal council business and other ways.

Words, kept secret like this, retain their power. He allowed me to give this one to his friends, but there were others we did not share. Like the one spoken teasingly, in his happiness at how the day went, about what we would do later when we were alone.

My mother brought us to Alaska when I was young enough to take for granted the similarities to this land and Idaho, where I was born, yet old enough to understand the differences that could cause problems—cold needed to be taken absolutely seriously, the mountains and creatures you could look at and not touch. Sometimes Jeff reminds me of this landscape.

In the night, his eyes tight closed, I watched him in moonlight. He'd just loved me as attentively as he navigated the waters. His face was like a mask you can see on museum walls, high cheekbones, slanted eyes, black hair. I folded my face into his broad shoulder, longing to understand the maps that guide him. He's always right here, next to me, even when I have to be far away. Yet he's of another world, and I keep putting out my hand, waiting for him to pull me forth into it. He doesn't.

How do you take yourself into another culture? I watch people already there, just living it. *Where do they get the comfort zone?* So far, Jeff hasn't given me the comfort zone for moving un-intrusively into his world. He seems to be waiting for me to take it for myself. Look but don't touch, don't harm, don't take advantage of, don't seek to influence—those words jam up my thoughts.

That summer when we went on an archaeology dig on the other side of the island at Karluk, Jeff and I dug for a week in the black oily dirt on a bluff overlooking the sea. Everyone's knees were coated with prehistory, what archaeologist Rick Knecht was careful *not* to call the Middle Ages, a Eurocentric reference, he said. Jeff was the only Sugpiak digging. An ancient kayak paddle, lip ornaments, lots of buried black hair—they hid their cut hair to keep it away from shamans who might cast spells—baskets, ancient fishing gear of all varieties.

"This site is like a library with a whole lot of books," the archaeologist told Jeff. "You can read it a layer at a time."

Jeff was reading his own history, buried by centuries of more dominant cultures asking them to forget, to change, to speak new words, and to pursue new ideas. After all that changing and for-getting, being a Kodiak Islander today means not knowing what to call yourself: Aleut, like the Russians called them? Koniag, like their enemies to the south called them? Indians—to make sure no one calls them Eskimos? Or Sugpiak, an all-but-forgotten name the Eskimos to the north remember, the elders remember.

On a grassy mound normally serving as the Karluk school's playground, we had set up our tent, and at night as we lay in the winds we tried to make hypotheses of our own, based on Jeff's knowledge of his culture. Archaeologist grad students chatted away the digging days while he remained respectfully quiet—not to the students but to the dead. It was hard to know whether he agreed or disagreed with their often elaborately constructed pre-history theories.

For us, no domestic or cultural detail was too huge. Or too small. Like how did men and women from distant places get together? The archaeologists would tell us about pottery shards as evidence of blending. Jeff was fond of the "stolen woman" theory.

"That's what you would be. I took you from someplace else," he said.

Yes, that's what I feel like. A stolen woman, but one not minding being taken.

☾

The clients knew what they wanted, and Jeff guided them to the streams and helped them get it. So far they had caught seventeen salmon and two huge halibut, all cut up now and frozen in the lodge freezer. When the freezer spilled over and couldn't handle more, we went to Jeff's parents' house and stored more in their freezer. Mike, the younger man, said they cooked the salmon during the winter, entertaining friends with the rich meat, trying all kinds of recipes, even making lox and smoking some. This journey, therefore, had practical value.

Marty helped me stock Martha and Victor's freezer with the stored fish. Jeff's parents were in Kodiak for a few days.

"Women's work," the men teased. But they meant it. Our job was to make sure the meat was put away. It's my cultural habit to watch for things that demean being a woman—in any culture. But here meat means something different when it comes from such mysterious waters.

Raising children also isn't cleanly divided into sex roles, especially for Jeff, a single father of five.

Still, I was self-conscious as his clients watched me curiously to figure out my relationship with the children. Was I going to make them a good mom? In short, would I make Jeff a *good woman?*

"I'll stay home with the children this morning so I can go see them at school," I said one morning, deciding not to go out on the water with him and his clients until after lunch. I felt bad about not spending much time with the girls and preferred their simple company to the more complex, unasked questions I faced with the clients as Jeff's "Indian woman."

Jeff stood in the doorway a moment, trying to figure out whether this was to his liking or not. He liked to be the one to say who does what. Finally he said, "Fine, good," and kissed my lips.

I recall that he told me he wanted a partner in all things—to hunt and fish with, to be home with, and to go to his many tribal and other council meetings with him. But during the summer, when I lived in the village, I was all too often shut out of all that. The implication was that I had so much to learn first.

At times I couldn't sort out what was what with Jeff. He seemed to be growing more distant, or was there a cultural habit of his I was not understanding? Did I really have that much to learn? His sudden inexplicable distance, and other complications, were enough to make me return to Anchorage to teach English courses at the university. At this point, we were going back and forth between village and city.

Now I wore my split spirit like my split identity as I drove horribly straight Anchorage streets in too much traffic.

After Kelsey climbed on the bus, Bean stayed with me until kindergarten started at noon. I swept the house clean of volcanic black rock that got on our bare feet, making it necessary to dust off with hands before getting into bed, and washed the dishes and put in a load of laundry. Then I walked Bean down to the school, with her talking the whole way there.

Kelsey's teacher, Olga Pestrikoff, was raised in Old Harbor, the only teacher back in her own territory. The village was proud of this, after two centuries of less-than-understanding teachers (to put it kindly) from other races, first the Russians and then the American missionaries. Olga let Kelsey out a few minutes early to eat lunch with me. The cafeteria was four long tables in a room the size of a big living room, with the kitchen off to the left.

"What did you bring?" she asked, after talking about a - picture she was making, drawing on air to help me see it better.

"*Sitkiak* in cream cheese sandwiches."

"Um!"

"I'm meeting your father to go out with the clients this afternoon," I said.

"He's 'Dad.' Why you call him 'father?'"

"I'm sorry. Your dad. I'm going with him."

I say too many words that don't mean anything to the children. Even to say "children" is stiff and formal.

After lunch Kelsey wanted me to watch her do a trick on the monkey bars, where she proved agile and monkey-strong. Then she "showed" me to her girlfriend and a cousin.

"You're a neat kid," I told Kelsey, as I kissed her before leaving.

Since meeting Jeff and spending time with his children, I've grown more sensitive to language. The grammar and rules we're taught all too often offend. Proper English is exclusive, not inclusive, in places like the village. In Anchorage, there are generally two or three Natives in each course. In Kodiak the ratio was higher. After using the old standbys, I tossed their words up on the blackboard at the university to show how language has a habit of taking two ideas to make one word; in Latin we have *philo,* which means love, and *sophy,* which means wisdom. In Alutiiq, *qunuk* means love, *lluku* tells who one loves. So to love him is *qunuklluku.* Or *agayun* is God and *wik* is place. Church is *agayuwik.*

Sometimes those Native students glanced over their shoulders to see if they were going to get caught saying these words here.

⑥

Out on the water, knowing this was my last time for now, I drank the sweet air and sun, tears from wind running shortly down my cheeks. The clients, the older man, sipped occasionally from a flask—gin, I thought. Jeff, out of politeness, perhaps, because he doesn't indulge much, took a bit and handed it to me. I too took a taste, which sealed our bonds with the clients.

We headed down Jim Creek, outside Old Harbor to the backside, where silver salmon and steelhead go to spawn, where cedar bark from Southeast drifts and gets caught in the mat of grasses as tall as us, good for firewood or the steam-bath banyas.

Bears were also back here, eating their fill of salmon and berries, but they usually shied away from humans. Kodiak has the world's biggest bears, yet there hasn't been a bear-human mauling in more than thirty years, probably because humanity hasn't diminished the bears' food resources.

The sun held, the day was warm. All around us, forming a U, were the emerald mountains with just a touch of yellow. The water was clear green, opening the view to silty brown bottoms, fish easy to spot. Like the photos I took, I wanted to freeze-frame us in this moment, in this place, and never return to Anchorage.

Today they were fly-fishing, a new sport for Jeff, but he was a fast learner. Green line whispered through still air, its pink sucking leech at the end, and he caught a trout before the clients began to catch their first steelheads.

I tried only halfheartedly to fish. After Mike caught a steelhead—he was off by himself on a bank—I hurried to help him bring it in. In the grasses the fish flashed silver, thrashing, not wanting to go. He took a club to hit its head, surprised when I grabbed both sides of the fish, holding it in place so he could club.

"Wait a minute," he said. "You'll get blood on your pants."

"I don't mind."

He hit, and blood squirted across the green grasses beneath us. "It's for food," I said.

"Still," he apologized. Then he stood up tall in the grasses to show the others his fish, big and bold, glimmering chrome in the pink fall sunlight.

Jeff, satisfied at the day, stood alone with me in the grasses not long after. "This is the kind of day you could just lay down in the grass and..." he said.

I watched his handsome features, his long lashes downcast, full-lipped smile, bronze cheeks, and black hair curling oddly, and I shook my head. What a thought. Yes, in this perfect air, in these grasses that hide their own—bears, us—yes. Against this river that gives banya wood and smokehouse wood and such perfect fish. Longing filled me. My plane was to leave in a few short hours. Just to just lay down in the grass. But already, I was not with him. His eyes that wouldn't meet mine said so.

We made one more stop on the river farther in. Everyone was wearing waders except for me. Jeff put me on his back, and I folded in half as he carried me to the grasses so I could use the *nusniiq.* Our word for bathroom. (Did I really say *our?*) Grasses hid me. Then I was back.

"Whitey, see him? He's heading back to town. Want to go with him?" Jeff asked, suggesting I take his boat so he could stay with the clients. Whitey, a village elder, could get me to my plane.

Whitey's boat was weighed down by wood he had gathered. "No, I want you to take me." Connections cut quickly, Jeff was pushing me back down that river, back to Anchorage.

I sat in front of Jeff on the short ride back to Old Harbor. We couldn't talk above the engine's roar, and what could we say anyway? What did the future hold for two people like us? Jeff wasn't good at saying good-bye—it was no time for a discussion. In Alutiiq, his language, there is no word for good-bye. Instead they say the equivalent of "I will see you again soon." Those words hold a beauty all their own, a rope to hold while planning our next move.

I curled against the window in the small airplane, watching Jim Creek below for signs of Jeff and his clients, filling my eyes with the sweet curves of the river, impossibly tall grasses soon to fade, purple-blue mountains, slam of wave on stone. When I'm alone and cold in Anchorage, it is this I want to feel inside me.

In Kodiak, I looked down and noticed my jeans as I stood among well-dressed tourists. Fish blood across my knees, scales down lower. I smelled of fish and salt as I went from small plane to a larger one that put me back in the city. I smelled like Old Harbor.

Out of Alaska

Jessica Maxwell

I had a room in Alaska at the foot of the Juneau Hills. The 60th parallel runs through these islands, one hundred miles to the north, and the room lay at an altitude of over sixty feet. In the early summer you felt that you had got up high, thanks to the midnight sun.

The geographical position, and the sleight of hand of the light, combined to create a landscape like nowhere else in the world. There was no fat on it, save for the local folk who had spent the long dark winter eating salmon and drinking beer. The odors were wet and raw. Even the trees had a light fragrance, the scent of which was different from that of the trees in the Lower 48: it flowed straight down the trunks where fishermen and hunters had marked their territory. Out on the adjacent waters there was a heroic if unromantic air, like the aroma of full-bellied fishing ships with their nets chewed up…by killers, Kommande confided.

"Killers?"

"Killer whales. Orcas. We Natives call them blackfish. But it's the humpbacks that are in now."

And not, I learned, because the coho salmon were also in and leaping like silver fleas all around our boat, but because it was summer and the mysterious warm-weather upwellings of the Gulf of Alaska had shot this water through with new life. Everything was eating everything, the largest of the wild animals there—the humpback whale—feeding on one of the smallest— krill, the tiny shrimply cousins of the family *Euphausiidae*.

But we were after salmon.

"You missed it! Try again!" Kommande commanded. He was a Native fisherman, a Tlingit (pronounced Kling-git), one of the great Alaskan fishing tribes.

Kommande was one of their best.

I was keen on fishing and had been out on many salmon safaris. But when I became a writer I put away my rods and reels. Still, I often talked about the trips that we had been on. On one of these trips, I had seen a school of salmon, 129 of them, come out of the motor mist under a Copper River sky, one by one, as if the bright and massive chromelike animals with the mighty horizontally swung tails were not approaching but were being digitalized before my eyes and set out in the water past the boat as their images materialized.

"That was a hit! You missed another one!"

From Kommande it was a word of warning, such as a loyal friend might give, to stop you in an angling proceeding unworthy of you.

From my first weeks in Alaska, I had been drawn to the Native people. But it was not easy to get to know them. Until you knew a Native well, it was almost impossible to get a straight answer from him. To a direct question as to how many salmon he had caught, there was often an elusive reply: "As many as I told you I caught yesterday." Once I asked a Tlingit taxi driver in Ketchikan if he'd ever shot a brown bear, and he told me no, but he'd shot a six-point summer buck and carried it home on his back and had brown bear claw marks on each hip to prove it.

And from my first days in Alaska, I had been drawn to the land. The views were immensely wide, and everything you saw made for greatness and freedom and unequaled mobility. Not via roads—there are no roads in Southeast Alaska—but by water and by air. Every coastal Alaskan owns a boat or has a friend who does, and everyone everywhere flies about in small airplanes whose doors are held on by coat hanger wire.

The chief feature of the landscape, and of my time in it up there, was the air. And the fact that there is still air up there, not the rheumy, petro breath that passes down in the Lower 48. Looking back on a sojourn in the Alaskan backlands, I am always struck by the feeling of having lived for a time up in the air. As for me, I once had the feeling of having died for a time up in the air.

"Take over," the pilot commanded. "I need a nap."

I had not flown a plane before, of any sort. And being a seaplane, this was a machine of special complexity, a fusion of bird and beast. I had watched them many times from my room at the foot of the Juneau Hills, taking off into the air from the water like great gaily painted metal ducks, with ossified wings immune to flapping. And I had watched them land, again much as garish seabirds, and skitter along the surface on their hard bellies, sending back sprays of Gastineau Channel water from each pontoon like long, spidery guard feathers. But making one come and go myself?

"What do I do?" I asked the pilot, feigning calm.

"Push in to go down, pull out to go up. Good night."

And so I flew, the rightful pilot snoring on my left. I had tremendous views as I got up above the Alaskan islands, surprising combinations of blue waterways coiling like snakes around brown eggs of land. Then fishing boats running straight over the water snakes like white foxes, splitting their blue backs in two. Then wide, round storm clouds lowering themselves protectively on the egg islands like great gray hens. Then I saw I was lowering down with them and would likely become an egg broken on an egg if I did not pull back the metal crescent in my hands—or was it push in? I tried one, then the other, succeeding, finally, both in a rousing impersonation of the Alaskan water snakes hissing beneath me and in rousing the pilot, who proceeded to offer up hasty prayers to a merciful God and pulled us out of the fall just in time. But he did allow us to fly low enough to see the whales and eagles and brown bear on the lands below and to feel toward them as God did when he had just created them, which, I was sure, explained the continued utterances of the pilot to Our Lord Jesus in all his variety of names holy and un.

I was, at that time, trying to arrive at Haines, Alaska, to see the eagles that gather there on the Chilkat River in the last two months of the year to enjoy a very late run of chum salmon. Three thousand five hundred of them, all bald and overfed and walking along the Chilkat's braided glacial silt like any number of cigar-smoking comedians.

I was aching to know that the eagle and salmon and big game were out there still, in their own country. When I was there, brown bear, black bear, and wolf lived in the Juneau Hills—and the very old Natives remembered a time when there were moose as well. I called the stiff peaks that rise like waterfront Alps behind the town the Juneau Hills, while the locals called them by their individual names such as Mount Juneau or, more generally, the Juneau Ice Field. I was always sorry that the whole of Mount Juneau was not enclosed in a game reserve.

I thought of all these things when times were dull back in my room. The big game was out there. Their nearness gave a shy playfulness to the atmosphere of the room, a welcome antidote to the human carnival that is summer in Alaska. When I stepped out, I would see herds of cruise-ship tourists traveling through dense Native art galleries, padding along as if they hadn't an appointment in the world. I had time after time watched their progression through the jeers and gaffs of the local drunks. These rotund visitors in their odd, vegetative gracelessness and vacation colors moved not as a herd of Homo sapiens but as a family of common, thick-stemmed, freckled, gigantic plastic flowers slowly advancing, wallets ajar.

Out with the big game and on the wild Pacific I had learned to be aware of abrupt movements. The land and sea creatures for which you hunt and fish are wry and watchful; they have a talent for invading you when you least expect it. As Kommande and I continued our salmon safari that day, a whole world opened up just beyond my right shoulder. It was really a room, a cavernous room not unlike my room at the foot of the Juneau Hills. Except for the smell. It smelt…like smelt smelt. Like one of the three-hundred-pound halibuts that Kommande regularly pulled off the bottom of the sea, left prone across the planking of his boat's floor, where it had for several months gone unnoticed.

"What's that funky smell?" I asked politely.

"Humpback," he snorted, and before the snort could graze the cool blue putrid air, a whale's tail rose unannounced only meters from the first whale's stadium of a mouth and began battering the surface of the water with resounding wet flat noises.

"They're hunting," Kommande explained. "Together."

Indeed, a mated pair surfaced. Hunters of the finest caliber. Team hunters, the female working the thin silver skin of the water with her great tail, herding the krill through the male's filtering baleen teeth. It was Alaska, focused down to the base reckoning of the place: Hunt or be hunted.

"Lazy S.O.B.," Kommande spat. "Get out there and fish for your own damn self."

In Alaska, abrupt movement did not present itself only in the form of wildlife. The elements were capable of shifting into a kind of animate force, and never was this mystery more apparent than on another day when we were fishing Outside, in the fitful indigo waters of the North Pacific proper, off Prince of Wales Island.

Kommande, as always, was in command. The boat was small—a cabin cruiser of some age—and a photographer was aboard to document the trip. We were after lingcod that day, and when we left port the sky was fine and blue. Kommande plaited our course through the fractured coastline, through its crinolined basalts and onioned schists that looked from the water not at all like eggs, but like the neolithic shrapnel that they were. Finally we were Outside, and the feeling there was one of great danger and thrill. The early morning air of the Alaskan islands is of such a tangible boldness and frostiness that this fancy came over me: I was not on earth but in dark deep waters, going ahead along the bottom of the sea. Except that in this case we were on the top of it, which made for an especially fanciful fancy. One wherein the variables were countless and clearly slippery. It was as if you were afloat in an open-ended system of climactic emotion, capable of rocketing at any moment between blissful joy and frank rage, and you could only sit by helpless if, indeed, you chose to remain in your seat in a theater devoted to utter chaos.

True enough, in a hummingbird's heartbeat it turned. Sudden war broke out between the weather and the sea. The day went black, as if by eclipse, as the sky battalions, dressed in charcoal gray, entered the battleground from the northwest. The ocean regiments stood at attention, rising up tall, all in blue, their whitecaps reaching now to meet their dark sky rivals.

"What the hell's happening?" the photographer begged of Kommande.

"Storm," Kommande replied, then flicked his cigarette overboard.

In all my years of knowing and fishing with Kommande I had never known him to startle. A great white could, I am sure, lunge at him without warning and he would simply say, "Shark," and shoot his pistol down its open red mouth. A monstrous brown bear could rise—and has risen—up in his path and he would surely say, "Bear," and press his rifle against its cinnamon chest and shatter its heart. Kommande never did but what he wanted to do and no great beast would stand in his way. It was a surprise to see shock run like a caribou through his clear brown eyes. And so it was that the storm on The Outside that day offered me the gift of Kommande's vulnerability, for I had not seen it before.

It was not the storm's handiwork alone, but The Moment's. One dreadful unlucky Moment that laid itself down at the confluence of Three Terrible Things, all of which we were obliged to suffer through to the end without solace. The First Thing was The Rock. Kommande saw it first, of course, and was startled. He knew this water. He'd fished it for decades. He knew the map. He'd studied it again that morning. And yet there was The Rock where it had never been before. And the wild sea was indeed washing us directly toward it, as if by the devil's decree.

"Start the motor!" Kommande commanded.

I leapt into the cabin, grasped the key and turned it, only to be confronted by The Second Thing: Our motor was dead.

"It won't," I yelled, "turn over!"

And it wouldn't. I turned and turned. Nothing.

"Try again!" Kommande barked.

"I already have! I have!" I cried.

The Rock remained so large and hard and close Kommande could have almost pushed us off it. But we all saw that the fitful rolling of the sea would only push us against it. Destruction loomed.

Finally The Third Thing arrived, fierce and inescapable, one of the most dreaded phenomena of the open sea—The Rogue Wave. Like an unexpected elephant, a mammoth column of tufted salt water levitated directly up and out of the ocean, leaned, then crashed on our boat—as it happened, directly onto the photographer, nearly casting him overboard. But, rather than The Curse of Death itself, when The Rogue Wave broke, the spell of evil broke with it.

The engine started, and as the sea shoved the boat's stern flat into The Rock, Kommande, who was now in the cabin, mumbled something about a "kill key" and pulled us away from it and the certain disaster its fearful pinnacle offered.

The photographer was none the happier, demoted as he now was to the likeness of a large clam, his equipment all but ruined.

"And did you get a picture of The Wave?" Kommande asked him, turning his back to us to leave his mark on this strange place. The usual clarity in his eyes returned and even elevated to a kind of glee. The photographer's response was little more than a deeper souring of his damp expression. Men, I think, cannot easily or harmoniously envy or triumph over one another, especially when luck was wholeheartedly with one and not the other. My own thoughts drilled deeper, flew higher, than the competitions of men, for I knew now that their truest tests lay not against each other but at the whim of The Way, The Grand Revelation, the eerie movement of The Forces with which we take our chances every day. And in that moment I knew that the most important thing was neither Kommande's control, which is his art, nor his knowledge, which is vast, but his uncanny ability to read the signals. And why we must have natural places to go to where the signals remain intact. For they repose not in the language of the media, the grid of televised and online culture that throws a net over our minds and blurs the mystery from our vision. There, we learn little but automated responses, and our subtle radars atrophy. We Americans need our Alaska wild and intact, big game, big fish, the land, the sea, all at home in their "countries." Our Alaska: where faith and humility serve equal sentences, allowing adventure to reign supreme. As for me, I serve no other master.

The Art of Grassroots, Alaska-Style

Susan Ewing

After a day of outboarding and beach-combing, Evon Zerbetz led the way back toward our Kuiu Island camp. Six of us and a big dog had crowded into an open aluminum boat, holding on tight as the speeding skiff slammed through the cold, gray chop of Sumner Strait. "I love going so fast the air goes up your nose," Evon had shouted above the wind.

Three dozen Alaskan artists were gathered on this island in the Tongass National Forest to create images for an art show that would raise awareness about the impending logging of Kuiu's old growth. Like many of the artists invited to participate in the project, Evon grew up here in Southeast Alaska—a loose alliance of land and water drifting alongside Canada like a flotilla of forested icebergs.

Evon, Mary Henrikson, Carla Potter, and I had jumped out of the skiff at the mouth of Salt Lagoon so we could stop at our satellite camp before rejoining the larger group up the beach. The tide wasn't all the way in and I slipped on wheezing rockweed, trying to keep up with the efflorescent Evon. Mary and Carla strung along behind, laughing and shouting, poking at piles of tidal debris and stopping to cheer the vaudeville in busy tide pools.

I was the guest here—non-artist and Alaska expatriate—but I used to troll for salmon in the waters around Kuiu in a gracefully aged wooden boat called the *Salty*. There wasn't much money in hand-trolling, but I liked losing myself in the fog and quiet; liked listening to whales breathe. I spent good years in Alaska, learning about life and my place in it. I was born in a different state, but in many ways, I grew up here too.

Our satellite colony of tents was nested under the sheltering arms of a huge Sitka spruce; weak light drizzled down with wet mist through the layers of forest canopy. Carla started a fire in a tidy ring of rocks and the artist friends perched around it like ravens, drinking fire-brewed coffee and enjoying the good fortune of being in these woods. A comment about the essential feminine nature of trees was floated, but this tangent wasn't pursued. More interesting were slugs, opera, spiders, perfecting raven calls, and keeping the fire going in the dampness.

With stray twigs and lichen in their hair, the women talked about what they might create for the art show. Evon considered focusing on the details, a linocut of a newt, or an orchid perhaps, or the hummingbird that buzzed our tents each morning. Trees may grow back after clearcutting, she frowned, but the old-growth nature of the forest is lost—the details erased.

Mary envisioned a wall-sized canvas thundering with straight-grained power. She threw her arms into the air and looked up the trunk of the tree on whose roots she sat. I followed her gaze and couldn't see the top.

We finished the coffee, reorganized braids and ponytails, and wandered up to join the other artists for dinner, wading through a wet patch of thigh-high chocolate lilies along the way. Main camp was an open-air cook tent, perpetual bonfire, and two freshly dug latrines. A colorful assortment of tents snaggled down the shoreline of the lagoon and bit into the tangled edge of moss-draped Alaska rain forest: the Tongass.

The Tongass National Forest is larger than West Virginia and includes within its borders not only the seven-hundred-square-mile Kuiu Island but a full 77 percent of the rest of Southeast Alaska—nearly seventeen million acres. Most valuable to the timber industry are the forest's two-million-plus acres of low-elevation old growth. Almost a million acres have already been cut. Unfortunately, the stands of commercially valuable old growth are also the most biologically valuable components of the forest. Covered with old growth and fissured by salmon streams, Kuiu is worth a biological fortune. In addition, Kuiu Island's protected bays, beaches, inlets, and coves provide some of the best human recreation habitat in all of Southeast. Like a face on which only the family's best features are found, Kuiu reflects all that is most beautiful and precious about the Tongass.

The mood around camp was relaxed, warm, and optimistic. In the cook tent, people picked at the remains of grilled halibut and snuffled through plastic boxes looking for more cookies. Others roasted marshmallows and bulbs of bull kelp around the fire, sharing stories of their day's adventures looking into Kuiu's eyes. They had skiffed, rowed, paddled, hiked, watched birds, hunted special rocks, stalked wildflowers, sketched, and shot rolls and rolls of film. They told of a tree six arm spans around, of eagle feathers and hermit crab orgies, of a mink eating a sea urchin, and of the real, goose-pimpling whisper of ghosts.

"There is so much magic here," Joe Sebastian told me, shifting in his seat on a drift log and scratching a stubble of beard. Joe and his wife, Joan, had conceived and organized the Kuiu artists' retreat. When they weren't out trying to make a living salmon fishing, the couple and their two young children lived in Point Baker, an isolated settlement on Prince of Wales Island, ten miles east of Kuiu.

Joe was worried about the future of Southeast's forests. Clearcut logging can destroy salmon habitat, but Joe was concerned about more than his livelihood.

"It's been hard living on Prince of Wales," he said, sweatshirt hood cinched around his tired face. Hard not because fishing is tough work or because Point Baker is removed from what we think of as standard amenities, but because the trees behind his house were being marked, cut, and skidded out of his life. Taking the trees takes the soul of a place. Changes it irredeemably; painfully. Old-growth forests are ecosystem community centers full of activity, where all manner of lives connect and interact. In them is a sense of entirety. Clearcutting razes the community center—breaks the windows, smashes the walls, impoverishes the neighborhood.

But how to stop it? How to explain what's at stake? How to make people care?

Touch them, Joe decided, with art. He got a grant for the artists' retreat from the Southeast Alaska Conservation Council, and now here they were. Artists and photographers from Petersburg, Port Alexander, Point Baker, Port Protection, Sitka, Haines, Gustavus, Cordova, Juneau, Ketchikan, and elsewhere had been flown out in floatplanes and ferried in on fishing boats and sailboats, sketchbooks and cameras in hand.

There are virtually no roads connecting one Southeast community with another, and this was the first time many of the artists had met. It was a polar fleece, wool, and rubber boot cocktail party. They may as well have been in their living rooms. Really, they were.

In the lingering gray light they talked about their work and listened to a blue grouse hooting from somewhere in the forest. They pointed out to each other the black bears ambling around across the salt chuck, visible from where we sat drinking Carla's homemade blueberry liqueur. There was a casual, voice-call inventory of the number of guns in camp (three).

They didn't yammer about the scenery; they were more like salamanders, taking the place in like oxygen through their skin. People who live in Southeast don't gush about trees like the rest of us don't gush about opposable thumbs. But it is clearly understood we'd be in a world of hurt without them. A world of hurt, without the trees.

Like a needle to magnetic north, talk swung to forest politics. Alaskans can blend liberal and libertarian views into a salty margarita of strong opinion they are happy to pour in your ear. Most Southeasterners aren't squeamish about getting out there and messing around: cutting some trees, catching fish in nets, hunting, trapping. Logging per se isn't what bothers them so much; it's the way logging is being gone about.

Two men heaved a driftwood trunk onto the bonfire and sparks flew.

Most people here shared the same vision for Southeast: no more clearcutting; an end to timber monopolies by large, multinational corporations; more small, independent mills; and the development of local, value-added processing. Gathered in a circle around the fire, the artists began asking Joe questions about his plans for the art show. The purpose had been clear enough: Through art, cause strangers to make an emotional connection with a place they had never been. Make them feel sad, get mad, write to their elected officials. Okay. But to whom should they send their finished pieces, and what were the expected venues?

Joe looked at the group and shrugged. "I just wanted to get it this far," he said simply. "Get you to Kuiu. People would have picked apart any plan, so we're just going bit by bit. See, there's nothing to worry about because nothing exists."

The artists looked blank, then looked surprised, then looked at each other. An announcement of such major loose ends in a stuffy meeting room could well have spelled doom. But winging it is a familiar Alaskan strategy and no one seemed especially shocked. Some were leery of being roped into yet one more thing, but it was clear that the rain forest road show would happen only if they themselves made it happen. As the fire cracked they thought about Kuiu, about the vulnerable old-growth nature of Southeast, and about their responsibility to the landscape that nurtured their lives and incubated their art. Eyes turned to Ray Troll, Ketchikan painter, T-shirt artist, book illustrator, and entrepreneur. Ray facilitated a free-form discussion of logistics, copyrights, audience, and coordination. They committed themselves to the project and set size guidelines and deadlines for artwork. The question of where to send finished pieces would be decided later, they agreed. A hopeful voice wondered if there might be grant money to pay a part-time coordinator. With grant money and duct tape, Alaskans can do anything.

They roasted more marshmallows and continued to sort things out.

"I don't think an art show will change anyone's mind, but it might soften their opinion," a watercolorist offered to no one in particular. You could tell the ones who lived in mill towns.

"Well, we should hope," another voice from the circle prompted. "If it's what we want to do, we'll do it."

Grassroots grew, the show would go on. Standing away from the circle, Joe had faith.

"The artist's vision can make wilderness real," he insisted. "People are estranged from the wilderness. That's why we have flat roads, square houses, central heating, and cars with windshield wipers." Understand that living in a place like Point Baker will lead you to contemplate things like the effect windshield wipers have on your life.

"I have a lot of time to think," Joe mused, "and I think there are no more Kuiu Islands out there. You can cut old growth slow or you can cut it fast, but you can only cut it once."

Two months after the retreat, through my two-line, electronic, speed-dial, redial, VariCom speakerphone in the Lower 48, I heard the telephone in Point Baker ring with a flat burr and click. A rotary dial maybe—black or green. How do we come to our choices? Joe picked it up.

"It's a real fluke you caught us here. We're still fishing—we'll be out for another week. A real fluke. We had an incredibly busy season and I just couldn't get to a phone to follow up on things. But a lot has been going through my mind."

In a couple of weeks, he said, the family was going to drive the boat down to Washington for the winter to get some work done on it. "But I'm going to get an address for people to send their art before I go."

Our conversation was momentarily lost in a burst of static. *KKkkkssssshhhhHHH-POP.*

"Darn phone. Anyway, SEACC heard from a lot of the artists," he continued. "I think the folks in Ketchikan are going to spearhead things, and we're going to work with friends to move through the first two or three towns. People in Sitka will take responsibility, people in Petersburg, Juneau. There's other places: Homer, Anchorage. Maybe we'll get it south to Seattle. The first show could happen as early as February, but I'm guessing March or April."

I said I thought the Kuiu timber was to be sold by then.

"Kuiu's been hanging by a thread for years," he answered. There was anxiety in his voice now. He needed to get back to his boat and catch some more fish; he needed for things to just work out.

"The old survey stakes that were set in 1979 are rotting in the ground next to the new ones that were planted a couple years ago. It's been scheduled to be cut for years, but one thing or another has interfered. The art show will either help prevent it or it will document what's been lost; the stupidity."

As we said good-bye, I pictured trees hanging on artwork. During the retreat, walking down the beach, Mary had been reminded of a sadly relevant Urdu saying, "Within the depths of history are instances when moments made mistakes and centuries were punished." I crossed my fingers for Kuiu, and for the art of grassroots, Alaska style.

On March 25, 1995, *Kuiu Island...a gathering* opened in Ketchikan with storytelling and celebration.

Thirty-six artists contributed forty-eight pieces of artwork including a cedar box, woodcut prints, sculptures, oil paintings, watercolors, photographs, quilts, and silk-screen on wool felt. The show moved from Ketchikan, to Petersburg, to Sitka, to Haines, to Juneau—the state capital. Organizers hoped to find further venues for their rain forest road show in Anchorage, Seward, Fairbanks, and beyond.

Ketchikan artist volunteers organized the show and got it moving, and transportation of artwork within Southeast and display space were donated at no cost. Volunteers and conservation organizations in each community pitched in to ensure the show's success.

As of January 1, 1996, none of the contested Kuiu old growth had been cut, although the island's future still hangs by the thread Joe Sebastian sees in his sleep. Senator Ted Stevens (R-Alaska) has vowed to escalate timber harvest in the Tongass and even tried to tie logging in the forest to Department of the Interior appropriations bills. So far, public pressure and a presidential veto, coupled with a lawsuit brought by the Southeast Alaska Conservation Council, tourist operators, subsistence users, sportfishers, and hunters, have run adequate interference in Kuiu's case. But the fate of the island, and of the Tongass itself, now hangs in the arena of national politics. A very thin thread indeed.

Jenny's Domain

Linda M. Davis

A single light sparkled in the white snow, two hundred miles west of Anchorage on the western side of the Alaska Range, three hundred miles east of the Bering Sea coast. The light escaped from an underground cabin, somewhat like a bunker, with only the roof above ground level. The cabin would have appeared to be just another mound in the snow comforter if not for the light and steam rising from an air hole at the roof's ridgepole. From the cabin the closest settlement (population forty-seven) was the Athabascan village of Lime, which lay sixty miles to the northeast across the tundra, across the Door Mountains, across several creeks. Downriver, when the water was open, the Eskimo village of Sleetmute could be reached by boat by taking the shallow, clear, windy Hoholitna River to the dark and placid Holitna, and that to the powerful Kuskokwim, ninety miles downstream.

It was Christmas night, and in the ten-by-ten-foot underground cabin, our family celebrated. Jenny sat quietly, her five presents on the table in front of her, facing the bed where my husband lay. With our dog curled beside me, I sat on the foot of the bed, on the sturdiest, flattest poles we'd selected for the bed's edge, so it could double as a work place. While the Coleman lantern hissed, my husband read. I watched Jenny. Behind her, light from the lantern bounced off the white snow crystals piled high to the ridge outside, then back through the clear sheet-plastic gables, flooding the room with its brilliance.

This was our second winter in the cabin. One time the winter before, we left the cabin for a week when it was ten below and traveled by dog team to one of our winter tent-camp sites. We left a coffee can full of water on the ground behind the woodstove while we were gone. When we came back, the water in the can was still water, not ice. It was a roasty warm cabin, snug and secure, even at forty below.

On the days of a new snowfall and trails to clear, or days when I'd extend my trap line, I'd come home and fall back onto the bed, letting the aches and tiredness drain from my body. Jenny would hop down from her bed, where she studied, and would unlace the hightop leather winter boots I wore, slide on my slippers, and hand me coffee. Heaven couldn't be better than that.

After the chores were done, I'd sit on the edge of the bed, sipping coffee. I'd look around the cabin and see Jenny lying on her bunk reading, my husband on ours reading. I'd see the dirt crumbling from the walls falling into and mixing with the mud on the floor; the organic smell of wet dirt mixing with other smells—bottled animal musks used for luring animals to our traps, long-unwashed down coats and sleeping bags, spruce and birch wood smoke and the grainy smell of wood ash, the sweet fragrance of boiled beaver, or moose and barley stew, of black and green mildews growing on the roof purlins.

Below us in the four-by-four-foot walking area lay three rough-sawn spruce boards tacked to poles, nearly smooth now. I brought the boards the second fall we arrived here by riverboat from our homestead, fifty miles away across the tundra on the

Stony River, about 150 miles by water. My husband shook his
head at me as I scrubbed those boards that were lying in the mud.
To me it seemed a natural need, for a woman to scrub what she
could, to try to feel clean.

Those boards were where I'd stand to fix dinner, using the
edge of our bed as a work space. Where we'd stand when we
bathed in the small washtub or when we washed clothes. Where
my husband stood to skin the animals we caught. Where we
kneeled to put wood in the woodstove made from one-third of a
fifty-five-gallon oil drum.

Multiple layers of cardboard held back dirt and moss chinking between the logs over the beds, added insulation, and provided a wall to pin up Jenny's artwork and calendar for school
projects. On the north wall above our bed I pinned a picture of
geese on the ice, maybe on Chesapeake Bay, from a Remington
calendar. As the sunlight moved from the back gables to the front,
the pinks and lavenders in the picture looked as though the geese
stood in the dawn, through midday, ending at dusk with the
sunset coming through the front plastic gables. Inside that picture
I felt great peace.

I'd see and smell these things and get an uneasy feeling,
thinking that if a social worker came, they'd probably try to take
Jenny away, saying it was an unfit environment, saying we were
not providing a good home, saying she was neglected. I knew the
chances of a social worker showing up there were as remote as we
were, but it still scared me.

I'd seen them in Lime Village. I'd seen them land on the
gravel runway by the river in a plane they had chartered from
Anchorage or Bethel. They carried briefcases and clipboards and
an expectation for everyone to fit their white-world images of
a minimum standard of living. As they walked around Lime
Village, their faces held many things: curiosity, bureaucratic
boredom, sympathy, disgust, caring, a need to "help." To the
Natives who'd worked hard, lived a natural life, competed with

other animals for survival, built log houses that were now gray on the outside and a rich rust color on the inside from years of wood smoke, they'd say, "We'd like to build you a house." The implication was, "Yours is not good enough for our standards. You are not providing for yourself adequately according to our standards. We will take care of you, and assume responsibility for your life, according to our standards."

I thought of them, and it scared me to wonder if it was possible for them to take Jenny away from me because of how we lived.

Jenny sat at her table, quietly looking at the presents in front of her, choosing which to open first.

Her little table was the only one in our cabin. She'd hovered over me as she watched me cut poles and shape them to mount the two boards. My husband had grudgingly agreed to force the boards from a short section of log we had left over from building the cabin. Extracted from a white spruce tree, the boards dipped and rose from the shaping by our swede saw and axe and from the uneven drying. I had taken a rasp to the gouges in an effort to smooth the surface, but the boards still showed where my husband's axe had taken chunks out of the living pulp. The grain of the spruce swirled where it changed directions around the knots, abrasive on one side, silky smooth on the other. The aging of the tree had colored the heartwood magenta, blue, and red. The boards were now polished from use, making the colors and swirls vivid. All had combined to produce humble boards of some depth and character. To me, the boards and Jenny were a lot alike.

Jenny would jam her down sleeping bag into its sack, place it carefully the right distance from her table, and with a regal air assume her tallest posture, the small of her back arched forward. Her taut little form perched on her bag, she ate and did school- and artwork, her five-year-old legs fitting snugly under the table. She'd spend hours forming perfect letters on large print-ruled paper, practicing adding using playing cards, and guiding herself, for the most part, through school workbooks. But mostly, she liked to read. In our one-room cabin, sitting at her table, Jenny was in her private domain.

The table was two boards, each about eight inches wide by twenty-five inches long, mounted over the foot of Jenny's peeled-pole bunk. Sitting there, she faced the head of the pole bed my husband and I shared. The foot of her bed, where her table was, met the head of ours right under the ridgepole. When she sat on her sleeping-bag sack at the table, her eyes were level with the ground outside the plastic gables, where the ever-roaring Coleman light reflected.

One foot above Jenny's head, poles supported a sod roof made of more clear plastic covered with tundra. Above the foot-thick layer of dirt and moss tundra was the white layer of snow that spread as far as we could see in any direction, and that curled around the hole where the light escaped.

Four-inch gaps between the peeled spruce poles overhead allowed glimpses through the plastic of a world that grew all winter under the snow: mosses of several colors and hues—ever-green, lime, rust, gold, and wine—and in the shapes of miniature trumpets, ferns, sponges, and trees; and in the mosses, tiny green worms, the sound of their gnawing as if through megaphones; in the dirt, shrews tunneling from one place to another.

Three rounds of stacked and notched logs separated Jenny from the dirt that banked the outside walls of the cabin. We had dug two feet down into the frozen ground inside the cabin, then thrown the dirt outside for more insulation against the cold. A six-inch-deep bed of moss and sticks held the log walls above the two-foot-high dirt walls that bent to make the mud floor. Through holes in the dirt wall, shrews entered and left—their homes and ours. We entered and left by sliding through a hole in the plastic gables, removing a window that was framed in rough white spruce. At the eaves, the wall was just under five feet tall; at the ridge, a little over six. Under the ridgepole my husband could stand up straight; I could stand, with my head cocked, at the eaves which Jenny could touch by stretching her arms above her head.

⑥

At least this Christmas we had food and we were together. Last year we'd been three weeks without food before Christmas, waiting for the plane that didn't come. We'd reboiled coffee grounds for a month and had to catch a beaver every other day to feed the three of us and our dog. Some days we didn't catch one.

Jenny had actually gotten heavier then and had been perky as ever. She'd bounce ahead of me on the trap line in her sturdy, faded blue snowsuit I'd gotten from the Salvation Army. While we walked, Jenny would jabber. Listening to my own thoughts, I heard her words only now and then, soothed to hear her happy chirping, voicing the world inside her. Her small blue backpack hugged her back, and Brownie, her only "toy," hung his stuffed puppy-dog head out the top of her pack, ears bouncing as she walked, swaying when she wore snowshoes in fresh snow.

Whenever we walked, we'd chant the days of the week, or count by fives, or spell new words, working her correspondence schoolwork into our days. On the trap line I carried two pieces of hard candy in my pocket, in case she got tired on the six-mile trail. When we reached the far end, she'd get one piece, the other when we got home. On some days, even the sweet candies didn't make her forget how tired she was, and I'd try to think of ways to distract her, wondering how often I pushed her too hard.

Like the time we'd gone out along Door Creek to set a new line. Absorbed in my surroundings, I went to work making sets. After a while Jenny said she was cold. I told her to walk around to stay warm and I'd be a little while more. Twenty minutes later she began crying, and I turned my full attention to her. A hard-headed five-year-old, insistent that she could dress herself; I had given up on forcing the issue and allowed her that responsibility. I looked inside her coat. A long-john shirt was the only thing there. I wore not only a thermal long-john shirt but a flannel shirt and a down vest under my coat. Inside Jenny's winter boots, her feet were bare. I quickly gave her my socks, vest, and coat, and we hurried the two miles home. After that she was hypothermic, then sick for four days. During those four days as she lay in bed, fifty trail-less miles away from a radio, I wondered if a social worker would be a better judge than I. Was I an unfit mother? How could I learn to be a good mother with no model? Should Jenny be taken from me?

Last year when we'd run out of food, the plane had come to take us to our supply cabin two days before Christmas. By then, Jenny and I were reluctant to leave my husband and our dog alone at Christmas, not knowing when we'd get a flight back, but we needed the food. Jenny and I had feasted on Spam and green beans on Christmas Day, although she'd suggested we wait until we got back home.

But this year we were together, and the game warden, Larry, had come by and brought us a turkey and oranges, like he did for other isolated families at Christmas when weather permitted. His wife, Pat, a teacher in the bush community of McGrath, had bought presents for Jenny. Three of the packages in front of her were books I'd gotten by sending in a card for an "introductory offer," and canceled after receiving the books. The other two, the brightly wrapped ones, were from Pat.

I had adopted Larry as my foster dad. Patrolling in his small plane, he'd drop by every month or two while doing his rounds to see if we were alive and well. I'd meet him at the plane. Smiling, I'd say, "How do I look? Am I okay?" Like Papillon on the French penal colony island, isolated, asking how he looked of any prisoner he chanced to see—looking for perspective, re-assurance. Larry would look at me seriously, knowing that though I laughed, I was serious. He'd say straight-faced, looking in my eyes, "Girl, you're as squirrelly as the rest of them," meaning the few other families who lived as we did. I'd laugh and he'd grin while we both felt a tinge of uneasiness inside.

Jenny set the shiny wrapped presents from Pat aside to open last. She carefully unfolded one wrapping after another, savoring each gift as it appeared. One by one she peeled away the paper, read each book that was from me from cover to cover, then set it aside. She neatly stacked the books on her table, then opened the presents from Pat. She ran her hand down the cover of the first when its wrappings were laid aside. The glossy cover held pages and pages of detailed Arthur Rackham fairy tale pictures to color. Jenny looked through it, then laid it aside also.

As I watched her, I thought of my own childhood Christmases in Florida and the intense aloneness I'd felt there, even sitting with my older brother and younger sister among three-foot-tall mounds of boxes and wrappings. We'd unwrap the heaps in a frenzy, sinking inside when we were done, wondering why there was still that painful hollow feeling. Was there anything more? The presents never did make up for not feeling free to talk about what was happening in our lives, about the drinking, about the anger. Our parents really loved us. They'd done the best they could.

Jenny sat up straight, opening her final present. I watched as the paper unfolded. When the gift was revealed, her back rounded down in a slump. She held the plastic package of thirty felt-tip coloring pens in both hands, folded open on her table in front of her. She looked without making a sound.

I watched her silently, knowing this was the final present. Grief for her world without kids, with no sister or brother, without oranges and green grapes, without mounds of Christmas presents and so many things that most people take for granted, welled inside me. Mostly, for her world without kids. The best that I could do for her was not good enough, not nearly, and would not be, ever. I said, "What is it, honey? What are you thinking?"

Jenny held the package in her hands and, sitting at her table, turned to look at me. Holding the markers up for me to see, she said, "Mom, I must be the luckiest kid in the whole world.... I have all these colors to choose from."

Mendenhall

Migael Scherer

The day was overcast and shad-
owless. I caught my breath at the first sight of the glacier. The
Mendenhall dominates an already dominating landscape of mountain, snow, and alpine meadow. It looms massively, its coarse
surface muddied with rubble and rock, its face broken into giant
shards of blue: navy, turquoise, pale aqua. Ice so compressed it
absorbs all other colors.

Every trip I make to Juneau includes a visit to the Mendenhall, but this time the glacier was a detour, not a destination. In
just a little while I would drive on to visit Dan, the first Alaskan
friend I ever made. What would he look like, in these last months
of his cancer? Would his face be hollow, as my friend Michael's
had been, the skin pressed like tissue paper against the bones, his
intelligent smile gone to jaw and gum and teeth? A skull, I had
thought instantly, as though he were already dead, and then his
eyes brightened, and I knew he was in there, alive, and I wanted
to pull him out.

Dan, I knew, was lucid, but I was still afraid of the pain I imagined I would see, the grief I would feel. Too full of my own feelings to be able to focus on him. I drove to the glacier on instinct, hands clenching the steering wheel, stomach tight. Drawn as to a shrine, as though the Mendenhall were a living spirit that could give me courage and comfort. I know it is an inanimate thing—gravity provides the impetus for its journey from forty-five hundred feet up in the ice field—but it feels alive. It exhales a frigid breath as it crawls on its belly down between the mountains. It poises its bulk, gracefully somehow, at the edge of Mendenhall Lake and patiently waits to calve. When an iceberg is born, the glacier moans with a primitive rumble that is felt as powerfully as it is heard and can never be forgotten.

I walked a narrow path that descended to the lake, found a place to sit away from the steady stream of tourists. For a long while I simply stared at the frozen, undulating river, letting its reality absorb all my thoughts. Comparisons skittered uselessly down its icy walls like cobbles, were swallowed into its crevasses. So heavy it crushes stone to flour, so huge it seems to be always close. The Mendenhall's face alone is a mile and a half wide and two hundred feet thick, the mouth of a river flowing so slowly that a ride down the full twelve miles of its length, moving at its pace, would take eighty years.

If the glacier seems alive, then it is also dying, melting faster than its heavy advance. Since my first visit only ten years ago, it had retreated noticeably. The pile of silt I once scaled in rubber boots, where I routinely posed my friends from "down south" for photos, was now a mere hump of sand. The waterfall of Nugget Creek to the east, once partially obscured by ice, was now fully visible. The bare hill above it was green; grasses and shrubs had found root room. Someday a forest will stand there.

Yet the glacier still seems undiminished. It was this stolidness, this permanence despite constant change, that I had come for. I tried to breathe this in with the thread of ice that was woven through the air like a scent. I wanted to be strong for Dan and his family. So I sat, on a slanted gray rock scarred with the ancient tracks of the Mendenhall, as though waiting for a sign.

Is this what friendship comes to, finally? A chance meeting, an immediate rapport, sharing family, friends, meals, and talk—then nothing at all? I looked around. If Dan were with me here, he would be squinting at the steep green of Bullard Mountain, searching for goats. Or describing the microscopic creatures that thrive in the dead ice. Or speculating about the condition of this trail, that stream. I caught myself smiling. He'd have me up exploring and learning in a way that felt like play. His passion, it seemed, was never to let anyone take Alaska's beauty sitting down. Dan was always outdoors or dressed as if about to be: plaid wool shirt, wool trousers, lug boots. Hands in pockets, he'd rock back on his heels like a boy, ready to bolt.

The gray sky thickened, the temperature dropped. I zipped up my jacket. Three helicopters, small and noisy as gnats, headed up toward the ice field. Some years ago I had strapped myself into one of them and had stepped onto the Mendenhall's crusty surface; a sharp chill had risen up through the insulation of my boots. Looking down, I had seen an alder leaf, dark brown from the previous autumn, leathery with decay. Absorbing more heat than its surroundings, it had melted the ice beneath it, etched a resting place into the glacier one inch deep.

What do you say to a friend who is dying? All I know is this: The final good-bye breaks the heart. And fills it.

I drove to Dan's house on Back Loop Road, taking in the tall trees, the log cabin perched on the edge of Montana Creek, the creeping plywood subdivisions. The fireweed still bloomed bright pink, a good sign; its turning white with seed would signal that summer—never long enough—was over. Dan's winding driveway was crowded with spruce, skunk cabbage, and alder. When it opened to the house, I counted four or five cars; just as always, this was a home filled with many lives.

Beth met me at the door, smiling, smoothing over the sharp edges of strain with hospitality. She showed me around; the house had been recently remodeled, but already the family had sprawled over the newly painted rooms. Books, papers, jackets were everywhere. Whittaker, an aging water spaniel, scratched in the kitchen. Brita, their second oldest daughter, wrote at her father's desk, exuding like her mother a robust friendliness.

To my surprise—the sky promised rain—Dan was outside on the new deck. He sat in a lounge chair that faced Auke Lake, the Mendenhall, all the surrounding mountains—an astonishing view. A wool blanket covered him to the waist; above, his bathrobe gaped open slightly. An IV bag hung from a shiny metal stand beside him, dripping liquid into a clear tube that snaked under his sleeve. Dan's head, once a confusion of gray locks, was now bald from over a year of chemotherapy. His narrow, lined face looked older than his sixty-two years.

"Hey, Migael," Dan said and immediately reached for my hand. His eyes and smile were startling and bright. "This is Tom, an old kayaking buddy. We go way back." He looked at Tom, a man I guessed to be about my age, in his mid-forties. "Migael here lives in Seattle. She and her husband built their boat. How long did you guys live aboard here?" Dan asked, gracefully inserting the traditional Alaska conversation opener.

I smiled at Tom like a fellow pilgrim and sat next to him on a chair at Dan's feet, my back to the Mendenhall. I hadn't expected this liveliness or my surge of happiness; I felt almost intoxicated. "Four winters," I answered, grinning. "I'm not as tough as all of you."

"Nonsense," Dan said. "Migael just completed the Admiralty Island race. Tell us all about it."

So before I had time to ask about him, I was describing the crew, the boat, the splendid weather, the light winds, and the rough spots. Ten years ago, at our first meeting, Dan had answered my almost-identical question. Leaning against the bulwark of his sailboat, he had described his voyage down the East Coast, through the Panama Canal, and up the West Coast, his voice filled with a mixture of exuberance and humility.

"So what did you learn?" Dan asked. It was always what he wanted to know whenever anyone talked about a new experience.

"Well, I'm certainly no racer," I said. "It's so intense, especially compared to cruising." What was I talking about? Here was Dan, living through one of the most intense of all human experiences. But there was unmistakable interest in his face; *Take me with you,* he seemed to say. So I babbled on about the demands of watch routines and sail changes, the drive to win that I apparently lacked. When I confessed to getting seasick, I stopped. How could I complain about nausea with Dan, who had been through weeks and weeks of it in chemotherapy? I noticed the gray circles under his eyes, the pallor of his skin, the thin shoulders that had once been square and full. "I guess the main thing I learned is what I can't do." I glanced away.

"I don't think you should generalize from just one race," Dan said. "It isn't a matter of what you can and can't do. Finally, it's a matter of what you know you have to do." His eyes flashed, glacier blue. "That's why this is so hard. What I know I have to do, I can't."

I leaned forward, struck by Dan's words, anxious for more. What did he mean? Was it dying that he had to do? Or living? Would it be okay to ask? I was trying to form the question when Tom broke in.

"Kayaking's all I've done," he said, taking the helm of the conversation, putting it back on a smoother course. I had almost forgotten he was sitting beside me. I felt as if I had been corrected, not rudely, but gently, for the sake of us all. "A different kind of torture. Remember that trip we made up Lynn Canal, Dan?" And they were off, eagerly riding the current of mutual memory.

Beth arrived with a pot of tea and Brita with a plate of smoked salmon, naming the friend who had brought it. I sipped and nibbled, let myself float in the present as I listened to Tom and Dan talk about the past. The future, for now, for all of us, had moved away. The IV fluid dripped, dripped into Dan.

"It's good to see you here, Dan," I said, after he and Tom had beached their story. "The last time we were together was in Seattle."

"I'm sure glad I left that place," Dan agreed. "Here, I can spend the afternoons at home. The hospital takes care of me at night, so it's easy on Beth." He glanced at her, and they connected, briefly and fiercely. "Besides, the doctors said there was nothing more they could do. I realize now that Seattle was doing me harm. My spirit was so *dry* there."

His eyes focused beyond Tom and me. I didn't need to turn around to see what Dan saw. It was the Mendenhall, solid and palpable though six miles away. Thousands of years ago, it had covered the spot where we were now sitting.

"But not here," he continued. "Here I'm filled up. I love this wildness around me. Even the cold." He shivered slightly.

"Can I get your cap?" Beth asked, standing up as she spoke.

"No thank you, Beth." Dan rubbed his bald head. "I like to *feel*."

"Yes," I said. "That's it exactly. Why I keep coming back to Alaska." I felt happy, though I didn't know why. I turned to the glacier: powerful, indifferent, neither malignant nor benign— beautiful and frightening at once. The happiness dissolved. "Sometimes the wildness is too much," I added, turning back to Dan. "It makes me feel so small."

Dan was watching me intently, as though my words had size and shape. *It makes me feel alive,* I thought, looking into his eyes. *Afraid, and alive.* And in the admission of my own fear I touched, just for an instant, a little of his.

Recoiling, I rushed to change the subject, as Tom had before. "And for sure," I said, forcing a hearty tone, "Juneau is never dry."

Relieved laughter, and the talk turned to the unusual sunny spell they'd had—almost two weeks in a row. How quickly we move toward the surface when the deep is close and real.

Tom left, promising to return the next day. Dan, Beth, Brita, and I eagerly retrieved our own memories, of potlucks and picnics, skating and cross-country skiing. Every memory was marked by the land and water that surrounded us: Eagle Beach. Auke Bay. Gastineau Channel. Mendenhall Lake. The names alone made us smile. Each seemed a monument now to our friendship.

This burst of remembering seemed to take the last of Dan's energy for, soon after, his shoulders sagged and his eyelids were drooping. I finished my cup of tea, stood to leave, and the sorrow I had been holding down rose with me. I was leaving Juneau tomorrow. The next time I returned, Dan would be gone. Without knowing what to say next, determined to be brave, I approached his lounge chair.

The words spilled out. "I was prepared to feel sad. But I wasn't prepared...for the happiness I've felt seeing you. Thank you." I turned to Beth and Brita, who were staring at me, eyes wide and unblinking. I could only imagine their suffering. My throat tightened.

"I'm sorry," I said, wiping my eyes. "I'm not very strong about this."

"No," Dan said. His voice was urgent. "Your feelings. Express them. It's your strength."

I nodded numbly. I squeezed his hand. It was warm but seemed to weigh nothing, and that lightness transferred to my very breath and bones. The lightness stayed with me—a deep calm—as I said good-bye to Beth and Brita. As I drove into town. Even as I cried. As I thought of Dan on the deck, barely moving, imperceptibly leaving. The Mendenhall in his eyes.

Letter from Nuiqsut

Mark Bergemann

January 21, 1996. The village of Nuiqsut, on the Colville River off the arctic coast of Alaska, one hundred and thirty miles southwest of Barrow, sixty miles west of the Prudhoe Bay oil fields. The countryside is the classic Alaskan expanse of flat white that you have seen in dozens of pictures.

I'm writing at a window seat, soaking up the first sun since Thanksgiving. The sun arrived back in this country only this past Thursday. Every day since then, I have taken advantage of the brief moments of light, absorbing it through my face and eyes. There's a caribou stew simmering on the stove, and bread rising in the breadmaker—just enough going on to hold me in the house for a while. Soon as I can, though, I'll get out and take a good walk. It's warm enough, about twenty below, that I could go out on the snowmobile. But my back needs the walk; so walk it will be.

Watching the sun come back to this country reminds me of a cheap roman candle. It begins feebly at first, a ball moving from the same place on the horizon each morning. Each day, it falls slightly farther from where it began, until some weird science takes over. A physics begins to push it back a little farther each dawn, and it gains strength to rise a little higher and set farther each day. By early March, its flat arc will encompass a quarter of the sky. A scant month later, it will float across more than half the horizon. A few short weeks after that, it will never set.

It has been fifteen years since I last lived north of the Brooks Range, and I like being back on the arctic plain. I'm recognizing it this time as a place where you are alone with yourself a lot. Not lonesome, just alone. I think it's a function of the flat, treeless terrain and the clothing: layer after layer of warm clothes, each one thicker than the last, and finally a parka. At forty below, I wear at least six layers, two of which are a ski jacket and a parka. When my hood goes up, I am essentially alone. Even with others around, I am fundamentally by myself. Communication is difficult, vision restricted. Talking is energetic, words forcefully projected to get through your and someone else's face mask, hat, hood. Usually we just stick to directions, compass readings, animal sightings, and simple arm signals.

We, the teachers with whom I work, do play—though being educators, our play is framed with a purpose. One of our first projects was an igloo, which by the time we finished looked more like a tepee. We did actually get the whole thing domed in though, and we were chinking the cracks when one of those things happened that makes you glad you decided to practice. Standing inside, I had shoved a small block of snow, about the size of a short two-by-four, into a crack. It went too far and began tumbling down the outside of the dome. Just the vibration of this little block of snow—it couldn't have weighed a pound—started the house settling. And then falling down. All of what we had assembled crashed over us and settled in a wreckage of broken blocks around our feet. I can still hear the snow block's hollow song, as it skipped away down the wall. Can see the snow dust sifting down in the momentary settle. Then the spiral of the blocks falling one after another. A week later, traveling past the site while hunting for caribou, a friend reported that there was no longer any trace of our work. The wind of a single storm, generating an inexorable dune of snow, had drifted it over.

A few weeks later, the creek bed we used as a major thoroughfare to the country south of Nuiqsut disappeared under the snow as well. One day a highway with virtual on and off ramps leading up to secondary trails, the next day an exhilarating narrow and twisting bobsled run of hanging cornices and gut-wrenching drops into wind-blasted holes. The day after that, just gone. Filled by the dune, nothing, not a dip or a swell to betray it was there. I liked to stand here, suspended above the spot, and watch the ground wind sweep the graceful eddies of snow along to their next landfill. Just off the pace, the occasional willow leaf scrapes along, trying to keep up. The sound of the snow is dry, like sand running over paper.

This is not a place to feel at one with nature. The boundary between you and it is too thick, and too important. The power of what's all around keeps you absorbed, constantly checking the status of that boundary. If you happen to fall outside it—a glove blows away, ice breaks and you fall through, you sweat too much—then you are probably going to freeze something. Or you might not get home at all. It sounds severe, but it's true. Your margin for error is inversely proportional to the thickness of your clothing. I see the proof every day, in faces in various stages of repair from frost-nipped cheeks and noses, and more seriously in the occasional black and bandaged ear or leg.

Frostbite of the face is particularly hard to avoid. It's not like you're in extreme facial pain and then you freeze. Generally, you're just cold and preoccupied with having fun. The last time it happened to me, we were out in the high drifts formed by the banks of the river. We were riding our machines up under the cornices of snow and enjoying the free-fall back to the river's surface. Heading home, somebody mentioned I had a flake of ice hanging on my face. Thinking to flick it off, I tried to hook my fingernail under the edge. It turned out to be my frozen skin, stiff as a scab. Warmed by my hand, it thawed, but a few days later, the real scab formed. It eventually sloughed off, revealing the beautiful pink of new skin.

The arctic is not a death-wish kind of place. It's just a place where you are always aware of keeping the correct amount of distance between you and it. It's a place where you are left alone to experience and ponder its absolute power and remorseless implacability. That experience is wonderful and frightening. It clutches at you, feeds paranoia, makes you want to run for home. In no other country I've been in can you be five miles from home and be in such quick danger of being completely and totally befuddled directionally. Even in good weather, for a newcomer like me, there are simply no landmarks. I can go out by myself, shut my machine off, and stand there taking in the beauty of the awesome expanse—and feeling the unreasonable fear begin to build. Quickly start the machine, just to be sure it still starts. Check the back trail, just to be sure I can still see it. Verify again in my mind, for the umpteenth time, the direction to the village. I'm always laughingly amazed at the mental checklist.

These days I'm experimenting with trusting my Global Positioning System. So far it's been very accurate, and I'm glad I have one. If I can keep the GPS warm, it works. That's been the only issue so far, keeping it warm. There has been a time or two I've turned it on, and by the time it's picked up a couple of satellites it has gotten too cold and begins to lose them before I can get a compass reading on where home is. It's a very panicky feeling to watch those satellites drop off the screen and know your only sure way home is to backtrack a trail that is being erased by the wind as you stand there.

Enough. I had better get outdoors before I lose the light. In the time it has taken to write this, the sun has risen and set. Time to go enjoy a long twilight walk.

The Bush Life

Ted Kerasote

Back in the late 1980s, the Haydens were some of the last unincorporated hunters in North America. Unlike the many hunting, trapping, and fishing families who lived in Native communities, the Haydens lived off in the bush, by themselves, 120 miles north of Fort Yukon, in the far northeastern corner of Alaska.

To be frank, they did this because the father, Richard, was a curmudgeon. He hated crowds, he hated cities, he hated towns, and most of all he hated people (read "Government") telling him what to do. What he loved was the bush, the thousands of square miles of Alaskan tundra, dwarf black spruce, bog, and braided rivers that he called his own and in which he raised his family.

He wore a filthy but dapper Australian bush hat, the color of faded roses, the brim cocked up. He wore heavy, plaid wool shirts, and he smoked home-rolled cigarettes all day until his teeth were stained the color of moose turds. He had blue eyes, pale as the arctic sky.

His wife Shannon was Tlingit, and more than anything else in the world she wanted a washing machine, to keep up with Richard and her five kids: Richard, Jr., seventeen; Danny, fifteen; Suzie, fourteen; Dwayne, two; and Judy, just born. Even though they were 120 miles from Fort Yukon and didn't have a generator, Shannon could have had a washing machine. But Richard said it wasn't in keeping with "the bush life," so Shannon didn't get one.

The Hayden family's eternal debate centered around what was and what wasn't in keeping with the bush life. They killed a dozen caribou and several moose each year, shot quite a few geese, and caught lots of salmon, all of which were definitely in keeping with the bush life. And they trapped marten and lynx all winter, also in keeping. They trapped them by dog, going out a hundred miles in the midwinter darkness and staying out for a week when it was fifty degrees below zero Fahrenheit, camping in little tents, with tiny woodstoves. These trips were definitely in keeping with the bush life. So was chopping through the ice of the Sheenjek River to fetch water, reading by Coleman lantern, and eating the vile-smelling marten carcasses when food ran out during bad winters.

Now using a snow machine—this was debatable. They had one and constantly hedged and hemmed and hawed about its use in the bush life—the kids for it, and Richard, Sr., ambivalent, knowing he should stick to dogs, but still sucked in by the snow machine. But it rarely started at below minus twenty, so the debate was really a nonissue during the deep winter, unless the machine was dragged into the cabin to start. This they sometimes did, filling the house with plumes of blue smoke and roaring away through the front door into the darkness.

Insulated coveralls instead of caribou clothing—these too were debatable. Suzie and Danny had switched to coveralls; Richard still used caribou-hide clothing. And the radio, with its convivial "trap-line chatter"—the over-the-air messages for bush families—was definitely in order, as was the evangelical program beamed from somewhere deep in the heart of Texas. But anything smacking of the names Darwin, Leakey, or evolution was definitely not part of the bush life.

"You believe we came from monkeys?" said Suzie in astonishment, as she looked at one of the many books I had brought along for my winter stay with them.

"Well, not exactly. We came from a common ancestor."

She screwed up her mouth. "Reading's worthless," she said. "A trapper doesn't need books."

"What happens when you have to go Outside?"

In Alaska, "Outside" means outside the state.

"I'm never going to go Outside. I'm going to be a trapper forever."

At this career goal, Suzie and her brother Danny were succeeding handsomely. Their mother had given up her campaign to make them bathe, and each of them was now in their seventh month of not having washed. Since Suzie and Danny also wiped their hands on their coveralls after they placed the various musk "attractor" scents on their traps, and since the scents had seeped through their coveralls and into their jeans and long underwear, which, in keeping with their no-bathing policy, they had also not changed for seven months, the smell in the cabin was definitely in keeping with the bush life.

It was, therefore, a great relief when we left the cabin, setting off north to tend the trap line one dark January day, the light, at best, dusky at noon. From November to January, the sun never rises over this northern part of the Brooks Range.

The four malamutes I'd been given as my team were now howling at the top of their lungs, lunging forward, turning their snouts to the few still visible stars and crying their agony at being left behind.

"Those dogs want to go," said Richard, Jr., in the flat voice that many Natives use, so you can't tell if they're stating a fact or being sarcastic. By the twinkle in his eyes, I knew it was the latter.

He leaned in the doorway of the cabin and watched me stow my cameras. He had been left behind—to chop wood, fetch water, and help his mom and younger siblings. Not much of a hunter or a trapper, he wanted to become a bush pilot.

"Really?" I said through gritted teeth. I had begun to struggle with the hook, two curved pieces of iron shaped like a rigor-mortised hand, to which the mooring rope of a sled is attached. It is thrown out while traveling, much like an anchor, and will stop the sled in firm snow. At a campsite, it is put around a convenient tree, or back at home snugged around a post. The only problem with the hook is that when you try to pull it away from its post, the entire team, made up of dogs who weigh 125 pounds each, is trying to yank it in the other direction. Of course, you can try to pull the hook off with two hands, but then you're not holding onto the sled with anything except good intentions when it rockets toward the horizon.

"Need a hand?" asked Richard, Jr., as amused as the rest of the family by my efforts at learning to drive dogs.

"How do you do this?" I asked, stepping onto the sled.

"Never be last," he said, hauling on the hook and setting me free.

We careened down the slope, smashed onto the river ice, nearly turned over, and flew up the river in pursuit of the other sleds as I reeled in the wildly flaying grapple. Where the track turned back into the willows, heading toward the dwarf spruce that lined the hillsides, the snow got deep, and fluffy, and deeper, and the four dogs sat down.

"Come on, Kobuck," I said to the lead dog. "Gitty up, Silver. Let's go, Bingo. Hey, come on," I shouted. "We've got miles to go before we sleep. And your family's way ahead of you."

Unimpressed, they gave the most halfhearted of tugs and immediately sat down again. In unison, they looked over their shoulders. It's too hard, said their eyes.

I yelled, "Let's go!"

Embarrassed for me, they looked away.

"Hey-ho, get a move on, gitty up!"

One by one, they pawed the snow, curled noses to tails, and made their husky nests. The wind began to blow, creating a small ground blizzard of powder. I sat down next to them. "Let's talk about this," I said.

Just as I was broaching the subject of healing their puppy within, Suzie drove up with her team.

"You gotta be harder with them," she said, looking at me with a mixture of pity and disgust. Dressed in a bulky green snowmobile suit, she was about five feet tall and three feet wide, with long black hair and big red cheeks. The summer before, I had seen her carry nearly eighty pounds of meat on her back and eat eleven caribou steaks at one sitting.

"And you need another dog."

She unhooked one from her team and wrestled it over to mine.

"Now be tough with 'em," she ordered. "Give 'em a good kick."

Giving nothing more than a cluck of her tongue, she was off. The only word I got out of my mouth was a yelp of surprise. My team dashed after hers, and I had to lunge at the crossbar of the sled to keep from being left behind.

At two-thirty, just as it started to get dark, we made camp, erecting the two dome tents and tiny woodstoves. Shannon had made us a week's worth of rations, and to keep things simple we ate the same course each day—one and a half pounds of moose meat and three huge, deep-fried donuts per person, all of which was, of course, now frozen solid. It was twenty-six below zero.

After chaining and feeding the dogs and chopping about a cord of dead spruce, we got into the tents—Suzie and Dan in one, Richard and I in the other. He immediately rolled and lit a cigarette, filling the tent completely with smoke in one giant exhalation. Coughing up a goober of phlegm and hacking it out the door, he said, "Keeps my lungs in training."

For the next four hours we melted water, defrosted moose meat, and talked. Blowing smoke in my face, Richard said, "You know, not many people from Outside would do this."

"It gets cold in Wyoming," I said defensively.

"How cold?"

"Thirty, forty below."

"Ppppp," said Richard disparagingly. "You ain't seen nothing."

He was right.

We rose at the crack of dawn, or what would have been the crack of dawn about three thousand miles farther south. The heaven glittered with stars. We fried some more moose meat and ate donuts and coffee, and then took about two hours to get the dogs harnessed and the tents struck. It was so cold that when I took off my lens cap it shattered in my hands. I was trying to photograph this epic departure by flash, but I was being stymied not only by the cold but by the caribou hairs that were everywhere. Despite Suzie and Danny's switch to polyester coveralls, the Haydens's sleeping rugs were still made from caribou, as were their mukluks, their mittens, and Richard's clothing. And caribou shed luxuriously. There were hairs, long stiff brittle hairs, jammed between the contacts of the flash and the camera body, caught up in the lens mount, and waving in the viewfinder. They had been on my toothbrush, and stuck to the moose meat, and floating on top of the coffee, and even up my nose when I tried to breathe amidst Richard's smoke. And now there was one in my right eye. Or at least I thought there was a caribou hair in my eye because as soon as I put in my contacts, Richard struck the tent, and I was outside in the dark, simultaneously poking at my eye, loading my sled, and trying to fix my camera by the light of my headlamp. Except my eye was killing me. I pulled the lid down. I pulled it up. I twisted it sideways, rolling my eyeball underneath. I pulled it every which way I could, which wasn't easy or very hygienic, since my pile gloves were also covered with caribou hair, moose grease, the powdered sugar Shannon had put on the donuts.

Dumping a hundred-pound bag of dog food in the sled in front of me, Richard slapped me on the back and said, "I don't know how you can be taking pictures in this cold." I didn't know either; I could barely see.

Shouting, "We've got a long day ahead of us," he drove his team into the darkness.

"See you down the trail," yelled Danny, and he, too, was gone.

Between stabbing at my eye, carrying gear to my sled, and handling my camera, I had managed to harness all my dogs, who now bawled and screamed, foaming at the mouth, their voices cracking and breaking as the harnesses choked them. The sled leapt and shuddered, straining at the hook. I had attached it to what had seemed a fairly sturdy spruce tree, about seven feet high and three inches in diameter. It was now bent over at a sickening angle.

Suzie asked, "Think you can handle 'em?"

In the deep snow of yesterday afternoon, we had wallowed into camp at a crawl. I didn't expect much more from my lame fivesome this morning, no matter what they were vocalizing, so I said, "No problem."

She shrugged, called her team into a trot, and I breathed a sigh of relief. At last, I could attend to my eye.

But the disappearance of all their companions sent my team into a new level of canine paroxysms. I was unfazed. "Shut up, you guys," I said. "We're not going anywhere until I'm ready." Taking out my Silva Ranger compass with the built-in sighting mirror, I shone my headlamp into my eye while peering at its reflected image. Nothing.

Taking off my glove and putting the headlamp under a bungee cord that lashed one of the duffels onto the sled, I now removed the offending contact. Cupping it in one palm and holding the mirror in the other, I tried to get my eye in the beam of the headlamp. Except it was bouncing around wildly as the dogs yanked and jerked at the sled. So I had to bob my head, try to hold open my lid, not drop my contact, and hang onto the mirror all at the same time, which, I guess, isn't an unusual test when you're living the bush life.

But I still couldn't see any foreign objects. So I put my contact back in. Or tried to. It was now frozen solid and felt like I'd put a rock in my eye. So I took it out and reached inside my snowmobile suit, inside my pile jacket, and inside the next pile jacket to the pocket next to my heart, where all those who wear contacts in the cold keep their rewetting solution.

At this point the dogs, frenzied beyond all hope of quieting, broke into a melee, biting, thrashing, and taking out their aggression on each other, and generally tangling their harnesses. I put the rewetted and still frozen contact in my eye, held the lid down until it melted, then blinked a few times.

Aieeee! What pain! What could be in there? I plucked out the lens and once again contorted myself in front of the bobbing headlamp. Peeling down my eyelid as far as it would go, I saw *it* at last—there in the very bottom of my eyeball, bowed comfortably—the telltale caribou hair. Reaching back through all my parkas, I snagged a bandanna and pried the hair out with its corner. Rewetting the contact, the dogs howling, the sled lunging, I leaned close to the headlamp while trying to hold the mirror far enough away from my panting so as not to fog it instantly. At that moment, I dropped the lens off my fingertip, directly into the bowels of the sled.

The dogs, mistaking my epithet for the command to go, lunged against the bent-over spruce with renewed efforts. The tree looked to have about a minute left in it. Trying to stay calm, the world as described by my headlamp now disastrously blurred, I peered down into the sled. I moved a duffel…and some dog food…and a burlap bag of moose-meat balls…and there, illuminated miraculously in the beam of my lamp, lay my contact, frozen onto a piece of rope. But it wouldn't come off. I squirted it with some rewetting solution, or tried to squirt it. The bottle had frozen solid. I stood absolutely still and thought. Then I reached under all my layers and found my contact case. Emptying its still liquid contents on the contact, I was able to release the lens. By the time I got it to my eye, it was frozen again. No matter. I held the lid over it until it melted.

I opened my eyes. And I could see. There was even a little bit of light seeping down through the trees. No time to waste. I put my rewetting drops, lens case, and compass in my parka, clapped the headlamp over my head, untangled the dogs, mounted the back of the sled, and gave a mighty tug at the hook. It wouldn't budge.

The dogs, knowing they were about to leave, redoubled their efforts, sinking the hook farther around the tree, which was heeled over as if blowing in a hurricane.

"Ease up," I yelled.

They pulled harder.

Nothing else to do. I got off the sled, grabbed the hook with both hands, and hauled back with all my might. As it came off the tree, I and seven hundred pounds of malamute team were suspended in sublime equipoise for one millisecond. Then I was jerked horizontally through the air and slammed into the rock-hard snow. All our walking around camp and the departure of the three other sleds had created an icy runway through the forest.

The dogs blasted off like a missile, and I, clinging to the hook, caromed behind them, striking trees and stumps, snow cascading over my head and into my eyes and mouth. Hand over hand, nearly blinded, I pulled myself back to the sled and with a gasp clambered on. Tugging the hood from my head, I gave a triumphant shout: "Mush, you huskies. Eee-haa!" An instant later, Big Red, the new dog, fell in the deeper snow beyond camp and immediately became dallied in his traces.

The other dogs stopped and looked at him with disdainful smirks. Sighing, I got off the sled and walked forward through the knee-deep snow, not realizing I was committing the ultimate mistake of the novice musher. I hadn't set the hook. The moment I untangled Big Red, the lead dog, Kobuck, lunged. The rest of the team followed. I grabbed for the traces, planted my feet—an utterly stupid gesture—and for the second time that dark morning was plucked into the air by seven hundred pounds of dog team.

With incredible, malicious speed they ran forward. I bounced among them, snow filling my mouth as I tried to shout, "Stop, whoa, hold on!" I could barely see, but I did have the presence of mind to actually look behind me before I let go. A thousand pounds of sled and gear was following us.

The decision was quick. It was instantaneous death by crushing or a long, slow, ignominious walk after my team. I let go and rolled to the side, and my team and sled vanished down the trail into the dawn.

There are those moments in life when you know that no matter what you think of saying it will not be good enough, so why waste the time even formulating an excuse. Especially when you have a long walk ahead of you.

Postholing for fifteen minutes, I finally came to a gully. The sled was augured in at its bottom and the carabineer that attached the traces to its front had been snapped off neatly. My team was gone. I climbed out of the gully and walked on, sweating as if I were in the tropics, despite the cold. After another mile or so, I could hear the sound of Suzie snarling and the thud of her caribou mukluks. My team had caught up to hers and was engaged in a free-for-all with her dogs. She was kicking the malamutes apart and beating them with a length of rope.

When I came up to her, all had grown quiet. Like the Colossus of the Sheenjek, she stood, feet planted firmly in the midst of the two cowering teams. Handing me my team's trace, she said, "Maybe next time you oughta read a book about driving dogs."

Wild Sentries

Geneen Marie Haugen

The Cessna lost altitude in preparation for landing, but we swerved over the tundra without touching down. Circling, we tried again, skittered low. The voice of the pilot crackled in my headphones—distant, disembodied, even though he sat right beside me. "Too windy," he said. "We'll have to land somewhere else."

Landing elsewhere was one prospect I had never considered while planning this arctic trip from maps in my Wyoming home. Maps convey many things—a sense of topography, altitude, and contour—but not vagaries of wind and weather. "Where?" I asked into the microphone.

"We can try landing farther up the Marsh Fork, or over on the main Canning, or maybe down near the confluence." As the pilot spoke, we flew low over the upper Marsh Fork of the Canning River. From the air, the river looked like a turquoise necklace strung between the bare cleavage of the Brooks Range. I had never scouted a river from the air, and without trees to give perspective, I had no perception of its size or depth. "Is there enough water in there to float?" I asked. The pilot, Don Ross, a former assistant manager of Arctic National Wildlife Refuge, shrugged. "It's your decision," he said, adding, "we can go over the ridge and land on the Canning."

I didn't have topographic maps for the upper Canning. Landing at the confluence would cut out about half the river miles and the most varied terrain. I had a few minutes to decide. "Up the Marsh Fork."

Don nodded, banked a turn. The runway was invisible to me. The Cessna bumped down on tundra, rolled to a stop. My friend Lisa Varga and I scrambled out and unloaded packs, stove, cameras, video equipment, and a waterproof aluminum box filled with dry food. Don climbed back into the plane, saying he *hoped* he would return that evening with my partner David, our raft, and the rest of the gear—if the weather held.

After the engine noise vanished into an enormous silence, Lisa and I looked at each other and burst out laughing. We'd suddenly dropped from the sky into an adventure we had planned and imagined for months. So far, nothing was as anticipated. The sun on our faces and the pastel scents of wildflowers were shocking, peaceful, unexpected. The formidable arctic landscape of my imagination softened, curved tender and green. It was July, and the brief northern summer had just begun.

Earth hums. Put your ear to the ground and you might hear it, or the padding of paws, pounding of hooves, or faint brush of wings. Arctic National Wildlife Refuge is the last frontier for some of the most significant creature migrations left in North America. Polar bears dig birthing dens on land. Birds from Asia, both Americas, and Europe flock to the coastal plain. Legendary numbers of insects provide food and torment. As many as 165,000 caribou of the Porcupine herd travel twenty-seven hundred miles each year, cyclically returning to ancestral birthing ground on the arctic coast in summer.

Arctic National Wildlife Refuge is the largest intact wilderness ecosystem left in the United States. Combined with adjacent Northern Yukon Park, the area becomes the largest supposedly protected wildlife habitat in the world. Dall sheep, musk oxen, moose, wolverines, and wolves inhabit the refuge year-round.

Earth hums. Arctic ears capture a constant low-frequency drone. Sometimes the humming merges with a distant jet or an aircraft setting down.

๑

By the time a helicopter landed unexpectedly on the ridge perhaps a mile away, Lisa and I had made several trips across the tundra, dragging and carrying our gear a half mile from the invisible airstrip to the Marsh Fork of the Canning River. Up close, the river was clear beyond imagining and maybe almost deep enough to float a raft.

We found a caribou antler, half buried, splattered with orange and green lichen; a Styrofoam cup stuffed down a critter hole; and a pair of muddy white Jockey briefs, size 28. We discussed the helicopter while we fired up the Coleman for a cup of espresso. Petroleum geologists, we guessed, or academic geologists whose field research is sponsored by oil companies. The paradox for many whose passion for earth's strata led them to degrees in geology is that extractive industries are the primary employers vying for their knowledge. Lisa—a carbonate sedimentologist in an earlier chapter of life—was once employed by an oil company.

The helicopter lifted, buzzed away, and we wondered how near other people might be—a dozen miles? A hundred? More? We wondered if David would be spending that night on the tarmac at Arctic Village with both his .44 magnum and the shotgun my Alaskan uncle had insisted we take to the North Slope.

๑

Firearms have a scent, a metallic death smell. I do not know how far it carries. Even without wind to broadcast it, the odor radiates, a hostile presence to which animals will respond. At least, this is what I believe.

I had not wanted to carry weapons into Arctic Refuge. I had a soft-focus vision of walking among the creatures without advantage, as if one of them. I doubted the necessity of firearms, but I had heard enough Alaskan grizzly tales that my feelings about bear encounters were not so clear. Lisa set me straight: *Geneen, if you see a grizzly chewing my head, I want you to shoot it.* Who could argue?

Earlier, in Fairbanks, while we had sorted our gear on the lawn at my uncle's home, he asked what we were carrying for bear protection. When we said a .44 magnum, his cheeks reddened and he snorted with laughter. *Whatcha gonna do? Throw it at a grizzly?*

Even though I did not believe in problem bears, I had asked my "sourdough" uncle if he had ever had to shoot one. *Oh yes,* he replied, his eyes round and solemn. Then he called his son to deliver us a shotgun.

We had packed the shotgun and pistol, along with cayenne-loaded bear mace.

But for now Lisa and I were weaponless, abundant with food, camped beside the river, plenty of bear-concealing willow at hand. No paws marked the sand, no bear droppings in sight, no clawed-apart rodent burrows. We forgot bears and walked upriver, focusing on the miniature wildflowers, the water-worn stones. Two Dall sheep came down to a tributary, not seeming to know of—or mind—our presence. We crossed the river and scrambled up the flank of a treeless mountain, where we settled on an outcrop in the sun. I relaxed for the first time in days, unwinding so far that I nearly fell into dreams.

Lisa's voice broke my reverie. *Whoa. What's that?* I opened my eyes. She pointed at two creatures lumbering upriver from the north, from the direction of our camp. Through binoculars, I watched their fur ripple and shift between blond and brownish-black. The humpbacked bears paced the edge of the willows, following the stony riverbed we had walked moments before.

Even from that distance, it was apparent that these were not the footstool-sized arctic grizzlies we had seen stuffed in the University of Alaska museum. We congratulated ourselves on our good fortune: Don Ross had told us we would be lucky if we saw bears at all.

As the grizzlies ambled closer, growing larger as they neared—three-quarters of a mile, a half, a quarter—my stomach turned and I felt a small, sickening thrill. Awareness of our circumstance simultaneously scared and excited me: no trees to climb, no trees to hide behind, no fallen trunks to hide under, no stout cabin, no doors, no disguise. Bear mace usefully stashed at camp, weapons somewhere between us and Fairbanks.

Aloud, Lisa and I wondered if the pair had come across our camp. Most of our food was stored in a thick-sided aluminum drybox—tough to open, even for grizzlies. Still, I had an uncomfortable vision of two weeks' food supplies shredded on the tundra, and our trip at an end before David even arrived.

The grizzlies paced with heads swinging low—pausing, pressing snouts to the ground. When they turned ninety degrees to cross the river where we had crossed, we wondered—briefly— if they had gotten our scent. Were they tracking us? Impossible, we decided, remembering that grizzlies unaccustomed to humans would probably be as cautious of us as we were of them. The bears rambled closer, so we figured they hadn't spotted us yet. If they saw us, we reassured each other, they would probably run. We stood and slowly contoured north, across the outcrop, heading in the direction we—and the bears—had come from.

The grizzlies turned again. Instead of coming toward us, they now paralleled our path. We stopped. They stopped. It's been said that bears have bad eyesight, but we understood: the grizzlies knew we were there.

Some people who know the ways of bears say that shouting at them is a bad idea, but you can decide for yourself when two grizzlies rocket toward you and you have no place to hide. When the bears launched in our direction, Lisa and I instinctively raised our hands, palms outward, and waved our arms. I felt almost embarrassed, hollering, "Go away bears! We are not caribou calves!"—but my comfort zone had shattered and I had to dispense with pride and polite form.

Our voices seemed to stop them. The sow and nearly grown cub reared upright and rotated their massive heads. I almost had a breath of wonder and relief before the bears plunged and came on, running. The fur glinted silver where the sun caught it. *Running.* Muscles underneath pumped like a bad dream. *Running.* Great claws raised dust, spewed gravel. *Running.* The grizzlies swelled into furred missiles, dark and huge as fear.

Lisa's eyes reflected my own terrible confusion. We prayed aloud for a plane, an oil chopper, noise, anything. We held our naked hands overhead in surrender or appeal. "We are not caribou calves! Go away bears! Go away bears!"

Was there a scent on the wind? A sound we did not hear? Perhaps a hundred feet—a few seconds—away, the grizzlies reared up like two-legged giants. They sniffed the north. Hesitated. We shouted, showed our pale palms. "We are women in Gore-Tex! Go away bears!" Squinting our way, then vacillating, the grizzlies snorted north again. Swung heads and peered at us. Then spun down on four legs and sprinted—away from us. Away.

My heart pumped with the beat of eight splayed paws thundering upriver, upcountry, away from the fierce joining of our lives. My knees buckled. For maybe an hour, I sat, unable to move, to do anything but watch the bears gradually move south, out of sight. I felt—did I imagine?—a communion pass between two human women and grizzlies. Unarmed, like them, except for instinct, we were powerless to harm. The guardians allowed us entry, and I gave thanks for their mighty grace.

On the tundra-covered high arctic desert, two or three hundred square miles might support one grizzly, except when caribou calve their young and food for predators is abundant.

On Kodiak Island, Alaska, where spawning salmon and berries are plentiful, one brown bear inhabits every square mile. Glacier National Park reluctantly hosts the highest concentration of grizzlies left in the Lower 48: one every eight square miles.

Farther south, severed from Glacier by highways and clearcuts, grizzlies pace the raw edge of Yellowstone, clinging to their last refuge below North America's 45th parallel. Perhaps two hundred or more still survive. A dubious future awaits the isolated bears who remain, whose gene pools weaken with each birth unless cross-breeding can occur.

Where I live, south of Yellowstone, south of Grand Teton National Park, there are no more resident grizzlies—even though the national forest is only steps from my door and food sources are plenty. I half-wish to see *Ursus arctos horribilus* loping through these aspen and lodgepole pine. But except for a rare—and quickly relocated—interloper from Yellowstone, grizzlies here have long vanished, casualties of barbed wire, roads, and firearms.

Now bears, wolves, bison, and eagles congregate north, in what little space we have left them, and we name subdivisions and automobiles for the wild that once was: Trumpeter Swan Townhomes. Bear Haven. Buffalo Valley Estates. Mazda Navajo, Jeep Cherokee. Dodge Ram, Eagle Summit.

The coastal plain of Arctic National Wildlife Refuge is the last 120-mile stretch of American arctic coastline not currently available for oil development. In the summer of 1991—while smoke from Persian Gulf well fires still blackened the desert sky—the oil industry, the Bush administration, and the governor of Alaska wanted the Arctic Refuge bad.

So did I.

I wanted—what can I say?—to possess a memory, to know I had walked that land before it was tamed or smothered by the industry of humans. I wanted to travel through the proposed oil field. I wanted to experience the coastal plain wild, before roads, pipelines, drill pads, trailers, and heavy equipment forever altered the tundra.

In the Brooks Range, the Marsh Fork flows north, joining the Canning River on its run to the Arctic Ocean. The Canning marks the western boundary of Arctic National Wildlife Refuge. The river also marks the western boundary of the proposed

Section 1002 oil drilling area.

When I had written for information regarding North Slope rivers, the refuge managers sent back a package enigmatically describing the Marsh Fork/Canning: "A seldom run river about which little is known." The information on other rivers was not much more detailed, but I already knew they were attracting increasing numbers of visitors.

An outdoor writer once expressed dismay to me that an acquaintance of his gathered shed elk antlers to carve into objects to sell. The writer opposed taking something from the wild and deriving income from it. I said, "Is that so different from taking a story?" The writer said, "I never thought of that. Once I wrote about a remote river in a national outdoors magazine and it became a popular destination."

From Arctic Refuge, I wanted a story that would do no harm, but I don't know if it's possible to publicly celebrate something without exposing it. There is risk in bearing witness.

So many wild rivers have been lost, so many canyons and forests. I can neither celebrate nor mourn the ones I never knew. I do not know, now, if acquaintance could ease the loss, but then I likened traveling in Arctic Refuge to spending time with a friend vacillating between critically ill and recovery.

I did not know who would be comforted by my visitation.

Lisa and I had quit expecting the Cessna and were in sleeping bags, alert for large mammals, when we heard the airplane engine about 10 p.m. While Don Ross and David unloaded, Lisa and I blabbed our bear story, still running on adrenaline and disbelief. The pilot nodded as he listened. "So they came at you, did they? They were probably just checking to see if you were going to run."

The next afternoon, David, Lisa, and I portaged the rest of the gear from the landing site to the river, groaning in unison as we rolled the deflated, tightly compressed raft over tussocks. Although we had planned to hike five miles up the drainage to the

Continental Divide—the north/south divide intrigued us, scrambled our entrenched east/west sense of flow—we could see that the marginal water level of the Marsh Fork was dropping. We were ten miles upstream from where we had planned to put in on the river, and as far as we knew, we would be the first raft descent from there. We chose to load the boat and take off.

We took two paddle strokes and scraped gravel, vaulted out of the boat and dragged it. Jumped in. Took a few more strokes and hit bottom.

This is how you raft the upper Marsh Fork of the Canning: Hop in. Paddle once, twice. Leap out. Grab a D ring. One, two, three, heave. Climb in. Float a few seconds. Hit rock. Stumble out. Drag and pull.

The managers of Arctic Refuge describe the Marsh Fork as "little known, seldom run" for good reason. Weeks later, when Don Ross picked us up, he told us he had flown over the upper Marsh Fork a few days after he had dropped us: the river had completely disappeared.

In the high arctic, what seemed a few miles elongated easily into ten—or twenty. Days flowed together, seamlessly joined by bright nights. Our circadian rhythms adapted to the constant light; we slept deeply, but not long. Some mornings, we'd wake to fresh bear tracks. No black bears inhabit the North Slope; the prints in the sand were always grizzly.

Purple asters splattered the tundra, mixed with dwarf fire-weed, phlox, and a hauntingly fragrant violet-colored pea. We climbed one unnamed peak, a series of false summits luring us higher, undulating flanks covered with moss campion, daisies, blue flax. Strawberries! Sage! Some say the atypical flora found on individual arctic peaks indicates islands drifted in from elsewhere before colliding at the top of the world.

At the summit, rock ptarmigan blended with lichen-covered stone. A golden eagle circled. To the west, glaciers and knife-edged peaks cut the sky. In the north, we could see the crease of the Canning River valley, though we did not guess it would still be days before we arrived there.

The broad, wind-scraped summit bore no sign of prior human presence, and we wandered over the top in a kind of fever, a delirium of imagining we were the first people to witness the world from that precise location. The moon, I think, has hosted more visitors than some arctic peaks, and we reveled in wildness. At the same time, we could not help but reveal our humanness. In the tradition of explorers, we named the peak for ourselves: Gen-da-li, the Magnificent One. But only we would ever know its location—and even we might forget, in time.

⑥

Everywhere, the land wore evidence of caribou. Water-tumbled bones on gravel bars. Palmated antlers bleached on the tundra. Hoofprints—hundreds, then thousands of hooves—marked the beaten earth between hummocks for as far as I could see. We were too late for the migration; we saw few caribou, and only occasionally, not the huge thundering herds we had hoped for. So many wild bodies in motion was beyond any event I had reference for, and I could not imagine how humans without experience of the migration could be entrusted with the fate of the arctic coast.

⑥

On the eighth day of our journey, wind lifted off the polar cap and blew hard to the south, carrying invisible crystals of ice that burned our hands and faces. The raft floundered, driven back upstream if we quit paddling for a second. Where the river braided, we ran aground endlessly. We dragged our boat along, prepared to jump in whenever the water deepened. Our feet and hands turned white, numb. Other senses deteriorated, succumbing to the cold.

We looked for wind shelter, a place to make a fire. After one futile attempt, we moved farther downstream and found a fair spot. We huddled in the lee of a small embankment, behind willows, burned diminutive driftwood, lit our stove, made instant soup and hot chocolate. Drained boots, peeled off layers of wet wool and neoprene socks. After a while, we could speak and even laugh again, though we tried not to think of the polar wind and water.

High on a steep, talus-covered ridge across the river, a movement caught our eyes. Momentary confusion of colors: red and blue. The unexpected image slowly registered: hikers. Here? In a nineteen-million-acre wilderness?

I lifted the binoculars at the same time the two hikers squatted, holding binocs to their own eyes. My neck hair stood attentively even before we heard the voice, nearly shredded by blasts of air: *Is that Geneen and David?* Our laughter blew up that mountain, on the breath of the frigid north wind.

Dr. Keith Watts, brother of a close friend and professor of geology at the University of Alaska, had rounded the blustery ridge, returning to base camp, joking with his research assistant, Russell Scott, telling him to look for a boat on the Marsh Fork, saying that he had arranged for some friends to pick them up and float them back to camp. Russ laughed at the notion but looked upriver anyway. Nothing. Then he looked directly below. The gray Avon raft on the opposite shore stunned them both.

They slid, skied, and jumped down the talus field while we repacked and navigated to the other shore, picked up Keith and Russ, gave them paddles. Five made better headway against the bitter wind. Their camp was not far.

The low water, the upstream wind, the gravel bars and boulder fields, the airplane drop ten miles upriver—all had slowed our travel so severely that we were beginning to wonder if we would make our charter flight out. But perhaps rivers know more than people.

Months before, David and I had invited Keith on our trip, but his schedule of field research conflicted. When we had spoken on the phone earlier, in Fairbanks, it was evident that our time and travel routes would not overlap. He had not planned to camp beside the Marsh Fork.

Wind rocked the tent so hard it seemed the ground vibrated. By two o'clock in the morning I had not slept, although I had lain in the tent for five hours, calculating the distance yet to travel, wondering how fast we could move against the squall. When I unzipped the door and looked out, I saw snow blowing sideways. I finally let go and slid into dreams. We could not travel anywhere.

The next morning, we unfurled slowly. The snow turned to sleet, then rain. Clouds passed, but the wind remained. We packed our boat, then huddled under the geologist's kitchen tarp to make pancakes and espresso. Waiting for weather, we spoke of rock samples, geological formations, and the possibility of oil fields under the coastal plain. We laughed ourselves sick over bad jokes and stories. Keith dazzled Lisa and me by using fuel to heat water so we could wash our hair; Keith and Lisa, newly acquainted, dazzled each other more than the rest of us were aware. The day's weather never improved, but we were all elated for the company of other people, for shelter just large enough to cover us all.

We unpacked and set up our tents again, on a sloping field of shin-high hummocks. David said it was the worst tent site he'd ever had, but I noticed he had no trouble sleeping.

By our tenth morning, we had covered no more than sixty miles, and the Marsh Fork was still dropping. We had four days left before meeting our charter flight and at least sixty river miles to travel.

Keith paddled with us almost to the confluence with the Canning. Perhaps out of nervousness, professorial habit, or a desire to impress Lisa, he took command of our raft for the duration of his float, shouting out instructions. David and I, accustomed to squabbling for the glory and shirking the blame of piloting the boat, paddled according to our own instincts. We left Keith on a gravel bar, all of us envisioning deep water, a single channel, warm wind coming from the south, pushing us *down* the river.

But the Marsh Fork opened up, spread out, became rivulets—none of which would float a boat or even a large piece of driftwood. Which one dribbled directly to the Canning? Through blue ice fields or through willows? We could not find a clear way, even when we left the boat and walked. Finally, what remained of the narrow channel we had chosen was blocked by a willow carcass we could not move. We dragged the raft onto gravel, groaned, lifted the stern, pivoted around the bow—over and again—performing a twisting dervish dance to get that boat back to water.

Nearly imperceptibly, we merged with the braided, shallow Canning, a river that had swelled to nearly mythic proportions in our minds, so hopeful were we for water deep enough to float us.

The Inupiaq name of the Canning River had been given to me by James Nageak, who teaches the Inupiaq language at University of Alaska Fairbanks. He had kindly searched his records to find the name, which he had spoken repeatedly. I tried to copy the sound, but I could not get my anglicized tongue around it, and the word did not stay in my memory.

As we drifted on water the color of sky through land untamed as a bare infant, I understood that names can disguise true nature. Like a dancer saddled with a heavy, graceless name at birth, the word *Canning* disappoints, falls short of reflecting arctic elegance and fury.

Years later, I listened carefully to a long conversation in Inupiaq and found that, to my ears, the language evokes the calls of creatures and the wild sounds of wind, water, and ice. I discovered, then, that I had wanted to possess the Inupiaq name of the Canning River so badly that I'd never heard the arctic river streaming through James Nageak's voice, the blue water that rippled off his human tongue and shaped that unfamiliar sound.

For days after the bears came, we had slept with loaded firearms outside the tent doors. David had occasionally been seen wandering into the willows with a roll of toilet paper and a pistol. We had kept the loaded .44 within reach on our raft. But finally, the guns unnerved us more than bears.

I wish to live with the dangerous freedom of wild creatures—but I am not one of them. Dropped by expensive air charter, provisioned by health food stores, clothed in high-tech synthetics, transporting every scrap of refuse, traveling by Hypalon raft, carrying PVC drybags and metal boxes, recording with microphones, video, and still cameras, protected by bullets: *What sort of creatures are we?*

The Brooks Range gave way to the Shublick Range; the colors of stone changed to red, green, brown. Glaciers rose off the horizon behind us; tundra sloped to the sea far ahead. A large white raptor flew from the cliff beside the river: perhaps a gyrfalcon, our first sighting. We paddled through canyons of shale and limestone. Now lupine bloomed in violet-blue profusion. Rocks with mineralized bodies of coral washed down from mountains—remnants of an ancient tropical sea.

We paddled and dragged the raft past upthrust, angled layers of schist. In small canyons, Dall sheep posed, still as ivory carvings, on minuscule ledges. Gourdlike nests of cliff swallows, mud mosaics fused to sheer walls. Nearly emerald green hillsides. River otters dove for urgent cover, startled to see us. Gulls dive-bombed our heads, shrieking—eggs or babies close by. And always, azure water that we never purified, that never made us sick.

The Canning widened and seeped across gravel, dropped in shallow terraces. We watched for the faint tilt of riverbed, searching for channels. We were still scraping bottom, jumping out, dragging, floating, scouting with binoculars against the glare.

Musk oxen huddled as we passed; ice age survivors, extirpated from northern Alaska, then reintroduced on the refuge in

1969. Small herds clustered around the babies, guarded, watching us. Dramatic horns swept low and curled, drapes of hair caught on tundra. I collected handfuls of the soft warm *qiviat*. Where musk oxen gathered and migration routes of caribou etched the earth, it was hard to remember the political battle raging—in a distant and detached city—over the future of Arctic National Wildlife Refuge.

Earth hums. Put an ear to the ground.

There is no line, no sign announcing the proposed oil development area, but when the frequency of helicopters increased, we knew we had entered Section 1002. Holes from test drilling scarred the gentle slopes to the west, just outside the boundary of the refuge, and although it was nearly impossible to imagine the tundra ripped open, penetrated, and girded with steel, I knew then, and know still, there are many willing, even glad, to do such work.

An oil company executive has told me there is plenty of cheap oil in the world; that people will not need to choose—in fact, will not choose—between energy and environment for one hundred years. The same man boasted of an impending trip to Burma, where he planned to shoot an elephant to hang on his office wall. The man insisted, when questioned, that the technology to use hydrogen fuel does not exist, in spite of prototype vehicles, in spite of electrolysis extractions done by private individuals, in spite of National Engineering Lab research, in spite of hydrogen-powered rockets.

Hydrogen is the most abundant element in our universe. When burned, it produces a by-product: water.

The last morning on the Canning, the sun warmed us while clouds of mosquitoes hung in the wind shadow created by our bodies. So near the coast, the landscape was nearly flat—we checked the topo maps frequently, looking for the slight mounds that signal the presumed location of the airstrip. The river finally held together long enough to float without bottoming out. We paddled all day.

An anomalous branch propped at the top of a cutbank announces the tundra runway. Miss that, and you lose your way in the Canning River delta, and drag your boat north to the Arctic Ocean.

By one o'clock in the morning, we had unloaded and re-packed our gear for the next morning's flight. David and I walked in the low-angled sun toward a rise where we hoped to see the Arctic Ocean. A brown wave cresting the ridge stopped us: musk oxen. We set down our tripod and turned the video camera on. The herd kept running our way, kicking dust. Reminded of bison, I wondered aloud, *Could they charge us?* David said he didn't think they had seen us yet. We kept still. The musk oxen stopped in unison. Bunched up around the young. Looked at us. Turned and ran off slightly to the north.

David and I climbed the ridge, an expanse of tussocks, mosquitoes, and birds. The sun coasting on the horizon backlit wildflower petals, illuminating the tundra like elaborate stained glass. The Brooks Range loomed over the plain. The river we had traveled braided in tangled shallows. In the vast Canning delta we could not navigate, slivers of water crept north, seeped toward the sea. On the northern horizon, the sky fell into the Arctic Ocean, and our binoculars momentarily captured the glint of polar ice.

Oil shot out of the ground into the pipeline and into tankers and onto roads, and the roads returned me to Wyoming. Like grizzlies, I cling to the edge of wild. Roads bisect my chosen homeland, sever it again and again, dissecting the most well-preserved ecosystem in the Lower 48. In spite of human efforts to simultaneously protect and exploit it, the Greater Yellowstone

Ecosystem still hosts all indigenous flora and fauna—even the wolf returns. But it's a precarious refuge: a volcano rumbles beneath this land, probably the hottest place on earth.

The fresh tracks of a large grizzly froze me on the trail to hot springs just south of Yellowstone National Park. Call me romantic. Call me irrational. I took those prints as a sign: grizzlies had again intersected my life, intercepted my psyche.

In the impressions of a lone bear squeezed so close to Yellowstone, I read the loss, the shrinking habitat. I recognized the highways, homes, and human habits that have overwhelmed grizzlies. I read between the tracks and saw the landscape as it had once been: undiminished by the whims of human beings. I understood the coded print: bears once roamed everywhere, as I do now, so freely. I could not ask bears—or other creatures—to forgive my ignorance any longer.

I like to believe that grizzlies know they must find mates from outside their own regions to preserve the genetic strength of their kind. I have visions of them prowling around by night, sprinting from Yellowstone to Glacier to Banff and Jasper National Parks, rendezvousing with Alaskan and Canadian bears in a conscious journey of Eros and survival. I imagine grizzlies reclaiming their ancestral homeland. It is a sentimental notion.

Will the great bears and others survive our occupation?

In the aftermath of the Persian Gulf war, Senate Bill 1220, the Energy Security Act of 1991, was introduced, calling for oil development in Arctic National Wildlife Refuge as one of its provisions. Senate Bill 1220 would have subsidized the oil, nuclear, and coal industries. It did not call for conservation incentives, increased auto fuel efficiency standards, or additional alternative fuel and energy research.

Many individuals and organizations focused efforts to educate members of Congress about Arctic Refuge. When the bill came up in early winter, it was voted out, largely because of the provision to drill the coastal plain.

The next spring, in a small attempt to curb our own alarming oil dependency, David and I bought a fifty-mile-per-gallon Geo Metro, a stripped-down mild-weather vehicle—a luxury purchase in an environment where we cannot get home in winter without four-wheel drive.

A few months later, in early summer, Lisa Varga and Keith Watts were married in a place overlooking the Snake River and the Teton Range.

As I write this, in the spring of 1996, the Arctic National Wildlife Refuge coastal plain is de facto—but still not congressionally designated—wilderness. Without official wilderness status—and without a genuine energy conservation plan for the United States—another industrial assault on the coastal plain is inevitable.

Earth hums. I cupped my ear to the ground and heard bones creak, stones speak, and underground rivers run past. I heard seeds vibrate and burst, the slither of snakes and worms, and a subterranean chatter.

I heard the voice of the arctic but I was not large enough to understand it.

If images of threatened wildlife arouse sufficient sentiment for humans to relinquish endangered land to the care of animals, perhaps that is enough. We cannot interpret the language of permafrost and peat. We cannot translate the planetary role of sedges and moss. We do not yet know what climate-controlling global function, what essential carbon absorption and release, is played out by arctic tundra.

Caribou, musk oxen, wolves, birds, and bears inhabit the untamed earth beside us, changing little, infringing little on human lives. They dwell quietly in the primary world, the home of their ancestors—and ours—guarding the fierce and fragile land like wild sentries.

Musk Ox Hunting

Jenifer Fratzke

"**I** want my own snowmobile,"
I said.

Fred looked at my husband, Arlin. Arlin looked back at me.

"I'm not riding behind your machine in a sled," I said. "No
way." I crossed my arms, looking at the ten-foot wooden vehicle
on runners.

"Native women ride in sled," Fred said.

"I'm not Native."

Arlin smiled, "Let her ride a machine."

I glared at Fred. He looked at the snow machine, then over
to the helper, then to me, and back to Arlin. "Okay." The conflict
reminded me of the telephone conversation between the two
men before the hunt even started, when Arlin had asked if I could
go along for the two-thousand-dollar guiding fee. Fred had remained silent for several seconds, until he acquiesced, "Okay,
your wife can come too."

In February 1983, I couldn't wait until the snow machine
lifted me over the snow-covered tundra and carried me to where

the Alaska musk ox lived, on the southwestern corner of Nunivak Island, near the Russian mid-sea border. This fifty-mile-wide, thirty-mile-long tundra reef protruded from the Bering Sea and was surrounded by icy water on all sides. The animals couldn't escape. Neither could we.

Arlin and I were going musk ox hunting. After boarding an Alaska Airlines jet in Anchorage, then making a stopover in Bethel, we had climbed into a bush airplane and flown to the village of Mekoryuk. There, we would hunt in isolation, away from the Yukon-Kuskokwim Delta mainland of Alaska.

I loved adventure, especially adventure in Alaska, where everything seemed so extreme. For me, every wilderness experience was a risk-taking, life-and-death ordeal, an adrenaline rush. I had lived in Connecticut, Washington, Arizona, Hawaii, Oregon, Florida, and California, but had always returned to my Alaska, where I belonged. No other state fit my personality. In my mind, I was Alaska. I could fly an airplane five miles from my home in Anchorage and be in total wilderness. Alone. If the engine quit, if Flight Service lost my flight plan, no one would find me for days, maybe weeks. True living involved adventure, each one bringing me closer to a real knowledge of self. This hunt would teach me something new too, especially how to overcome my fears of hunting with a stranger.

Since I was nine years old, I had enjoyed hunting with my father in Washington State. My sister and I would walk ahead of him, flushing birds in the early-morning frost, our hands brittle cold, our ears covered with stocking hats of red and blue. Being in the wilderness, smelling the pine trees, and listening to my father plan a hunting strategy sparked my love for the outdoors.

The whole process of hunting fascinated me: analyzing weather, learning terrain, assuming responsibility, thinking independently. As a woman, I learned how to take risks, something that later prepared me to handle the pressure and competition of being a commercial pilot and then a professional writer. In time, I met other Alaskan women who loved to hunt, and the sport provided a special friendship between us as we practiced at the range and cleaned our guns. I don't know the statistics, but I have a hunch that more women hunt in Alaska than in all the Lower 48.

I walked over to the snow machine with the bright red cowling, a covering like a car hood that protected the engine and that latched tightly shut. Feeling Fred's eyes watching me, I aggressively pulled the starter cord twice until the snow machine engine cranked.

Arlin and I wore our matching light-brown parkas with the goose feather stuffing. We looked like a married couple: matching wedding bands, beaver hats, white boots. My husband's blond hair was matted down on both sides of his face. His blue eyes looked down at the map, and I noticed frost particles forming on his mustache, dangling like small icicles. I estimated the still-air temperature at fifteen degrees below zero. This was our one-year wedding anniversary.

"You have musk ox permit?" Fred asked.

Arlin put his fingers inside the down parka and pulled out the yellow piece of paper.

I visualized the arctic musk ox, with its long, coarse, hairy coat and curved horns, and thought about the Anchorage Zoo, where I had witnessed a musk ox baby feeding from its mother. The furry animal looked so cute, like a shaggy Shetland pony with stubby legs. From across the fence, mama and baby seemed shorter than my belt buckle. I wanted to call them, to pet them through the fence, but the sign read, "Stay Back."

"I'll only shoot a bull," Arlin said. "One that wouldn't make it through winter."

Somehow, I felt better knowing it would be a male—a male destined to die. Winter kill. I thought about the younger bulls, after the bull with the biggest horns fell. Now they would have a chance to mate.

Now, at eight-thirty in the morning, the noise of my own snow machine roared loudly in my ears.

"You ride behind me," Fred said, pointing to Arlin.

Arlin looked behind at me, shrugging his shoulders, with that crinkled-worried look around his forehead and eyes. I looked at him and mouthed, "I'll be all right. Don't worry." I could handle last place.

My biggest fear was getting lost on the tundra, where everything was flat. With only four hours of sunlight during the winter months, I was afraid of freezing in the frozen expanse. Gripping the handlebars tightly, I kept my eyes peeled for arctic fox. Even though some of the Natives felt they were an omen of misfortune, I had my own arctic myth: I viewed them as my heavenly protectors, clearing the path ahead of me and behind me of danger.

I kept the helper in sight at all times. I could see Arlin glancing back every few minutes until it was clear I had grown accustomed to the snow machine and new surroundings. I started to relax; the visibility was clear, at least five miles, and I had control over the machine. Over the little berms, I used my thigh muscles, lifting up so the impact would be absorbed in my legs instead of my back. I felt like I was going on just another recreational snow machine ride with friends. With admiration, I watched Fred weave back and forth around the little bumps in the terrain, impressed by his navigational skill.

Riding over the tundra, I could feel my hands getting numb, even through the heavy mittens and inside wool liners. I started to feel pain, real pain. In front, I saw a white fox dash to the side of the helper's machine. For a split second, the Native guide looked to his right, then slowed down. I caught up to the helper for the first time and noticed Fred and Arlin looking over their shoulders, turning around and circling back.

"The fox," the helper frowned.

Fred nodded. Arlin looked at me. "Are you okay?"

I shook my head. "My hands are freezing."

Arlin climbed off his machine and looked at the hand-warmer switch. The light was on, but no heat came from the handlebars.

"No wonder." He fiddled with a couple of electrical wires, pulling off his gloves to feel for warmth. "Why didn't you say anything?"

I lifted one corner of my mouth, like when I felt disgusted but not angry. "Right."

I looked at the three men facing my machine, engrossed with the wires, and asked, "Would you guys turn around?" They looked up, hesitated, then turned around. I probably should have been more direct: "Hey, I have to pee." There weren't any trees to hide behind. In nature, I had to forget privacy. The hardest part of being a woman was yanking the blue snowsuit down over my thighs and pulling the hood far enough away. In the cold, everything was survival, and getting wet was the worst enemy.

The men were anxious to get going. I took a few gulps of water, took a huge bite from a health food bar, and climbed on the snow machine. Once again, we raced over the snow in a formation line, with me at the rear. I wondered how many more miles my hands could have remained numb without getting frostbitten. Even if I had realized the hand grips weren't heating properly, I couldn't have caught up to the helper for help. In my heart, I knew the arctic fox had intervened on my behalf. *Thank you.*

We had been riding for three hours, and my shoulders and back had started to ache, when suddenly the snowmobile launched over a rock and became airborne. All I could remember was to keep the handlebars straight so when the machine landed, it would maintain longitudinal control and not roll over on top of me. My arm and hand muscles squeezed together tightly to overpower the machine. The sensation reminded me of horseback riding, when the horse decided to go one way and I had to kick the animal's sides for control.

If I had been paying more attention, I probably would have noticed the helper launching into the air ahead of me. Maybe I could have steered my sled to the left or to the right in avoidance, but for me, driving head-on into a known problem was better than launching into the unknown. What if the bump to the left was higher? What if there was a cliff or hole in the tundra to the right? After flying through the air, I remained on top of my machine, upright.

In another five minutes, the engine drone started to put me to sleep. Perhaps the rush of adrenaline going over the bump was wearing off, like the grogginess I felt after eating lots of chocolate candy. The helper started to slow down and parked behind Arlin's snow machine. Fred and Arlin walked to a small knoll with binoculars in hand. I was happy to just climb off the machine for a while and rest my back. Stretching to the right and left, I slowly walked to where the men stood.

"Musk ox," Fred said, pointing.

Arlin turned his head and binoculars to the left, scanning for the stocky long-haired animals, which have changed little since the Ice Age. I waited, standing behind Arlin. He handed me the glasses.

"*Ooomingmak,*" Fred said. "The animal with skin like a beard."

I assumed the word was Yup'ik Eskimo for musk ox, but I wanted to ask Fred more questions. I kept silent, knowing he would tell me things when he was ready, only when I had earned his respect on the hunt. I thought about my numbing hands, about not complaining, about launching airborne over the rock. How many more trials by snowmobile would I have to endure before he gave me another tidbit of information?

I saw three more musk oxen standing a few hundred yards from the first.

"Not big," Fred said.

Arlin nodded. I couldn't help looking at the irony of the situation: four snow machines juxtaposed with four musk oxen. The machines were shiny-new and built in the early eighties. The animals were prehistoric machines with blood and fur for survival. I looked at Fred, wondering why he was guiding us for money.

I had overheard Eskimo hunters tell of their belief that the animals gave themselves over to the hunt. These animals didn't look like they were walking into our rifle sights willingly. In fact, the three largest bulls started to walk away, toward the cliffs along the Bering Sea. At that moment, I wondered about capitalism. If Fred didn't accept the money as a hunting guide, there would be another Native in Mekoryuk who would willingly take us.

Guiding for a living reminded me of all the flights Arlin and I had taken as commercial pilots for the sake of more logbook time. Flights we had no business flying. Weather we wouldn't walk in. People we didn't like. Cargo that smelled. Dynamite that could blow up on hard landings. The more time pilots logged, the more likely they would get a high-paying major airline job.

I had heard how Natives thought it was revolting how white hunters put trophy heads on the wall. To them, it was like bragging, *See what I did*. To the Eskimo, animals were to be used as food, for subsistence. To hang a head mount on the wall was disrespectful and dishonorable to the animal kingdom.

I loved having the trophy mounts in my home. I thought of Sheba the Ram, a beautiful older male, as head protector. His eyes gazed from the highest point of my living room wall, some eighteen feet high. My head ram protector watched people drive up the long driveway, where my small castle-like home stood perched on a small hill. From the driveway, visitors could see Sheba's eyes, watching, his one and a quarter curled horns winding toward the sky. The ram's beautiful white fur glistened in the afternoon sun, shining through my bay window.

Because Sheba was in my house, other rams would have an opportunity to mate. In all likelihood, Sheba wouldn't have made it through the rut. The butting of horns, the tearing of body, the coming of winter, all contributed to the inevitability of death. Without the hunter, the body would have remained for the scavengers, for the elements of weather. No, nature couldn't have this ram. I claimed him.

We started our machines and flew along the southern shoreline, below the dunes of frozen sand. The terrain near the beach was flat and almost level, except for a slight grade down to the water's edge. I saw floating icebergs scattered in the slate-colored water. They rose and fell with the waves, in a rhythmic fashion. I wanted to climb on top of the largest one, which looked like it could hold a thirty-foot RV, and bob up and down with the current.

The men stopped again, this time their eyes focusing on something large running across the ridgeline about four hundred yards from the frozen beach. Reindeer. Hundreds of reindeer funneled over the hill, down the other side, their beautiful antlers swaying with each body movement. Their fur must have faded to a lighter color for the winter months because they didn't look as brown as the pictures I had seen in books. Camouflaged, they ran, their rumps and tails raising slightly in the air as their hind legs cleared the snow-covered tundra.

"Jenifer," Arlin yelled. I looked at him. His arm motioned for me to start my machine and follow.

I had to concentrate. The cold and the tundra and the isolation started weighing heavily on my mind. We didn't have to ride very far until I saw the large herd of musk oxen. The little societies of hairy animals banded together, hurriedly circling into a wagon-train formation for protection. Sometimes there was strength in numbers, when the animals put their heads down and drove their horns into the flesh of their enemy. This defense strategy might be highly effective against most predators, but certainly not against hunters with high-powered rifles.

The animals looked so funny bunched together. Their eyes stared at us as one by one we dismounted our snow machines. I had read that the females grow to four or five hundred pounds. The males weighed six to eight hundred pounds and looked a lot larger. The musk oxen looked like bent-over dwarfs, carrying huge fur coats over their shoulders. I said Hi to them with my silent lips, but they weren't looking at me; they were staring at Fred. *Traitor.*

"Over there, left." The helper pointed.

I saw Fred and Arlin crawling on their bellies over a little hill, toward three musk ox bulls.

"Down," they said.

I fell to the ground on my stomach and inched forward on the snow, my blue snowsuit protecting my body against the frozen tundra. I must have crawled, wiggled, for seventy yards, until I was right next to Arlin.

"Look," he said.

I looked toward the right, where his finger pointed. A huge bull with gray hair all around his horns stood alone, chewing grass from a small patch of cleared snow.

"He's a big one," Arlin said.

I whispered in his ear, "Would he die this winter?"

"Yes, Jenifer," he said, giving me that you-bleeding-heart-you look.

I didn't care. I had read how battles between bull musk oxen during the rut were violent contests of aggression. Sometimes the bulls would charge from fifty yards at top speed and collide squarely on the head. Sometimes the clashes would last for twenty charges. One of the Anchorage Fish and Wildlife biologists had told me about how each time two bulls clashed in combat, it was like a car hitting a brick wall at twenty miles an hour, head on.

I thought about this trophy in my home, as a protector of the family room. *Musty, no Musky Musk Ox. That's it.* I put my arm on Arlin's shoulder and nodded my head.

My husband remained on his belly and pulled the butt of the 300 Winchester magnum to his shoulder, the barrel resting on the small mound of white snow. I held my breath, waiting for the bull to charge us or run away. The animal stood alone. His fur was the largest, his horns the biggest, his eyes the most defiant. BANG.

The animals looked toward the noise but didn't move. I looked at Arlin and crinkled my nose. "Did you hit him?'

Arlin shrugged. The hairy animal stood. We waited for another fifteen seconds, another fifteen seconds, another fifteen seconds. *Where did the bullet go?*

Fred leaned over. "Good shot, but you might have to shoot him again."

Arlin raised the rifle to his shoulders. Before he pulled the trigger, the musk ox fell to his knees and toppled over. Dead.

Fred opened his parka and unsnapped the holster strap, revealing a .44 magnum pistol. The barrel looked really long; I couldn't imagine riding a snow machine over the tundra with something so rigid against my thigh. The four of us crept toward the bull, ready to run back if the animal stood up and tried to charge. I looked around, trying to locate the other animals, wondering if they planned an ambush. But apparently, the other three bulls had been spooked by the noise of the falling carcass of the loner musk ox.

Musky Musk Ox didn't have any help or protection from the herd. Walking toward the huge bull, I noticed how feeble he appeared, dead on the tundra. The musk ox body spanned five feet, with his nose resting on a small patch of cleared snow. I touched the cloven hooves; they were cold and hard, curved inward at the tips. The feet were sharp and worn down from scraping the frozen tundra for grassy food.

I felt so sad when I touched this mounded body, still warm, resting sleeplike on the tundra. I thought about how in the mid- to late 1800s, musk oxen were overhunted by Native whalers and hide hunters. The Alaskan animals disappeared. As a group, they were strong and invulnerable, but as soon as the animals stam- peded, or one or two left the protection of the group, they were easy targets for wolves and hunters.

Ironically, in 1930, the white man captured thirty-four musk oxen in East Greenland and brought them back to Fairbanks. According to Alaska Fish and Wildlife, five years later, many of the animals were transported and released on Nunivak Island, where we now hunted. Supposedly, musk oxen were adaptable creatures. Their thick fur kept them warm during the long winters exposed to the chilling wind of the Bering Sea. With permit-only hunts, with man-over-animal regulations, one hoped the animals would never reach the brink of extinction again.

The wind started to pick up to more than fifteen miles an hour. The distant sun was falling quickly below the horizon.

"Got to go," the helper said. "You, hold legs."

He was looking at me. I watched his eyes and saw them looking at the hind legs of Musky. Fred, Arlin, and the helper rolled the musk ox over on his back. I started to help them, knowing it was a privilege to be asked to hold the legs. I didn't want to push my luck on the hunt, so I waited with patience—a patience I normally didn't have. I thought about how Native and white men normally seized the opportunity for risk-taking adventures like hunting, and how for the most part, Native and white women stayed at home with the children, waiting for the meat. The wind seemed to swirl my ideas and stereotypes over the tundra, just out of my grasp of knowledge. I normally could figure out problems, any problem in nature.

I pulled the back legs apart as the helper made a clean

incision around the bull's chest, a circular cut that divided the animal in half horizontally. Then he made another cut from the middle of the sternum down to the testicles, two bulging sacks. I wondered how the musk ox had walked with his legs together.

Fred and the helper tugged the fur from the meat, using a knife to peel away the skin. Arlin watched more than helped. Even though we had both gutted large animals, we knew the two Eskimos could do a better job. They probably figured that was part of their job, part of the fee. The men rolled the huge animal onto its side and gingerly cut the fur away from the body. It was an expert capping job. Their knives and hands moved quickly.

In no time, they were ready for the head. Carefully, they cut around the horns and around the eyes, saving enough skin for the taxidermist around the nose, eyes, and lips to work with in the shop. I knew nothing made a professional trophy person madder than having little to work with around the eyes and lips. Glue and synthetic materials never come out as well as the real tissue, left by a careful butcher.

For the first time, I really studied the helper. I had met a lot of helpers during my hunting travels; most of them quit after the first season. After butchering the meat, loading the weight, and carrying the trophy mounts, the men usually determined there was an easier way to make a living. But this assistant guide-helper seemed different. The hunt on the tundra seemed to be the most natural job for him, like breathing. I wondered if he, like the white man helpers, would log each hunt, take a written test, take a practical test, and apply for the guide license. I wanted to ask him if he had aspirations to be like Fred someday, but I kept quiet.

"More," Fred said loudly. He was talking to me. I threw my weight into the legs, stretching them farther apart. They were working on the face, why would they care about me pulling the legs? I'd probably never know.

"Strong wind," Fred said. The helper looked at Fred, at Arlin, back to me.

The men worked faster. The knives neatly cut the back-straps. They didn't take the time to neatly scrape each rib, so they threw the whole rib cage in a large sack.

"You want heart?" the helper asked.

I didn't look at Arlin. "No."

The helper didn't say anything. He threw the heart behind him, on the tundra for the scavengers. He took the liver and put it inside a game bag, throwing it beside the rib cage. The brain he wrapped in a plastic bag and put in his sled. He didn't ask us if we wanted it, and I wondered about the significance of an animal brain.

"Honey, put your face mask on," Arlin said. "It's going to blow."

I dug in my largest pocket and pulled out my goose down face mask, the blue one I wore whenever it started to blizzard.

The men fastened the hide and meat in the sleds with bungee cords and filled each machine with gas.

"Stay close," Fred said. He looked directly at me.

If you're worried about me, then don't make me ride in back.

The line of machines pulled ahead, jockeying for position.

At first I started to look for our snow machine tracks from our trip, only a few hours before. But there were no tracks. The wind blew twenty-five miles an hour now, the snow drifting in front and around the snow machine, filling in all the cracks and ridges any machine had made on the surface. For an instant, I saw my body hunched over like the musk ox, frozen solid with the wind beating against my back and head, the men riding away from me. I determined not to be left behind.

Thank you, Arlin. My cheeks would have certainly become frostbitten without a face mask. The wind went into my eyes and I started to feel the moisture freeze. The helper slowed his machine and stopped for just an instant, with his left hand extended. I looked at his glove, palm up, holding something with a strap. I hesitated.

"Use this."

I reached over my snow machine and grabbed the durable, plastic motorcycle goggles and lifted them to my face, securing the strap over the back of my beaver hat. The eye coverings were large for my head, so the beaver hat's thickness worked in my favor. Before I could thank him, the helper quickly pulled his snow machine forward, back into formation. I added throttle, flying across the ground to catch up to Fred and Arlin.

I didn't think. I didn't turn my head. I kept right on the helper. For the first time, I felt anger. *Okay, you jerks. I'll ride over you if you slow down.* I felt the blood race to my face, the anger of once again having to prove myself worthy to be included in this hunt, to once again have to prove myself to a man.

The helper launched into the air, over a snowdrift. I followed and kept the handlebars straight. We didn't stop. We didn't slow down. I put my head down into the wind and even leaned over until my breasts almost touched the gas tank, trying to be as aerodynamically efficient as possible without falling off. The wind kicked up to thirty-five, forty miles an hour. I could tell we were in a blizzard because the visibility was obstructed right in front of my face. I could barely make out the taillight on the back of the helper's machine. If I collided into the sled, then at least that would be better than heading off into the unknown and sinking into the icy Bering Sea.

Fox angel, help. I didn't know if I was behind the helper or not anymore. I couldn't see. I started to drive by my senses, by my intuition and connection with the environment around me. I felt the direction with my heart, I smelled the direction with my nose, I saw the arctic fox with my peripheral vision. At that moment, my guide was not human. I started to feel my shoulders and neck, like they were no longer attached to my body. I took a deep breath and felt the water inside my nostrils trickle down inside my face mask and freeze.

Even with the goggles, I couldn't see very well. The snow was blowing sideways, with a force so strong I would easily get knocked backward if I sat on my sled erect. I concentrated on leaning into the wind and clutching the hand grips. In the dark, I could sometimes see the faint light of the helper's taillights flicker up and down, back and forth, in front of me. I wore insulated underwear next to my skin, then a wool sweater and wool pants over that. My blue snowsuit was rated to minus forty-five degrees. I estimated the wind-chill factor at minus sixty. I remembered the little chart in the Bethel Airport terminal, warning newcomers. At sixty below, human flesh would freeze in thirty seconds. I had read many stories about freezing to death and how people started to get sleepy, then numb. The cold ache in my body reminded me of the second stage of numbness, of how I could die on this hunting trip.

I don't know how long I rode, perhaps minutes or hours, until I almost ran into the back of the helper's sled. Three or four feet to the left of me sat Arlin and Fred, on their sleds.

"Second place," Fred said, pointing to me.

I nodded. I didn't feel relieved; I didn't feel proud. I felt numb. Fred urged his sled forward. I fell in behind him. Then Arlin. Then the helper. I rode without fear; my husband would surely run into me if I strayed from the course of Fred's leading. I started to feel protected by the pack. The goose bumps started on the tops of my arms and worked their way toward my back and toward my legs.

In the darkness we rode for over an hour, following one behind the other in caravan. With my snow-machine light, I could occasionally see Fred's beaver hat bob up and down, when the visibility picked up to twenty feet. Finally, I saw the shadow of a building. I felt respect for this Eskimo man, for his navigational experience.

We pulled the machines up to the trailerlike box structure we had left a little over twelve hours earlier. Nothing ever looked so good.

"We'll pack meat," Fred said.

Arlin and I nodded, waving good-bye. We quickly opened the door and fell on top of the beds. I unzipped my blue snowsuit and took my damp pants and clingy underwear off. Without any clothes, I walked around the room and drank close to a quart of water.

My husband walked behind me and put his arms around my shoulders. "You did good. Real good."

I hugged him for a long time. "I was really scared," I said.

"I know. I could feel it."

He undressed and we lay on our backs naked on one of the twin beds.

"Would you go again?" he asked.

"Ask me tomorrow."

I don't remember when I fell asleep, but the next morning I heard a loud knock on the door. "The airplane leaves in two hours."

I quickly covered my body with a blanket, thinking the man would come into the room. Arlin was still snoring. I nudged him.

We dressed quickly and choked down some oatmeal with powdered milk. When Fred knocked on the door an hour later, we had our gear and rifle packed for the trip back home. The Eskimo man didn't smile.

The three of us rode to the airport in Fred's pickup truck, with the meat neatly packed in the back. The Twin Otter kept one engine going to conserve fuel and engine cycle maintenance. I wanted to say good-bye to the helper and thank him for the goggles, but he wasn't around. The Natives talked with their eyes and rarely spoke, something I was learning to value. I looked at Fred and nodded, thanking him with my eyes.

Arlin and I sat in the same seats as we had coming to Mekoryuk, and this time I sat away from the window. Even though Musky Musk Ox was with me as a powerful reminder of the hunt, I didn't want to say good-bye to Fred, good-bye to my fox angel. I held Arlin's hand tightly.

Road Reflections

Stephen Binns

Getting from where you are to somewhere else is an adventure. This is true of physical movement but also of emotional, spiritual, or other travels. Going "to" implies dynamics, more possibility. To me, the word destination (in Latin, *destinare,* to fasten down, secure) sounds a thud of finality. I'd rather be on my way "to" and have potential, than "at," where discussions are in the past tense. Alaska accommodates me very well in this because destinations—physical or otherwise— are seldom nearby.

Alaskans are travelers. This is probably because we're so far removed from contiguous America that traveling to another state involves distances difficult for "outsiders" to grasp. It's about the same distance from Fairbanks to Dallas as to Glasgow, Guadalajara, or Panama; Hong Kong, no farther than Rio or Nairobi. A three-day, thousand-mile weekend is not outrageous. I do them as often as I can.

CIRCLE HOT SPRINGS

Every winter I try to spend a weekend at Circle Hot Springs. I like the lodge, and the 160-mile drive from Fairbanks allows opportunity for introspection, solitude, and adventure. Driving up on my first winter weekend, I had only a few miles of white-out near Eagle Summit. At the lodge, everyone was friendly without being nosy and didn't mind me poking around. I'm not much on swimming, but I tried the natural hot-spring pool and liked it. With the air temperature just a little below zero, trotting my chubby butt from the shower room to the pool caused my feet to make a sticky sound as heat was vacuumed from my toes, freezing them briefly to the ice. No stars or northern lights were visible because of clouds, but the 103-degree water made lots of steam and felt very good. I spent the evening with my head on an inner tube, floating belly up like a dead carp, comfortably warm in the water, while my hair froze into punk rocker fashion.

After the swim, I hung out in the bar waiting to eavesdrop on interesting conversations, but none occurred so I went for a walk. Away from the few lights of the lodge and the almost un-noticed diesel generator sound, only heartbeats and breath could be heard. During such silence, thoughts become loud enough that one may believe they are audible, and one wonders if others can hear or if telepathy isn't but acute hearing. I exhaled into the black sky, my breath dissipating slowly. I imagined I heard moisture molecules pop as champagne bubbles do. Surely it was my imagination, but a pleasant imagining nonetheless.

In the morning, driving back to Fairbanks, I came upon a rattle-trap pickup stuck in the snow just outside Central. The driver was attempting to extricate the truck; I recognized him from the previous night at the bar. I stopped. He seemed a little embarrassed. I'd seen his face in Fairbanks on occasion, didn't know his name, and neither of us expressed any desire for anything other than total anonymity. He probably felt vulnerable because he needed assistance, but knew that accepting it would obligate him to some form of social interaction.

He did not have to worry. Our conversation went like this:

Me: *Gotta chain?* Him: *Yep.* Him: *Thanks.* Me: *No problem. See ya.* Him: *Yeah, see ya.*

Somehow, I felt we had just become friends but would probably never speak to one another again—a mutual agreement of respect without expectation.

KENNICOTT

I crossed the Copper River bridge and continued up the Edgerton Highway from Chitina, stopping occasionally to photograph and listen. There is a bird, I don't know what kind it is, that makes the most eerie sound—hollow and haunting, more like an echo of a sound or the call of a peacock from inside a closed mayonnaise jar. Its direction of origin is indeterminable. Maybe the birds work in pairs to keep the listener guessing. One area of several hundred acres was flat and open and covered with tall marsh grass of even height and density. It looked like a crop of some kind, although I'm sure it wasn't; it had the look of something cared for, like a cat that is well treated, and like a cat, it purred a visual green.

Sixty miles from Chitina the one-lane, potholed road ends. There were a dozen cars parked, with license plates from Massachusetts, West Virginia, or Ohio, but no people were visible. I didn't notice any steamy windows or evidence of anyone sleeping in their cars. I assumed they were all hiking or at the lodge. I got out and started looking for my bottle of insect repellent. Mosquitoes were expected and seemed quite happy to greet any visitor. The sky was overcast, and being after 10 p.m., the light was waning. I stuffed a sweatshirt, wool sweater, army poncho, and camera into a rucksack and walked to the platform where the tram waited to carry me across the river.

The tram was erected by McCarthy residents and seemed to be sturdy enough. Two at a time is maximum capacity, and both riders have to work. Going solo wasn't bad, though. The cable droops in the middle, so no matter which way you're going, it's downhill...halfway. The middle section puts you five feet above the roaring, cement-colored Kennicott River. That's worth noting when wind and spray rock the little tram. I pulled myself to the other side. A fresh dose of insect rep was in order.

I started up the road. I could hear children shouting and dogs barking. A short walk brought me to a second tram. It held four kids, ages, I guessed, from four to ten years. A man was pulling them in like a fishnet full of arms, wild hair, and huge grins. A black lab and a golden retriever swam below the kids, fighting currents and silt and barking. The dogs ground ashore sixty yards downstream, barked some more, and trotted up to the rest of the family. The kids untangled from the tram, and they and the dogs attached themselves like starfish to a flatbed truck that already had two washing machines, a dryer, and another major appliance onboard. None of the machines appeared to have been in working order any time recently. The man helped pull me across the river. In my trying to observe so many things, I almost forgot to thank him.

The road, recommencing, diverged in two directions. A sign read "Glacier Lodge," with an arrow pointing the direction. I wasn't going to Glacier Lodge, so I went the other way. A 1960s-era hippy van with Oregon license plates sat near the road. The registration tags had expired. I assumed the van had too. I wondered about its owners. Were they still here? Did they drive to Alaska with McCarthy on their mind? Or did it work out that the van would become part of the landscape, and they would move on with a different philosophy or just different transportation?

Alders blocked the view, so I concentrated on the sounds of mosquitoes whining by my ears and the crunch of my boot steps on the gravel road. It's not really a crunch, more of a *scrush*—like spooning a Slurpee into a plastic cup. I walked quickly. After an hour, I started to doubt I had the right road, but then I came to a sign that read "Please Drive Slowly, Children Playing." Two dogs barked as I went by a house. The barking stopped when I passed the property line.

The alders stopped, and the surrealistic moraine of the Kennicott Glacier appeared. Sand and silt and gravel had been pushed forward, chewed, and digested by the advancing glacier.

Then, receding, it had left a valley of undulating mounds with unexpected crevasses and dropoffs, overhangs and caverns, sink-holes and danger. Listening, I heard the irregular and intermittent clatter of small rockslides and saw evidence of constant change as glacier runoff nibbled at the moraine. Trying to cross such an area would be similar to an insect crossing a sandlot infested with ant lions.

The road was, at this point, fifty or more feet above the moraine and the distance between was littered with rusted boiler-plates, pipes, wheels and cogs, levers, rollers, barrels, flywheels, bolts, motors, railroad track, and unidentifiable objects. It gave the impression the glacier had chewed up Kennicott Copper Mine and left a second moraine of metal and memories. The gray sky added no depth or life, and an unsettling difficulty arose in trying to separate, again, visually this time, metal from rock, man from nature, winner from loser.

I continued walking and soon saw several reddish buildings; the first was the lodge. A sign stated the room rates and that supper was served until 10 p.m. It was after midnight and I was hungry. The spattering of rain was tolerable, but the air coming off the glacier was decidedly cool. I put on my sweater. The single narrow street was deserted. All buildings with the appearance of occupancy were closed. No lights anywhere, nor did I hear a generator. My steps were quiet. I felt like a burglar stealing sights that were not authorized and not for sale. I was unexpected. Uninvited. But I was there anyway.

The buildings were mute, but the equipment—its size and complexity—spoke of labor and productivity, sweat, smashed fingers, cursing, laughter, and the whistle of the train bringing supplies, mail, pipes, bolts, clothes, and statements of profits.

The main building stair stepped up the mountainside four-teen stories. Its windows, many vacant, looked like a choir made up of the open mouths of toothless old men. The entire scene reminded me of Edward Munch's painting *The Scream*. I wondered if, when the wind screamed down the glacier, these windows whistled like lonely, empty, Coke bottles.

I went into a building. The floor was rotted in many places, and I felt a spongy give to some of the boards. I stepped carefully. Many tools and parts were scattered about. It looked like everybody had gone out for coffee one day and never came back.

I went behind another building and discovered drill bits and shafts, barrels of nuts and bolts, pieces of God-knows-what, and stuff. I stood, listening. The eeriness of silence amid machinery that surely was deafening when in use was incongruous. The very sight of giant gears and boilers made me want to cover my ears. The boards beneath my feet had once trembled from the daily crushing of hundreds of tons of rock. But now, after midnight, in the rain, only a pebble losing its grip on the moraine could be heard.

I continued along the backside of the buildings, following a path of boards and i-beams and boilerplates. It seemed to be a path, anyway, perhaps for a cursory maintenance inspection or for guided tours. One rock, not far from the path, in the halflight, seemed greener than the others. I figured it had a higher concentration of copper. I left the path and grabbed the rock as a souvenir. Then I noticed there were no other tracks in the sand. Maybe the rain had obliterated them. Maybe one wasn't supposed to walk out there. Maybe this rock was pointed out on guided tours so people from Ohio and Kansas and Germany and Florida would know what copper in the raw looks like. I can see it now: in a few hours, the first guided tour of the day stops, and the guide points to an empty spot (with tracks leading to and from) and proclaims it typical copper ore. I stuff the rock into my rucksack.

It was raining in earnest, so I stopped at a department store doorway. The display window glass was cracked, and a sign warned me not to trespass. I didn't wish to compound my crimes and stayed outside. I took out my poncho and pulled it over my head and rucksack. I smiled thinking how I must look—a hunchback in the rain, stealing rocks at one o'clock in the morning. I started back. Rain drops thumped on the poncho, and I pulled my head down low, like a turtle. I was dry, and exhaling into the poncho warmed it up. Condensation didn't seem to be a problem. The dogs at the cabin were still up and barked perfunctorily.

I didn't look up; I knew they were grinning at me.

Pulling the tram back across the river seemed harder. I was getting tired. It was almost 3 a.m., and I still had a three-hour drive to Chitina ahead of me. I was to meet friends there and go salmon dipping. The rain stopped and the sky was lighter than when I arrived. Clouds were breaking up. Sunshine was on the mountains and reflected off snow. It was an orange sherbet color. I was starving, but I pulled off the road and slept.

DAWSON CITY

The road from Fairbanks to Dawson is not difficult, just dusty. I enjoyed driving, and time passed quickly. I parked on a summit and walked to a neighboring ridge. Along the way were blueberries—lots of blueberries. I squatted down to pick a few and tossed them into my mouth. I noticed my tennis shoes were purple. The berries were good but very soft. I looked in my rearview mirror and could see my face was freckled with purple spatters. My fingers had a more uniform stain.

A caribou skeleton hid in the tundra as if it were embarrassed and trying to cover bare bones with moss and lichens. That was only fair; the caribou had spent its life putting moss and lichens inside, some on the outside seemed appropriate. Balance of nature.

I made a side trip to the town of Eagle, where I observed polite but reserved people. I bought a Snickers bar. The clerk eyed my purple shoes and spattered face, then dropped my change into a purple-stained palm without comment. I bought gas, too. There weren't any self-serve pumps, and the middle-aged lady attendant washed my windshield. She seemed pleased to do it, saying, "Still got water, may as well," as she smiled and knocked ice around in the wash bucket.

Not much to see in Eagle. The museum was closed for the season, unless you had an appointment. I didn't. Fort Egbert was interesting but not inspiring. And the Indian village was disappointing.

I didn't stay long because I wanted to cross the border that evening, and it closed at eight. I roared through the town of Boundary, but I don't think I woke the dog. The Canadian Customs Office consisted of two small buildings and a flag on a hillside as barren as a bathtub. What a lonely spot. A sign read, "Wait Here." I did. Several minutes later, an older guy came out, buttoning his coat. He was polite enough and believed my story about not smuggling cigarettes or being a bootlegger or drug runner, and with his beef-stew breath, he wished me a good day.

The Canadians build roads along sensible routes—across the summits of the ridges. Americans dip down into the valleys and slug their way back up through bottoms rough with bedrock and gold miners.

Dawson City, Canada, looks like Dawson City should—that is, after the tourists are gone and a patina of white frost covers the town. The streets looked like gold-rush streets and the buildings like people named Sluice Box and Nugget Nate or The Iron Pirate should be in residence. The contemporary occupants have the aura of previous inhabitants. Small, cramped quarters crowded together with junk piled in front, on roofs, in cars, everywhere. Fundamentalists. The spirits of Jack London and Robert Service were almost palpable. I was pleased. But there wasn't much to see or do. After Labor Day and the disappearance of tourists, many shops closed.

The frosty air carried a heady smell of baking bread, and its source was not hard to find. I declined donuts and opted for jalapeño cheese rolls. They were still warm. It wasn't very cold outside, maybe ten or fifteen degrees, but I cradled the rolls, one in each hand, and soaked up their warmth. Several schoolkids walked the wooden sidewalk single file, heads down and silent, their breath forming puffs like tiny steam engines.

On the road again, back toward Fairbanks. I felt like stealing an insulator from the obsolete telegraph poles connecting Dawson and Eagle. This was the original line to Fort Egbert—part of Lieutenant Billy Mitchell's effort and a slice of history—and I wanted it. I stopped and looked, schemed really, but lacked the proper tools for larceny. A recent tundra fire had blackened the hillside. The morning air was refreshing and the not-unpleasant smell of spruce smoke lingered. I thought maybe flames had weakened poles or cross arms enough that brute force and bare-handed bullying might earn a prized insulator. But that was not the case, and I left empty-handed.

I stopped in Chicken to buy a hunting license. They didn't have any, but the store was closing for the season and would I like to buy some chips? I never, well, hardly ever, buy potato chips. The short, heavy lady explained she was going to lose weight this winter and didn't want all these chips around to tempt her, and they're only one dollar a bag. I sympathized and heard her deter-mined words, but saw the helplessness and hopelessness in her eyes. I was convinced she would never lose weight—would prob-ably gain more weight with every attempt. But I love a bargain and bought five bags. Several miles from Chicken, I opened a bag of green onion and sour cream flavored chips and discovered I had been duped. The expiration date was July 15. I should send that lady a case of Snickers bars for Christmas. What a con.

Back at Tok, I sat in the Bull Shooter parking lot, looking at the road. Where to next? I decided to take the Denali Highway from Paxson to Cantwell. I'd traveled that way several times before, but each time the weather was nasty and clouds hid the mountains.

I intended to camp near Paxson, but the evening was too pleasant to waste driving, so I pitched my tent a few miles out of Delta Junction, in the shadow of Donnely Dome. That's where it would warm up fastest in the morning. The sky was unblemished and darkened remarkably toward the eastern horizon. Stars tenta-tively peeked through a curtain of indigo and rose. The moon, slightly diminished from yesterday, appeared in the northeast and watched me set up my tent. Using the timer on the camera, I took a picture of me and my buddy, the moon. I was distracted and goofing with something when the exposure was made. I ended up blurred.

It got cold, so I and my sleeping bag, pad, stove, pot, and clothes climbed into the tent. I lit up my little stove so that I could heat some water and managed to break off the spent match head. It glowed beside the gas jets. I hate it when that happens. The flame didn't burn uniformly and discolored the pot. I opened a bag of MREs ("meal, ready to eat, one each"). It was ham chicken loaf. I wasn't in a mood for ham chicken loaf, so I ate a candy bar and opened another MRE, beef stew this time. I decided to have it in honor of the Canadian border guy. I threw the pouch into the heating water, then decided I was really hungry and tossed the packet of ham chicken loaf in the pot too. While the water heated, I arranged my sleeping bag and put on a Synchilla jacket and thick wool socks. A hat too. I usually didn't wear hats because they make me look stupid, but I wasn't anticipating company. I ate a cracker and a freeze-dried pear square while emptying instant coffee, nondairy creamer, and cocoa mix into my cup. No sense fooling around. I ate the ham chicken loaf from the packet. It was hot on the bottom and cold on top; the beef stew was the same way. I rinsed the packets and drank the water. I poured steaming water into my cup and stirred the mixture with the plastic MRE spoon. A string of beef floated on top. Pretty tasty stuff. Mocha con carne.

I started to get a headache and opened the overhead vent to let out carbon monoxide and moisture. It was almost dark. The moon was bright, and everything had the look and feel of frosty anticipation. I zipped the tent shut and amused myself blowing steam rings. I learned to blow smoke rings in high school, smoking Hava Tampa Jewels and Roi-Tan cigars I stole from the Texaco station where I worked. I didn't like the taste, but blowing smoke rings was entertaining. The same *embouchure* is required for blowing steam rings. No problem.

I woke up about 2 a.m. The air seemed warmer. I unzipped the tent and wriggled out like an inch worm, sleeping bag and all. The moon was bright, and the northern lights were glowing in a single band straight across the sky.

By morning, frost had touched everything with icy white velvet. A raven complained. I lit the stove, and the tent quickly warmed. I was glad I had filled the cooking pot with water the night before; it's no fun getting ice out of a canteen. I put the pot of ice on the stove and fetched more coffee and cocoa packets, reading the labels carefully. I was quite comfortable in the tent and in no hurry to break camp or deal with frozen tent poles. Dressed, I sat on my rolled-up sleeping bag and watched ice turn to water about to boil. I had some crackers and a packet of peanut butter too cold to squeeze out, so I held it over the flame. I could feel the oils within start to bubble as if coming to life. I oozed some onto a cracker. The aroma of parched peanuts filled the tent, and I recalled pleasant times. The flavor was excellent. I felt good.

The world outside was spectacular. The mountains looked like chalk washed up from a sea of blue paint onto a shore of gold. It was a beautiful day. It took a few minutes to break camp because I was constantly holding my hands under my armpits. It was cold. I started my car and watched frost melt off the windshield. The brown paint quickly gathered heat from the sun and, like a chameleon, lost the white frost color. The part in the sun anyway. I speculated if it was possible to cast a hand shadow on the frost and have that image retained as the rest melted. That would be neat, the original cold finger.

I continued to Paxson and turned west on Denali Highway. The highway is paved for 22 of its 136 miles and offers scenery much like that found within Denali National Park: wide vistas and a feeling of openness. The view of the "backsides" of Mounts Hayes, Deborah, and Hess is fantastic—unbelievable size and stabbing whiteness, and there's nothing between them and you. Just a broad expanse of tundra and this incredible wall of rock and ice rising higher and higher. I can't describe it. I give up. It's neat.

Nothing of import happened during the rest of that trip, but I always feel uneventful miles are preparatory miles for another adventure. Years later I bicycled Denali Highway, partly because I'd had such pleasant past experiences and partly because I like going "to."

Out There

Mary Hussmann

It wasn't until I'd shown my Alaska photographs to friends a few times that I began to notice how I had photographed our tents or one of us to establish perspective, to place us in the landscape. Looking at the pictures, the tents dots of green, khaki, yellow in an immense firmament, or a tiny person against the glinting or cloud-shrouded mountains, I realized how I'd unconsciously sought to prove our presence in such a wild, unforgiving land.

In a photograph of one of the first campsites, I noticed that the foreground shadows are a wild cobble of head-sized rocks, mostly granite with varying striations and gray-blue hues. Then there's me, almost mid-photo, squatting next to the overturned white hull of one of our kayaks, studying (though the camera can't see it) a large wolf print in a sandy spot between the rocks. To my left the rocks end in a swatch of marsh grass, giving way after six feet to an impenetrable tangle of alder and willow. Behind me and off to my right, the sun spills across a tidal plain, desert-colored now at low tide. Glowing like a tiny, golden dome at exactly mid-photo is Karen's tent, no higher than the sun-brushed tops of the grass behind it. Farther back and slightly to the right, a speck of barely visible unnatural green, our cook tent looks as if it's nestled snugly against the craggy greenery covering the rocky hill a mile behind it. And towering above it all, the snowy spires of mountains miles and miles away poke into the wide blue sky.

Four of us had journeyed to Alaska's Glacier Bay to sea kayak and camp for two weeks, hauling all our gear and food aboard ever smaller aircraft, until, flying north from Juneau, I sat in the copilot seat of a tiny, single-engine plane whirring above sun-dazzled water and into the sudden shade between the snow and granite faces of the mountains. A cheery woman in a rusted van with half-flat tires picked us up from the tarmac at the airport in Gustavus and hurtled us down a dirt road to the national monu-ment lodge and headquarters at Bartlett Cove. There we spent an uncomfortable night wedged into a six-bunk dorm room the size of my bathroom at home. Early the next morning, we repacked all of our personal gear into waterproof bags lined with plastic, stuffed two weeks of food into bear-proof containers, checked out our double-person kayaks (slow, ponderous crafts aptly called Belugas), and boarded the tour boat, the *Spirit of Adventure,* that was our ride upbay.

I was the rookie. My three companions were experienced canoe paddlers and wilderness campers. What they had in com-mon was a love of whitewater and the wilderness. They'd been on month-long trips on remote rivers in the Northwest Terri-tories and had canoed above the Arctic Circle. None of us had been to Alaska, and sea kayaking was new to all of us.

On a ski trip in the Boundary Waters the previous winter, Sue had asked me if I wanted to kayak in Glacier Bay the fol-lowing summer. I knew these women rarely asked others to join them, so I was flattered that I had passed a test I'd been unaware of. But I didn't agree to go right away. Although I love the outdoors, and ski and hike and camp, I'm not a water person; in fact, I can barely swim because of a hole in my eardrum that makes it painful and disorienting to be underwater. Some of the bays we'd be kayaking on were over fourteen hundred feet deep, and the glacial water was so cold we'd have hypothermia in minutes if we capsized. I imagined the twin sensations of freezing and drowning as I sank deeper and deeper to the bottom, where I'd be food for the blind, luminescent creatures that live at such black depths. For weeks I teetered between the extremes of re-solve—a chance of a lifetime!—and horror—I don't even like water! Finally, Sue called me at work to say, "I've got to make the plane reservations next week. Are you in or not?" "Okay," I said, surprising myself, "I'll do it."

> *Thursday, July 28*
>   *We crossed a fair piece of open water today that had waves we really had to pull through, though Sue chuckled at me when I asked if the water was rough. "Just a little chop," she said, but it was enough to make me scared of going out into the open bay. Wind and weather change so quickly here, it's unnerving. I know we have to do it, but maybe I'll be more relaxed and willing later on. After all, it's only the first day of paddling. So far I'm not as terrified as I thought I'd be, but we're starting pretty slowly.*

In a photo Karen took as we were hiking to the Hugh Miller Glacier one day, my eye focused immediately on the whimsical grouping in the foreground left: Kate, Sue, and me with our backs to the camera, sitting high on a hillside in the rain. Kate and I in bright-yellow slickers, holding, respectively, a red umbrella and a black umbrella, flank Sue, dressed in red. Soggy backpacks are strewn behind us, the hillside dotted with tiny red and white flowers. We're gazing toward the misty background, where a gla-cier crests down a valley between two green and rocky slopes, then breaks into a maze of braided streams crisscrossing in the valley far below. Beyond it, a series of snow-covered peaks march off into the white sky.

It felt as if the landscape shrank and grew in Glacier Bay. When the clouds hung low, it felt gloomy, but in a gray and cozy and tucked-in kind of way. Then, when the clouds scattered and the sun highlighted the peaks, the view opened up again as if the landscape itself had enlarged. I had to keep readjusting my perspective. Although it was humbling to be in such a large space knowing we were the only humans for miles and miles, it bred an odd sort of intimacy too. I was operating for the first time without an infrastructure: no roads, no houses, no jobs, no stores, schools, or churches. Most social customs just weren't applicable. It was as if suddenly the whole world were my bedroom, my kitchen, my bathroom, my study. While I could look around me at the glaciers fingering down the mountains and feel acutely how infinitesimal I truly was in the landscape, so too could I feel myself expand to fill all the space around me at times.

Perspective operated on a purely physical level. The first week we spent exploring the back bays and estuaries of the Hugh Miller Inlet. We camped two nights at the head of Charpentier Inlet, a narrow fjord about five miles long, and paddled one day to the huge tidal mudflat at the end of it. Coming back, we were paddling against the tide, which wasn't difficult since the day was calm and overcast. We stroked steadily, chatting and laughing at the harbor seals that popped up all around us, watching for a minute with their great brown eyes, then diving below the surface. I was the first one to spot the tents in the distance, faint dots of color against the browns and greens. It was astonishing and sobering to discover that it took us forty-five minutes of steady paddling to get to shore. How easy, and how dangerous, it would be to underestimate distances.

I was used to camping in the Midwest—campgrounds you can drive to, or rustic sites a half-mile down a well-trodden path. Although we had tide charts, none of us was quite ready for the ten- to twenty-foot tides that swept back and forth every six hours. Invariably, we'd pull into a likely campsite at low tide and have to haul the ninety-pound kayaks and all of our gear several hundred yards over slippery seaweed and barnacle-covered rocks, skidding and twisting in our knee-length rubber boots. The boats were hauled up and tied to trees or rocks a hundred yards from the sleeping tents, which were in turn a hundred yards from the kitchen tent we called the "big top," and the bear-proof food canisters were yet another hundred yards farther. Merely trekking the rocky shoreline from tent to kitchen area was laborious.

Tuesday, August 2

This morning Sue and Karen went off in an empty kayak to do some scouting for the tidal channel out of this bay; Kate and I stayed in camp. I wanted to baby the cold I felt coming on and Kate had cramps. She comes from a huge Catholic family and I think that's partly why she's so quiet. I can imagine how easy it is to get lost in a group of rowdy older brothers. It was nice to have a conversation—just the two of us. Her father died not long ago, so we talked about that, and I talked of how weird it felt to have both of my parents dead.

We're rotating who we tent with at each site. Sue said they always do that on these trips, so people don't form pair bonds that affect the group dynamics, I guess. I had Karen for the first time last night, and I can tell she's going to drive me crazy if I don't find a way to deal with her eccentricities. She's so compulsive that not only does she floss her teeth every night out here, but she packed rubbing alcohol and cotton balls and every night she wipes off her fingertips with the alcohol. So she doesn't have germs on her fingers? And every little thing is packed in its own little Ziplock bag. I'm trying to sleep and there's all this rustling and puttering. Why do I let her bug me so much?

It's so nice to simply sit and let time go its own way. Being out like this, unbound really, lets me know how artificial the constraints of hours and days really are. I can't think of anything better than to get to live out here and write. I'm finding that I don't mind the so-called inconveniences, such as all the hauling gear, purifying water, heating it for cooking, for dishes, bathing in glacial streams, or going to the bathroom in the intertidal zone. Our group dynamics aside, I guess up here only three things regulate activity: weather, light, and tides—and weather is the least of these.

As the days went by, we talked less and less about the "real" world and more about what we were seeing. Once, as we came out of a small tidal estuary, distracted by the calling and diving of gulls and terns, we heard a rush of noise and turned in time to see a humpback whale spout and dive in the channel about three-hundred yards away. I could see the ridge lines along the mouth and one wild, unblinking eye as the whale arced by, blowing and diving.

Drifting by a mussel shoal one day, waiting for high tide to lift us across, we watched as a wolf came out of the underbrush along the shore. It trotted a ways, then caught wind of us and stopped and stared as we stared back, rocking silently on the water. Then it turned and vanished into the brush. Another wolf trotted up to the tents one night and looked in at Karen and Sue before ambling off. I liked to think that the more animal-like we became, the more animals we saw.

One evening, at a secluded site deep in a tidal estuary, I watched as a pair of black-tailed weasels popped up from behind ever-closer rocks until one stood upright, staring at me with its beady black eyes. They were so curious about what we were that the pair scampered off after Sue as she walked around the bend to brush her teeth. The next night, a hermit thrush hopped right into the campsite and obligingly stood on Karen's bird book. At Reid Inlet, we were startled by the call of the willow ptarmigan, laughing like a crazy person in the middle of the night, and the red-throated loons bobbing out on the bay, crying like lost kittens.

Late one afternoon, we found ourselves at the end of a large tidal estuary facing an immense gravel fan and mudflat, created by runoff from the glacier hanging off a mountain in front of us. We'd had a long day of paddling and were hungry and tired and ready to find a campsite. Karen and I pulled close to the shore, and I got out, sinking calf deep into boot-sucking mud. Trying to scrabble to firmer ground, I noticed grizzly prints less than six hours old since the tide hadn't yet washed them away. Karen got out too and came over to look.

"I don't want to stay here," Karen called out to Sue.

"I don't either," I said. "Not with fresh bear sign." I knew Karen and I were the most afraid of bears. But it was always Karen who walked around clapping her hands and calling, "Hey, bear," over and over, even after it was apparent there were no bears around. Sue, Kate, and I would smile at each other, with looks that said, That's just Karen. Living in such close proximity made it hard to keep our quirky little habits private. Though Karen clearly had the most obvious eccentricities, we all had to learn to give each other room.

"We're never going to find a bear-free camping spot," Sue said. "There's water here and a place for the tents. What about you, Kate?" I knew they were irritated with us.

But Karen said she still wasn't comfortable and offered to scout other spots. Relieved that she was the one giving a second voice to my fear, I got back in the kayak and we paddled away, Sue and Kate following silently behind.

We finally found a spot a quarter-mile back up the bay, with a small stream, and more importantly, no fresh tracks. Later, after dinner, I asked Sue how the group usually operated when members disagreed on a course of action.

"We usually let the comfort level of the most fearful person in any given situation be the guide for the group," she said.

"Like Karen and me this afternoon?"

"Yeah," Sue said. "I mean, we're never going to be sure there aren't any bears around. But you guys were really insistent, so we went with your wishes."

"And I'm glad we did," I said. "You didn't see the span of those claws."

Thinking about it later, I realized how easily we slipped into roles out in the wilderness—roles that reflected, though not exactly, the parts we played back in our regular lives. Sue seemed to be the natural leader, due in equal parts to temperament and experience. Calm, careful, generous, and funny, she seemed to embody the same qualities in the wilderness that made her a successful university administrator. Kate was quietly competent, her paddling and water skills second to none, and somehow, no matter how tired she was, she managed to good-naturedly pull together a gourmet dinner every night out of a hodgepodge of dry mixes in Ziplock bags. That same kind and efficient determination undoubtedly made her a wonderful physical therapist, massaging limbs and cajoling muscles into compliance. Karen always remained staunchly separate, unshakable in her own internalized code of beliefs. Scrupulously fair although tethered to her own code, she was open and curious about others' stories. Nonjudgmental and encouraging, she listened and prodded others to give their best, balancing empathy and fairness against the rules. From this perspective, it made perfect sense that she was a lawyer and a judge.

What about me? I wondered. "You've got a good head. You're smart," Sue had said to me more than once, after I'd seen the solution to the problem facing us, whether trying to pack the kayak or navigate into a tricky hidden inlet. I tried to be amiable, easygoing, yet competent and brave, observant and smart. Great qualities for an editor, I thought with a smile as I fell asleep.

There's a photo I took one brilliant, clear day at a mile-long tidal channel between Scidmore Bay and the main bay. The left third is a close-up of weedy marsh grass, tapering at the tops into wisps of golden seed. Mid-photo Sue reclines in shorter, yellow grass. Her backpack butts the wall of marsh grass and pillows her head, a faded chartreuse baseball cap pulled low over sunglasses. She's napping. Hands folded over her red polypro top, one red-clad leg resting over the other. She's pulled off her heavy rubber boots, her woolen socks. Her blue umbrella's popped open on the ground beside her, shielding her face from the sun. Behind her stretches the flat tidal basin, yellow spongy seaweed drying at low tide, shallow, washed-out blue where the channel still holds a few inches of water. Behind her, across this tidal valley, green hills rise against a backdrop of higher mountains, granite-colored, speckled with snow fields, pressed against the slash of blue sky.

We'd heard that the channel was navigable at high tide and had risen early and paddled to the opening only to find barely enough water to float an empty kayak. We unpacked all the gear, hauled as much as we could carry for a quarter-mile, then went back and half-carried, half-floated the boats, repeating these cycles until finally, after several miles and four hours, we were in sight of the big bay. It was an uncharacteristically sunny day for Southeast Alaska, but with a wicked wind that whipped the open water into cresting whitecaps.

I was glad it was Karen who admitted she didn't want to go out there with the full boats in the wind. I didn't either. Sue and Kate agreed that it was best to wait until the wind died down, since we'd be heading straight into it. So we settled in to wile away the afternoon.

Since we hadn't planned on being stopped, we'd carried water only in our individual bottles, and we'd already used most of that during the hot and sweaty hauling of the morning. Although there were no streams on our topo maps, Karen and Kate set off in hopes of finding a small runoff stream. Sue dozed, and I tried to read to keep my mind and imagination off the windy rustlings in the grass behind me. Karen and Kate came back reporting no water but plenty of bear shit. I'd awakened that morning with swollen glands and a sore throat, and by now I really was starting to feel ill, so I stayed behind, this time with Kate, as Sue and Karen tried to find water in the other direction. Again they came back empty-handed.

By now it was 8 p.m. and the wind still wailed around our ears; the bay was wild as ever. By 9:00 it was apparent that we were stuck for the night. We couldn't cook since we had no water, so we ate a few handfuls of trail mix, sipped the last few swallows in our bottles. We were all anxious and depressed at not having water and not being sure when we could find more. It made me feel claustrophobic in an odd way. In silence we put the tents up, backed against the marsh grass, and tried to go to sleep.

"Grizzly bear," said Karen, and I bolted upright to stare out the tent door into the gathering dark. I'd wondered if I could tell the difference between a black bear and a grizzly, and I knew the second I saw the hump behind his head, the burnt honey–colored size of him, not twenty feet away.

The bear walked a few steps beyond the tents, then turned to look at us, swinging his head. For several seconds there was a frozen silence as we sized each other up, then he swung his body around and walked on by.

"What should we do?" whispered Karen.

"Let's get out of the tents," I said. I felt hemmed in and defenseless in the cramped tent. I could hear the zipper from the next tent, and we all crawled out and stood together. The bear had walked about 100 feet away, then turned back to face us. Now he looked, from his hunched posture, as if he was defecating. On one level I could think for a moment how ridiculous we must appear. Four women watching a bear shit. We stood clumped together with our hands above our heads. Look big, the literature had said. We had taken the safeties off our three pepper spray cans, but we were facing into the wind so they couldn't shoot very far, and worse, the wind would carry the spray back into our faces.

"Talk loudly and sternly," Karen said. "Tell him to go away and leave us alone." She was right. The rangers told us not to yell or scream, but to make noise, talk loudly, stand together, and raise our arms. Sometimes bears can be tricked into thinking there's one big creature out there.

So we stood there, shivering and talking, as the bear considered what we were. I have never been closer to death, I thought, oddly detached for the moment, as the bear rose up on his hind legs to get a better look. He must have been more than eight feet tall. My stomach felt as if I'd swallowed a metal bucket; I could tell we were all shaking. Our voices sounded weak and paltry as we kept repeating, *Go away bear.* Again, time seemed to stop as the bear pondered us, swinging his head to get a better look, then finally he dropped to all fours and cut into the brush perpendicular to us. By now it was after 11 p.m. and too dark to see clearly, but after a few minutes, we could hear the bear in the brush behind our tents. That's when we knew he was too curious or else we were in his bedroom, so we decided to leave.

One by one we scurried into the tents to grab warm clothes, our sleeping pads and bags, and personal packs. Next, we threw our stuff into the kayaks and paddled across the tidal channel. Although we were only a couple of hundred yards away, it gave us a psychological distance. We huddled together on the ground, bear spray out, each of us facing a different direction, eyes straining to make out the difference between shadow and substance. Eventually, I dozed off for about forty-five minutes, until Sue woke me at 4 a.m., when it started to get light again.

As quietly as we could, we waded across the channel and pulled our tents from the ground, then carried our food containers and other gear back across. We were still about a third of a mile from the open bay and it was dead low tide. Though my swollen glands and sore throat had magically disappeared (does fear's extreme adrenaline rush slap down an illness with a "not now"?), I felt exhausted and weak from hunger and thirst. Slipping on the muddy seaweed as I carried gear and hauled kayaks, I wondered why I'd ever come along. No one else seemed to feel as bad as I did. Karen and Sue tromped on ahead, loaded down like mules, and Kate moved only slightly slower. I hated them, hated myself. My arms ached and my tongue felt swollen. I was ready to sit down and cry. Feeling ashamed and angry, I told the others that I couldn't carry anything else until I had something to eat. I found the trail mix and sat on a rock chewing and chewing as the others went back for more gear. Finally, at 6 a.m., we had the boats packed and were ready to head out onto the open water. It had turned into a beautiful, calm morning, and we found a stream less than two miles away. As we drank and splashed our faces after breakfast, we vowed never again to travel without water.

After the grizzly episode, we agreed that we'd had bad feelings about the place, but none of us had voiced those fears because there was nothing we could have done. But we devised a mythology. As a group, we forbade Karen to floss her teeth at night anymore. She'd been flossing the night the wolf walked by the tents. She was flossing the night of the grizzly. Though we laughed at our superstitiousness, we were serious too. By now we operated as a little society, and we wondered if that's how traditions and taboos get started: No one in this tribe may floss her teeth at night. In fact, the tribal warriors go out hunting armed with rolls of floss. Sit quietly and floss and the animals will come.

> *Tuesday, August 2*
> *Karen talked about how we land at a spot that looks so totally wild, then we set up our little tents and suddenly it feels like home, like a tiny village. It's true, my vision of what constitutes "home" has changed, shrunk, and grown clearer. Home is my backpack, a warm place to sleep, coffee in the morning, and dry socks. Home reduced to the essentials, yet clearly marked as "mine." While our home is whatever tent I share or the common "kitchen/sitting area" under the tarp, it's found on a more personal level too. My water bottle, my coffee cup, my backpack with my personal items and the few toiletries I have here. Funny how just having my pack around makes me feel secure. I notice that everyone seems to feel that way about their personal packs. Curious how our perspectives change. While the landscape has grown immense, my own personal space in it has shrunk to just about what I can carry.*

My personal possessions and my backpack took on an almost talismanic value; they were my security and my routine. None of us brought many "things," since space was so limited in the kayaks, and I, as the rookie, wound up bringing the fewest. I did figure out that the less one has the less one needs. My Polartec sweater made a comfy pillow at night, and camp soap worked fine for my few head-numbing shampoos in the glacial streams. I even invented a way to wash the crotch and pits of my long underwear while it was on me, suffering through only a few cold and clammy hours until my body heat dried it. Every night in the tent, I arranged my few belongings, laid out my clothes over my pack, and kept a bandanna, headlamp, and bear spray within arm's reach. Simply having my things around me helped me feel safe enough to sleep: huge, long draughts of dreamless sleep, ten or eleven hours a night after our exhausting days.

Paddling around Ibach Point one day, we could see across the mouth of Reid Inlet and spot the remains of a ramshackle cottage, the only man-made structure in the whole area. What caught our eyes immediately were the three spruce trees growing behind the cabin, the tallest greenery since the forest at Bartlett Cove to the south, and far ahead of their ecological time. In 1925, Joe Ibach and his wife Muz put ashore at Ptarmigan Creek and struck gold. For the next thirty years they traveled up the bay each summer to work their claim. In 1949 they built their cabin, and Muz hauled ore sack after ore sack of dirt upbay until she could plant a vegetable garden, the spruce trees, and a few wildflowers. The couple last came in 1956, then died within a few months of each other the following winter. One rainy morning, I got up early and wandered over to look at the cabins. Rock walks were carefully laid out in front of the ruins at the base of the mountain amid a few pieces of machinery so decayed they seemed part of the soil. Looking through the doorway, I could see some rusty coffee cans, an old *Life* magazine, the remnants of white curtains at the only window. I imagined Muz's perspective looking out, the harsh, scoured landscape softened and manageable framed by the gauzy whiteness. Out in front again, I noticed wildflowers I hadn't seen anywhere else we'd been, plants that looked vaguely familiar, perhaps the descendants of those that Muz had so carefully planted. I thought of how lonely it must have been, with Joe gone over the pass to pan in Ptarmigan Creek every day. How the white curtains at the window weren't enough to make her feel at home. Instead, she had given in to the settler's urge to alter the landscape. I imagined her coming upbay every summer when the ice went out, standing on deck, eyes straining to see the waving beacons those spruce trees had become.

Looking at a photo of our last campsite at Ptarmigan Creek, what struck my eye first is the quality of the light. A hazy brightness highlights the snow-speckled mountains hanging below the faded blue sky. The sun angles in stage left, from the west, washing the cliff faces in gold, casting a deep brush of shadow on the eastern slopes. The mountains edge into greenery along the shoreline, cutting the photo in half horizontally. The blue of the bay at sunset is the same watery blue as the sky. Mirroring the few scattered clouds above are the white drifts of icebergs. In shadowy relief, in the foreground, lounge huge slabs of granite, as bumpy and crosshatched with lines as elephant hide. There's a red speck on top of the rocks: Sue stretched out on her back.

On one of our last nights, jolted awake by the sound of something big crunching across the gravel, I sat up and looked out at Sue and Karen hauling a kayak past the tent.

"What are you doing?" Kate asked groggily.

"I woke up and noticed that the tide line was really high," Sue said. "So when Karen woke up, I checked the tide table and thought we better move the boats up since the tide's still coming in. You guys can go back to sleep."

Which we did until we heard Karen calling us to wake up. Unable to sleep, she had walked down to the rocks where we'd stowed our kitchen gear and food canisters but couldn't find them. Now in the murky halflight, we all stood around dazed, wondering what had happened. Everything was missing. Food canisters, maps, chairs, cook stoves, water purifier, thermos, water bottles. Vanished. I looked at the high-tide line and dug out my tide chart. Sue had been looking at the wrong month. We'd already had the highest tide so far—an eighteen-footer at 2 a.m. Our things had now been drifting out on the bay for two hours. We had no food, no water.

As Sue and Kate took their headlamps and a kayak and struck out in the dim light, Karen and I climbed to the highest rock and scouted. I knew Sue was furious; she, better than any of us, knew that mistakes in the wilderness can be costly, or worse.

At 5:30 a.m., Sue and Kate came back, having recovered three food containers, the stoves, and the water purifier. Unbelievable. My notions of scale and perspective were continually tricked by this landscape. Just as lowering clouds cut off familiar mountain tops, the tides rearranged the shoreline every six hours. How surprising to have found most of our gear, those tiny pieces spread across miles of dark water. Our net loss: the container with our lunches and trail mix, four camp chairs, the maps, and the thermos.

Sunday, August 7

I was all for calling it quits this morning, standing on the rock in the chilly fog, thinking we'd be all cutting down now to eating two times a day, lumpy Cream of Wheat and something else that could be eaten from a bowl, just like every other meal I've eaten for the past two weeks. I want something I can cut with a knife and fork, not simply spoon into my mouth like an invalid. I know I'm crabby and tired. All this beauty and grandeur, knowing I've done it, pulled my weight out here in the wilderness, and all I can think of is a restaurant and a shower.

I know we were all tense this morning, but when Karen snapped at me, I turned away because I started to cry. That's not like me, and I hate it that I let her have that kind of power. How strange that it's Karen that I knew best when we started, and it's Sue and Kate that I get along with better out here. Maybe I have mixed feelings about Karen because she's so vocal about what she wants, what she's afraid of, that I let her be the voice of my fears, rather than admit my own to the group.

We all felt demoralized this morning after the tide fiasco—chagrined and embarrassed and foolish. Especially after we met two rangers who said a tour boat had spotted one of the food containers floating downbay and used a long hook to fish it in. Sue's name is on it, so the naturalist had used our group as an example of carelessness in his lecture to the passengers. I know how much that galls Sue. She says it's called the "home free" syndrome, when you think you're almost at the end, so you slacken your vigilance. We've decided to make do on two meals a day and stay 'til our scheduled departure two days from now. I think I'm ready to leave, but I don't feel I can say it aloud.

From our base at Ptarmigan Creek we made day paddles, luxuriating in the ease of paddling empty kayaks, able to cut and glide through the water, rather than wallowing along as we did when fully loaded. We paddled to Lamplugh Glacier, where the icy wind whipped the water into a gray churn and I had to clamp my hat down to keep it on my head, then into the inlet of Johns Hopkins Glacier, the most imposing of them all. The day was too hazy to see anything clearly, and we had decided to turn back when a huge cruise ship, longer than a city block and six stories high, came around a corner, bearing down on us. We'd been told ships that size couldn't see us at all, so we paddled furiously to the closest shore, an area closed to campers because of a rogue grizzly. As we jumped out to wait out the swells, we saw fresh grizzly prints, each long claw outlined in the sand. Karen and Kate decided they'd rather ride out the swells on the water, and after ten minutes of watching the brush for movement, feeling like the proverbial sitting ducks, Sue and I followed their lead.

On our last night we assessed how dirty and smelly we were and decided to heat water and use the last of our camp soap for shampoos and washing. After two weeks of icy streams, my small bucket of warm water seemed like a hot tub at the Ritz, and then I put on the pair of clean underwear and socks I'd been saving to wear back on the boat. Later, after dinner and our baths, we gathered out on the rocks overlooking the bay. It was a trip custom, Sue said, to sing an old English sea chantey. As we struggled to learn the verses, Sue speaking them, then the rest of us piping in with a tentative melody, we watched the sun touch the snowy peaks, one by one, each sparking in a dash of final brilliance before night's shadow crept across the water from the east.

Twilight was an active time for shorebirds, oystercatchers especially, medium-sized black birds with long orange beaks and legs. They were crotchety and vocal, nesting pairs clearly establishing shoreline territory and driving off intruders. We were surprised, as we sang verse after verse, to notice a couple of oystercatchers, then a few more, then a whole flock winging in to hop around us on the rocks, calling and squabbling, but not really driving each other off. It was as if they were singing with us, all of us calling together across the soft gray water.

I looked at Sue and Kate and Karen around me on the rocks, the evening shadows highlighting the planes and ridges of their weathered faces. Glancing at my own cracked and swollen hands, I realized we were each a living landscape, subject to our own tides and shiftings, and affecting the motions and moods of those around us. We each had our hidden channels, our sudden storms. Just as we had learned to adapt to our surroundings, we'd also learned to survive the weather of each other. Despite Karen's odd habits, Kate's reticence, and Sue's occasional bossiness, I realized that they'd become as familiar to me as my backpack, as I had, no doubt, to them. For the first time I had the sense that we'd come through something together, squabbling and testy as oystercatchers perhaps, but together, all of us perched there on the rocks.

I took my final picture on the beach, waiting to be picked up. Looming out of the background shadows is the unmistakeable shape of the double-hulled *Spirit of Adventure*. Three men stand on the bow, ready to lower the ladder and throw lines down to reel in the kayaks. The water looks calm, except for the white crest of surf, stopped by the camera in mid-roll. Karen's closest to the water's edge, dressed neatly in slacks and sweater, erect and eager, holding the rope to her kayak, her backpack tightly strapped to her. The other kayak sits farther from the shoreline. Sue stands behind it, dressed in red windpants and windbreaker, hands on her hips, watching the boat come in. Behind the boats and in front of Kate, our gear is scattered on the sand in a heap of blue and red and black and orange and yellow plastic and rubber bags and the metal food containers. Kate stands to the left and behind the pile, wearing black pants and a purple windbreaker. She's looking off-camera, her arms folded across her chest, waiting. Standing a short distance back and out of the frame, I'm the one behind the camera, trying to focus, trying to take it all in.

Upside Down with Borges and Bob

Frank Soos

From here, I see my truck as a big red rock thrown into the lake of my life. Thirty-five feet down the bank, its dusty entrails exposed to the sky, the driver's side door cocked open at an odd angle so the dome light casts a weak peach tint onto the snow, it looks worse than maybe it is. I see the bright silver casing of the newly overhauled transmission with less than a hundred shifts in it, the new front brake hoses; everything exposed to me looks to be in perfect working order if only it were right side up.

It is not. And no amount of wishing on my part will make it so. The wrecker is on its way; and, while I wait, I consider the ripples my rock has made. Things could have been worse, my wife, Blalock, tells me. I have to agree. One possible rippling wave out to the future does not contain me at all. Rather than standing on the shoulder assuring passing drivers that I am all right despite all indications I ought to be otherwise, I could be history, gone, out of here.

"Did your life flash before your eyes? Did you see any interesting sights?" my friend Farnham asked me a few days later. I saw my truck sliding up the road wildly to the right, then after some furious steering, sliding wildly to the left; I saw it head back to the right again, and this time as the road curved to meet it, there was not enough space to execute any more desperate maneuvers. I say "I saw" because it seems to me now that I can actually see this wreck as if I were hovering above it in a helicopter, no longer a participant but a witness.

In his book *Labyrinths,* Jorge Luis Borges suggested we can live thousands of parallel lives of the imagination, an idea that appeals to me just now. In one of these lives I am efficient, organized. In another I ski like an Olympic medalist. In another I am a fabulously successful writer. In another I have chosen a different route, a different time, a different kind of weather for myself. Not one of these alternate versions would have me standing by the roadside shivering and waiting for the wreck truck.

When I try these Borges premises on a class of undergraduate Alaskans, they dig in their heels and tell me what hooey it is. Who would trade in the life we are living for any imagined life, even if that imagined life contains no vehicles in the ditch, no insurance adjusters, no smart-aleck wreck truck drivers, and no leisure-prone auto body men? Nonetheless, I am still attracted to the idea of following myself along, being myself in two places at once. I am both driving the truck and watching myself, or watching the truck with me in it. And I feel compelled to run this repeating film loop again and again. Here comes my truck down a slight incline. To the right is a kid on a snow machine hugging the shoulder. I say "kid" because I knew he was a kid before I ever saw him. I saw his snaky track playing into the road, crossing over into the left lane, making spins and squiggles for a couple of miles before I came upon him. Only a kid would play in the road that way. Not that adults don't play on their snow machines. But an adult would have a truck, maybe even a trailer, and pull the snow-go out to the nearby hills where you can play without worrying about the traffic. Somehow the kid hears my engine through his crash helmet, over the sound of his own engine, and pulls to the right so I can pass him.

I wave, and he waves back. At least I think we exchange these waves. And I think it partly because as I struggle to orient myself in the upside-down cab, it is the kid who is outside my window digging through the snow and down into the dirt trying to help me free the door. While nothing else quite makes sense, bottom is now top, left is now right. I know my rescuer is this high school kid.

How did this happen? Sometime after I passed him, maybe a couple hundred yards, on the uphill climb, accelerating to pick up the momentum I lost when I slowed to get around him, I begin sliding. Quickly enough, I have come to a stop.

Inside my capsule, the light is dim. I can see nothing out the front; the windshield is shattered and pushed into the snowy ground. Around me are familiar objects in unfamiliar places, schoolbooks, boots, a scattered mess of clothes that have escaped the unzipped gym bag that was on the seat beside me. An axe. It had been behind the seat. So was a heavy canvas bag of tools pulled out only yesterday to fix a broken spoke on my bicycle. I had meant to put it back.

At some point, at a time before the kid came to dig at the window, I punched the button on my seat belt and fell softly into the ceiling of the truck. It wasn't a long fall. I had already conducted an almost instant inventory of my own systems and had convinced myself I was okay. I had the sense to turn off the radio, which was running a feature about red wine and French cooking. The point of this feature seemed to be that if you ate all that rich food it would eventually kill you, regardless of how much red wine you drank with it. I had suspected as much.

About this one thing, Borges is undeniably right. We are born and then, after a while if we're lucky, we die. It's how we manage what's in the middle that matters. But unlike the characters we meet in Borges's story "The Garden of the Forking Paths," I cannot accept with equanimity a future that excludes me. I cannot imagine a world without me in it. Even the rippling wave of possibility that runs on without me still contains my conscious presence. I imagine Blalock grieving, and because she is strong, I imagine her surviving all right without me. She lies on the couch surrounded by her cats, as always. Sadder. The cats pick up on this sadness and snuggle closer to comfort her. But after a while, she gets up; she eats, prepares for her classes, and even does the ugly work of taking up the loose ends of my own classes. But through seeing her act this way, I remain a constant presence. Blalock's future life spools out of my head. I may imagine it one way this minute and another the next; maybe she is more angry at my foolishness than sad, more organized herself as a result of seeing me off with so much left undone. Maybe she uses the insurance money for handmade red-and-black cowboy boots. But it is still my imagination at work. And it is for this reason I literally cannot imagine a future that in some way does not contain me.

I had not expected to be hearing the news of death by French cooking quite this way. I always suspected something was going to kill me: maybe cancer, maybe heart failure, maybe an accident of one kind or another. But I had not believed it and still do not believe it. If I did, would I have just spent the past few Sunday hours differently? Wouldn't I, like the hero on the old TV show *Run for Your Life,* have started on a hell-for-leather adventure involving beautiful women and a quest for peace, love, or justice? Instead I had spent my time driving to school, talking to a few students, driving to Birch Hill and skiing, and while skiing thinking alternately about my form, particularly why it was so bad, and about politics, people, my up-coming sabbatical, when I planned to put my life in order and get oodles of work done. Would I have driven to Fox to get some springwater for our coffee and tea? Would I have stopped halfway there to look in the bed of the truck for my thought-to-be-missing ski gloves?

Would I have spent the last almost forty-four years any differently at all? Would I still be waiting for my upcoming sabbatical to put my life in order? No and yes. Based on the evidence—me—what other honest conclusion could I draw?

My neighbor Bob Bell puts his hand up to the top of my head. "I just wanted to see if you were any shorter after your wreck." When I am driving, I can sense the presence of the roof less than an inch above my head, feel, when the weather is right, the pull of static electricity drawing my hair up to the roof liner. And to the left, also very near my head, is what car crash people call the A-unit—the part of the frame that supports the roof, that the doors nestle into. In collisions, it's common for people to get thrown against the A-unit. Such a wreck usually doesn't kill you. But it mushes up the left side of the brain, the cell clusters that control language and speech. Hitting the A-unit turns you into a noncommunicative idiot with a healthy appetite and a seventy-five-year life span.

I know this. I knew it all along. But only rarely has the proximity of my head to the roof liner and the A-unit caused me to drive more slowly. Bob Bell tells me about a wreck he had while driving a heavy dump truck at the gold mine where he works. The brakes failed on his first run of the day, and he went head first over a fifteen-foot bank. "It was like an invisible hand held me back. First run of the day, I didn't even have my seat belt on." While we lean against the fender of his pick-up, Bob's daughter sits inside and reads a magazine by the dome light, oblivious. "It was a miracle. I believe in miracles."

I wish for miracles myself. And I wonder what constitutes a miracle these days. In Bob's case, he is unbruised, uncut. The speed of the brakeless truck throws his twenty tons of gravel out ahead of him, cushioning the fall instead of rushing against the bed and crushing him. This is miracle enough for a man who believes in miracles.

And for the guy who doesn't? Bob's wreck is a model of Newtonian physics. I think of a little car we rolled across the lab table in my high school physics class. Pull the pin with the attached string and a steel ball is launched mortar-style out of the top of the car. Left alone, car and ball continue on their separate ways until the ball falls back to earth and is caught—miraculously?—in the metal cup that launched it. Stop the car and the ball goes on without it. Stop Bob's truck as it tilts over the embankment, and the gravel flies over the bed, passing the truck. Momentum.

Or loss of control. "I made a mistake," I tell Bob. "No," he says, "you had an accident." It's all a question of control. My own or somebody else's. When Bob runs over the bank in his dump truck, the faulty brakes are outside his control. Somebody in maintenance didn't do his job. And then God, or something very like God, stuck a big hand out and kept Bob Bell from slamming through the windshield of his truck.

"Going too fast, weren't you," the wrecker owner says, fixing me with his bloodshot eyes. He's seen it all; he knows. "Two-wheel or four-wheel?" I admit to him, "Two." He looks away. I am just too stupid for words. A slick road, fresh snow on top of a little ice, snow blowing, and cutting down on visibility. Here I come in two-wheel drive like it's Sunday in July.

In Bob's view, a miracle might be the presence of God and the absence of control. God will take care of things in whatever way suits him. All of us agree with Bob on some level. If I go back in time, I feel no need to take steps to alter my grandfather's failing health. To do so is only to postpone an understood inevitability. I can't stop his death from happening, only delay it. In this way, I accept for others what I will not accept for myself. I fight against it like a fish against the surprising hook and line.

What if, as Borges suggests in "The Secret Miracle," time might come in bubbles like notes of music given different values and filling up different bits of time? I slow my life to adagio. And I know for a fact I can make this happen, having traveled along the Blue Ridge Parkway at high speed, the radio tuned to a classical station where a string quartet slowed the world through the windshield down to a majestic crawl. Within these notes, full and fat as grapes ready to burst their skins, I have rolled along well beyond the posted speed limit, believing in the power of my synapses to direct my feet properly to accelerator, clutch, and brake. And believing no deer, possum, or skunk would pick such a moment in time to saunter out of the laurel and into the road. Nonsense and stuff. A 360-degree spin in the wet road was enough—for a short time—to convince me. Despite neurons sending their pulses racing literally like lightning, my poor muscles and bones are long and slow. The music is mere artifice, illusion.

My momentum carried my truck right down the bank. Wheels cocked to the right as the truck began its descent caused the thing to begin to lose its balance to the left. Slowly, slowly, it began to roll over. I say "slowly" because although I couldn't keep up with the images flashing through the windshield—they were coming in too fast for me to see myself going over—I could tell what was happening. I could tell the struggle was over. Maybe I felt it in my inner ear. Maybe my brain really did process the images but didn't know how to tell me what it was seeing. Something like this must have happened: As I began to roll, my body relaxed. The inertia of the truck pulled it down while I leaned away from the fall, almost laying my head against the back of the seat. Then my head swung back straight. Only I was upside down. I knew this in the same way I knew I was unhurt. The power switch on the radio was exactly where it should have been, so I reached out and turned it off. Only then did everything stop making sense. Only then did I start trying to put words to it.

Let's just say I could stand on the roadside and make a hole in time, a tear in the cloth, and crawl through it. Wouldn't I do everything differently this time? I would not, for example, sleep through most of my eight o'clock classes as a college freshman, through many of my nine o'clock ones as a sophomore and junior. I would sit in front of that brown calculus book and fight with stolid courage until I got it, until integrals and derivatives actually meant something real to me. I would not waste electives on sociology; I would go to the May Day antiwar rally and put myself in the road, stop traffic on the bridges from northern Virginia to D.C. Maybe I would even ask that red-headed woman for a date and not look at my shoes. In short, I would be smarter and better and more self-assured.

We expect—at least I expect, and every science fiction movie I have ever seen on the subject has confirmed my expectation—to carry what we know backward with us. Unlike Plato, who believed we start off knowing everything in our immortal souls but forget it all at birth, then spend our whole lives doing remedial work, I would go back in time armed with the knowledge of what would be out there in my future. I already like to believe I have a perfect, retrospective knowledge of my life, having a pretty good memory and having paid careful attention up to age forty-three years and eleven months. All I need is a chance to fix it, to revise.

What is that ache to return all about, if not to go back and take a kink or two out of time? Maybe not worry with the little goofs—dozing off in the middle of the scholastic aptitude test, say, or dropping my almost new Zebco fishing rod into a muddy lake—but taking corrective actions against the biggies—no concussions, broken bones, or stitches. Get rid of my first marriage. But if it weren't for the pitiful mistakes of the first, how would I ever have had enough sense to manage the second?

Simply going backward in time wouldn't work out. How could we sort out who we are from what we've done and still expect to be the same? No, what I want—what I guess we all want when we crawl back through a hole in time—is to recover time itself. Back behind us should be vast, open tracts of empty, lost time. Standing in lines, filling out forms, getting trapped in meetings with no means of escape. Television. Card games, board games. Crummy novels. Crummy movies. Meandering after-dinner arguments with people I didn't want to eat dinner with in the first place. Roll all that wasted time together, and I could surely make some good use of it. I would have the kind of resume people envy, a scroll full of accomplishments and the awards that go with them, what passes for proof of a full and productive life.

I once spent three years of long-distance driving to see a woman who didn't love me. I wore out a car and just about wore out my knee from sitting cramped up so long in the driver's seat. But once she and I went canoeing and trailed a little blue heron up the Potomac River. And once we went to an Australian movie neither of us had heard of and saw a pool scene where these guys did an Esther Williams number, synchronized swimming with inflated rubber sharks. I wish I could remember the name of that movie. I guess it doesn't matter; I think I remember the best part.

And once Blalock and I went fishing on the Chatanika River on the far side of Murphy Dome. We caught only two fish, and she fell in the river and had forgotten a change of clothes. Along the way, we had seen a moose and calf and a little black bear. Who would have wished it otherwise?

That is the trouble with time, that is the way Borges catches us out. He knows that to be human is to want it both ways, to want it all ways. We want the now and the some-other-more-convenient time, the safe and predictable and the accidental moment full of surprises. And if we can manage it, we will have all of them at once. My students, too stubborn to admit their fantasies of other times or of the same time in different places, only need to stand outside in the minus-forty-degree cold for a while to let out what they really think. Yet minus forty is the very time when living in the here and now might matter the most. Maybe what Borges knows best is our wish to take hold of time and use it to change things, to evade life's ultimate unhappy ending, or at least to put it off as long as we can. To revise and revise and never make an end.

Though in the larger scheme of things, it is relatively minor, a speck of lint, this last moment is what I would like to revise the most right now. To just run the film loop in reverse, the way we did the old eight-millimeter reels shown on a bed sheet in my parents' living room. The last thrill of the evening, to watch ourselves undo all our actions, to back right off the screen into nowhere. My truck flips back onto its left side, then up onto its wheels and rolls back up the bank, out into the roadway, swerves wildly backward down the road until it reaches the bottom of the hill. There. Let's leave it at that.

Biographical Notes

David Abrams lived in Fairbanks, where he pursued a Master of Fine Arts in creative writing at the University of Alaska Fairbanks. His stories have appeared in *The Greensboro Review, Permafrost, Nebraska Review, Belletrist Review,* and *South Dakota Review.* His nonfiction essays have been published in *Grand Tour* and *Snowy Egret.* He now lives in Texas.

Mark Bergemann has lived in Alaska for the past twenty-one years, seventeen of them as an educator in Alaska's public schools. Nome, Atqasuk, Anaktuvuk Pass, Fairbanks, and Seldovia have all been home. He is currently principal at Trapper School in Nuiqsut, Alaska.

Stephen Binns grew up in Oregon, Montana, California, and Arkansas. In 1984 he moved to Alaska and in the process got divorced, lost one hundred pounds, and became a different person. He has worn out two trucks, a backpack, several bicycles, and a crappy hat but not his appreciation for adventure. He works as a federal civil servant in Fairbanks.

Jennifer Brice was born in Alaska. She holds a Master of Fine Arts in creative writing from the University of Alaska Fairbanks. Her essays have appeared in *Manoa* and *Permafrost,* and in the anthologies *American Nature Writing 1994* and *From the Island's Edge.* A collection of her essays is forthcoming from Duquesne University Press.

Steve Chamberlain teaches English at the Kuskokwim campus of the University of Alaska Fairbanks. He lived in the bush of Alaska for twenty-two years and has worked as a commercial fisherman. His fiction and poetry have appeared in various literary journals, and he has had nonfiction essays about Alaska published in *Mother Earth News.*

Sheryl Clough lives in Washington, and in Alaska whenever possible. She holds a Master of Fine Arts from the University of Alaska Fairbanks. She counts among many blessings poetry study with Nelson Bentley at the University of Washington and the adoption of her dog Starbuck. Her writing appears in *Arnazella, Bellowing Ark, Women's Outdoor Journal,* and other publications. She has completed a book-length poetry manuscript and is working on a collection of nonfiction essays, which will include "Scab on the Chugach."

Linda M. Davis was raised in a Florida beach town. She moved to Alaska at nineteen and spent fifteen years in the bush, homesteading, trapping, running dogs, and flying. She left the bush and plunged back into "civilization" at the age of thirty-five, and has been "catching up" ever since. Her essays have been published in *We Alaskans, Northern Lights,* and the anthology *North of Eden.*

Susan Ewing is the author of *The Great Alaska Nature Factbook, Going Wild in Washington and Oregon,* and a children's book of verse, illustrated by Evon Zerbetz, titled *Lucky Hares and Itchy Bears.* Her work has also appeared in *Sports Afield, Gray's Sporting Journal, Fly Rod & Reel, Spur, Alaska Fisherman's Journal,* and other publications. She left Alaska in 1987 and currently makes her home in Montana.

Jenifer Fratzke is a creative writing student at the University of Alaska Anchorage, and an erstwhile bush pilot. She and her husband are hunting and fishing enthusiasts. "Musk Ox Hunting" is her first major publication.

Melissa S. Green is pursuing a Master of Fine Arts in creative writing (poetry emphasis) at the University of Alaska Anchorage. She works as a publication specialist for the Justice Center at the University of Alaska Anchorage, and designed the Justice Center's Web site at http://www.uaa.alaska.edu/just/ljustice.html. Originally from Montana, she has lived since 1982 in Anchorage.

Geneen Marie Haugen has traveled, worked, and celebrated the rivers and backcountry of the West. Her work has appeared in the anthologies *Another Wilderness: New Outdoor Writing by Women* and *Solo: On Her Own Adventure,* and in *Northern Lights, Caldera,* and other journals. She lives south of Wilson, Wyoming, with her partner, David, and their ninety-five-pound dog, Furry Flipper Fourpaws.

Mary Hussmann has a Master of Fine Arts in creative nonfiction from the University of Iowa. She has published poetry, essays, book reviews, and interviews in *The North American Review, The Iowa Review,* and *The Kenyon Review,* among others. She is coeditor of *Transgressions: The Iowa Anthology of Innovative Fiction* (University of Iowa Press) and is the associate editor of *The Iowa Review.*

Ted Kerasote has written about nature and outdoor recreation for many publications, including *Audubon, Outside,* and *Sports Afield,* where his EcoWatch column follows wilderness and wildlife conservation issues. His two latest books are *Bloodties—Nature, Culture, and the Hunt* and *Heart of Home.*

Naomi Warren Klouda taught English at the University of Alaska Anchorage as an adjunct professor. She frequently contributes to *Alaska* magazine, *Outside, Women's Sports and Fitness,* and other magazines. She has published her Master of Fine Arts thesis, a collection of short stories entitled *Road Kills and Other Stories,* and has recently finished a novel. She now makes her home in Old Harbor.

Kay Landis visited Anchorage in 1976 and somehow never moved for the next twenty years. She received a Master of Fine Arts in creative writing at the University of Alaska Anchorage in 1995, and has recently moved to the Netherlands.

Mary Lockwood is an Inupiaq writer from Unalakleet, Alaska. During her early years she experienced the final days of the traditional village culture. Her shaman grandfather was the last chief (headman) of her village. She was granted a four-year regents scholarship to the University of California, Santa Cruz, in 1970. She was an invited participant in the historic 1992 Returning the Gift conference in Norman, Oklahoma, has published in anthologies, and has had her writing featured on National Public Radio.

Jessica Maxwell has a farm in Oregon at the foot of the McKenzie Hills, where she writes "gonzo frou-frou adventure stories" when she's not fly-fishing, practicing her golf swing (and using a putter with a straight face), or zydeco dancing until the steelhead come home.

Migael Scherer is a Pacific Northwest writer and teacher. She is the author of two books, *Still Loved by the Sun: A Rape Survivor's Journal* and *A Cruising Guide to Puget Sound,* and numerous articles. *Still Loved by the Sun* received a PEN/Albrand Special Citation for Distinguished Nonfiction and also won a Pacific Northwest Booksellers Association Award.

Sherry Simpson grew up in Juneau, Alaska, but now lives in Fairbanks with her husband. Her essays have appeared in the anthologies *Another Wilderness: New Outdoor Writing by Women, American Nature Writing 1994,* and *Teaching Us to See.* She won the 1995 *Sierra* magazine Nature Writing Contest.

Frank Soos teaches English and creative writing at the University of Alaska Fairbanks. His recent short stories have appeared in *Cimarron Review, Writers' Forum,* and *The Bellingham Review.* His essays have appeared in *North Dakota Quarterly* and *Now and Then.* His current projects include a novel and a collection of essays.